101
practical
ways
to make
money
at home

GOOD HOUSEKEEPING BOOKS

Editor MINA WHITE MULVEY
Art Director WILLIAM LEFT
Art Consultant JOHN ENGLISH
Senior Editor PATRICIA DEMPSEY
Copy Editor JUANITA G. CHAUDHRY
Assistant to Art Director LYNN THOMPSON

FOR GOOD HOUSEKEEPING MAGAZINE

Editor WADE H. NICHOLS
Publisher RAYMOND J. PETERSEN
Executive Editor JOHN B. DANBY
Managing Editor BENSON SRERE
Art Director BERNARD SPRINGSTEEL
Director, The Institute WILLIE MAE ROGERS

PUBLISHED BY THE HEARST CORPORATION

President RICHARD E. BERLIN
President, Magazines Division RICHARD E. DEEMS
Executive Vice-President, Magazines JOHN R. MILLER
Vice-President, Magazines WILLIAM S. CAMPBELL
Vice-President-Director, Book Division JAMES B. FISHER
Production Manager, Book Division HENRY L. WENZ

101 practical ways to make money at home

by the Editors of Good Housekeeping

Drawings by James Andrews

Good Housekeeping Books

New York

CONTENTS

WHAT
THIS
BOOK
IS
ABOUT

This book is for the woman who needs extra money—and which of us doesn't?—to help pay off the mortgage, save for a child's education, raise the family's standard of living, or simply provide a few luxuries (that long-dreamed-of trip, a movie camera for the man of the house, or some fashionable new clothes). In these days of high prices and rising expectations, it's hard for any family to get along on a single paycheck, however good a provider the husband may be.

Yet, for many women, taking a job outside the home is not the answer. Some women (and their husbands too) feel deeply that children need a full-time mother, one who can be counted on to be there when a crisis arises or a confidence needs to be shared. Others fear that the additional expenses connected with an outside job—clothes, carfare, lunches, baby-sitter fees—may mean that they would be working for almost nothing. Still others are simply allergic to the idea of a nine-to-five routine.

Fortunately, there are ways to use your interests and talents to make money right in your own home. In fact, there are many, many ways, and this book outlines 101 of

1

them in detail. Not every way is for every woman. Some demand very little in the way of background and experience, some quite a bit. Some can provide only pin money; others, depending on your skill and how hard you want to work, are a source of substantial income. The chances of success of all vary with the nature of the community in which you live. There are ideas for women with only a little time to spare and for those with a lot; for stay-at-homes and for women who, so long as they can arrange their own hours, can stray from home base as much as necessary. Among all these, there are certain to be a number of promising opportunities for *you* to choose from.

The 101 ways listed here are practical ones; all have been successfully used by someone, somewhere. They do not call for extraordinary business acumen possessed only by the lucky few. Most discussions of making money at home dwell on success stories like those of Hazel Bishop, who, not finding a lipstick to suit her, compounded her own, and thus took the first step toward what became a million-dollar business. Or Pepperidge Farm, which started in the kitchen of Margaret Rudkin.

These are true accounts, and show what heights a home business can reach. But it's not necessary to have the makings of a woman tycoon to work successfully at home. What you *do* need, though, is considerable self-discipline, resourcefulness, and the ability to maintain your initial enthusiasm for your project over long periods.

You also need good health and plenty of energy, since it takes stamina to do *two* jobs—and every wife and mother already has one.

Third, it's absolutely critical that you make a realistic appraisal of your skills. If there's an idea that appeals to you but it requires more knowledge of the subject than you currently possess, you must be prepared either to give it up in favor of one more suited to your present abilities, or be willing to put in time and work learning before you plunge in.

Just as important is preliminary research to determine whether a market for a particular idea exists in your community. A business can have made a fortune for somebody else and fail for you, depending upon the circumstances. (The reverse is also possible, another reason for good market research.)

WATCH OUT FOR FRAUDS

One word of warning: Beware of the many pitfalls for the unwary in this area. The National Better Business Bureau estimates that there are hundreds of fraudulent "earn-money-at-home" schemes, and that they take over a half-billion dollars annually from several million people. Here are some of the examples given by the Bureau:

> A show-card painting scheme was receiving over 2,500 letters a day in answer to its advertising and took in over $500,000 before it was stopped. The victims bought work materals only to find that the promoter would not purchase the finished product. Regardless of its quality, he rejected it all.

> In a scheme to sell employment of photo-coloring, over 15,000 people paid in over $500,000, but got no work.

> A scheme to promote the idea of decorating and selling Christmas cards took in over $100,000.

The Bureau finds that there are as many as 11 different categories of fraudulent earn-money-at-home schemes. All of them have one thing in common: they take money in instead of paying it out. This fact is almost never evident in the advertising. Instead, your services are said to be badly needed, and you are offered huge earnings. Usually these ads appear in the "Help Wanted" columns of newspapers and magazines.

One of the commonest schemes is to lure you into buying instructions—which turn out to be worthless—on making money at home. A claim is made, for example, that you can make up to $25 a week addressing envelopes. When you answer the ad, you are asked to pay $1 or more for instructions to "get started." Often the instructions simply tell you how to address an envelope and get a list of names. (The fact that you already know how to address an envelope or you would not have been able to answer the ad does not bother the conscience of the promoter!)

There are many variations of this basic ploy. Sometimes, under the pretense of offering you work, the promoter tries to sell you pamphlets, home-study courses, or books on making money at home. Sometimes the purpose is to sell you instructions and equipment or materials for making products, which the promoter promises to buy from you. Strangely enough, however, nothing you make ever proves to be "up to standard." Or you find that, despite the promises in the ad, you yourself are expected to sell everything you make.

Other schemes promise to sell short stories to TV and movie studios for fabulous sums, or to set poems to music and publish them as popular songs. Still others claim a fortune can be made from breeding minks, chinchillas, rabbits (or even bullfrogs). A fortune is made, all right, but it is made by the promoter, not by the victims who answer his ad.

The best policy, therefore, is to look carefully before you leap. Some of the same areas particularly favored by the tricksters—manuscript typing, newspaper clipping, and envelope addressing—can be a legitimate source of income for women working at home. But when an offer of such work is made by others, make sure the offer is genuine, and not a scheme to make money from *you*. If you have any doubts, check with your local Better Business Bureau.

A WORD ABOUT PRICES

A final word about the prices and fees quoted in this book. They aren't, and can't be, valid for every set of circumstances and every community in the country. Home products and services are fewer and less widely distributed than commercial enterprises, and information on them is much harder to come by. Moreover, prices fluctuate so rapidly that even by the time this book is printed, the situation may have changed somewhat.

Nevertheless, it has been thought worthwhile to include current price information, where available, in order to give you *some* idea of what kind of money is involved. Just remember that the quoted prices are guidelines only. Always check them against those actually prevailing for similar products and services in your own community.

THE PLEASURES AND PROBLEMS OF WORKING AT HOME

No one has to tell you what the advantages of working at home are. It's convenient—no traveling to and from a job; it lets you keep an eye on the kids and meet the convenience of TV repairmen and others who work only during prime time; and it's "free"—at least you don't have to fork over rent for your premises or pay extra for electricity, heat, or a telephone. In fact, when you use your home to produce income, part of the expenses for maintaining it can be written off as tax deductions.

The disadvantages of at-home work are less obvious but just as real. Looming large among them is the matter of interruptions. These can come in any number of varieties, the main ones being clearly recognizable as tradesmen, neighbors, husband, and children. The milkman stops to chat as he delivers the bill, the woman next door drops in for a cup of coffee, your husband wants you to come hold the ladder ("just for a minute, honey") , and the children—when have children regarded Mom as anything but their devoted slave? When you work at home, time will become your most precious commodity, and you will find yourself scheming to beg, borrow, or buy it.

THE PROBLEM OF FAMILY

How much time you will have for your business, and, in fact, its ultimate chances of success or failure, will depend heavily on your family's attitude toward your activities. Necessarily, any venture you undertake must be, to a great extent, a group project. Though no one but you may do any of the actual work, everyone must cooperate if you are to be able to manage.

Your husband will of course be the key figure. Some men are delighted to have their wives undertake work that both interests them and brings in extra income. They are encouraging, supportive, and in some cases so enthusiastic that they may want to become a partner in the new venture.

Others have no objection to a wife's work so long as it doesn't disturb their daily routine or require them to make any sacrifices. If your husband is one of these, you will have to proceed with care. Not for you is a business that brings customers to your door in the evenings or on weekends, or that usurps considerable space in your home.

Most husbands fall somewhere between these two extremes, and can be pushed into either camp depending upon the way the situation is handled. It is worthwhile going all out to get a husband's cooperation, for he can help in innumerable ways. First, since you are bringing in extra income, your spouse may be willing to help with the children and even the housework, as well as put up with any personal inconveniences your activities may cause him. Second, his skills may come in handy—in building a greenhouse for a home nursery, for example, or in taking pictures for an advertising brochure.

Even if your husband hasn't the time or desire to participate physically in your business venture, you may find him a gold mine of information about business practices. You may also be able to profit from his personal or business contacts. A member of the bookkeeping department in the company he works for may pass on tips for keeping your books, a lawyer acquaintance may offer free legal advice. A husband, in short, is a good man to have on your side, so take care to involve him in your hopes and plans from the start.

Children (we're speaking now in a strictly technical sense) can be both an asset and a drawback. When they're small, they are invariably the latter, and all you can do is plan your work around them. For one thing, they don't understand what you mean by "work." Daddy works. He picks up his briefcase or tool kit, kisses you good-bye and goes off to the office or shop. But Mommy working? That's pretty hard to digest. You're right there at home with them.

By the time children are in primary school, though, they will be out of your hair most of the day. In addition, children of this age group can staple, fold letters, stuff envelopes, and perform many other simple but helpful tasks. They can also take the younger children off your hands occasionally, and do extra household chores.

Teenagers who can type are invaluable for correspondence and paying bills. In addition, they can file, answer the telephone, make posters, hand out advertising flyers, and, if they drive, handle pickups and deliveries for you.

How do you get all this help? That's simple. If your kids are young, you tell them it's fun, and they will believe you and enjoy sharing in your activities. If they are older, you pay them. Whatever their age, you do your best to make them feel partners with you in a family enterprise, rather than victims of a situation that deprives them of much of your time and attention without any compensating benefits.

It will pay you to make things as easy on them (and on your husband) as you can. That may mean, for example, relaxing some of your highest housekeeping standards. You can only do so much, and if your business absorbs much of your extra time and energy, it will be better to let the floors go unwaxed or the silver unpolished occasionally than to work yourself to the point where your temper is short and your nerves frazzled. At that point, however much you try not to, you're bound to take it out on those nearest to you.

Also try not to let your activities disrupt family life too much. As interested in your enterprise as your husband and children may be, their enthusiasm will begin to flag if they can never bring friends home because it would interrupt your labors, or if your business paraphernalia are always in everyone's way.

"AT HOME" VERSUS "FROM HOME"

Much, of course, will depend on what kind of work you choose. Various types of business can be run from a home base. Generally, these fall into two broad categories: "at-home" jobs and "from-home" jobs. The first covers businesses featuring products, such as food, handcrafts, home-grown flowers and plants, and custom sewing. It also comprises a host of services, including child care, telephone answering and soliciting, giving instruction, and clipping newspapers and magazines.

From-home jobs use the home largely as a base for functions performed elsewhere. Among these are services provided by wedding consultants, party planners, interior decorators, market researchers, real estate and insurance agents, and child photographers.

Then there are jobs, falling somewhere between these two, in which most of the work is done at home, with some time spent outside in consulting with clients, tracking down materials, or making deliveries. Making slipcovers and draperies is one of these; so is free-lance bookkeeping, operating an enterainment bureau, or running an antiques shop.

THE PROBLEM OF SPACE

Besides calling for different personal schedules, at-home and from-home jobs differ in the amount of space required. For a from-home operation you will probably need not much more than a desk, file, and telephone, all of which can be tucked into a reasonably quiet corner.

At-home jobs are another matter. If you turn out a product, you will, in most cases, need a separate room, where you can work undisturbed and where materials and inventory can be safely stored. Inviting the public into your home for services or sales will also require you to set aside a special area. In some cases, such as giving lessons or doing alterations and mending, the space thus allocated can be returned to family use outside your business hours. But for others, including any kind of home shop, and ventures such as a dog-grooming salon or a mini-restaurant, part of the family's living space will have to be given over to your operation full-time. The size and physical layout of your home or apartment should therefore be an important consideration in your plans.

THE PROBLEM OF LOCATION

For businesses that require customers or clients to visit you, the location of your home is also critical. In considering any such enterprise, ask yourself these questions:

1. Are there other businesses in your neighborhood?

2. Is it heavily populated? Or is it reasonably near a heavily populated area?

3. Is your house easily distinguishable from others on the block?

4. Is the address clearly visible from the street?
5. Is the area where you live easy to find?
6. Is it close to public transportation?
7. Is there much foot traffic near your house?
8. If customers will be coming to you by car, will they be able to park easily?

If your answer to most of these questions is no, you will probably do better with a business that permits you to go to the customer (either directly or through a middleman), rather than the other way around. With ingenuity, some obstacles can be eliminated. You can, for example, always call attention to your house with a coat of bright paint! But a dearth of potential customers nearby cannot be so easily overcome. Each case, however, must be considered on its merits. If you have a really unique product or service, people who live miles away may beat a path to your door.

A vital factor in your plans will be the zoning laws that apply to the neighborhood in which you live. Check these well in advance, for they may rule out certain types of home business, or restrict them so severely that their chances of success are limited. If such restrictions do apply in your area, it may be possible to obtain a variance from the zoning board. In any case, it is well to know exactly what the situation is before you make any definite plans. Some types of at-home work—telephone selling, for example, typing manuscripts or creating needlework designs for sale elsewhere— are not subject to zoning regulations (if any) so long as you do not identify your home as a place of business.

DO YOU HAVE WHAT IT TAKES?

No matter what type of work you plan to undertake, your chances of making money from it will also be determined by your own personality and character. The Small Business Administration suggests that anyone thinking of operating her own business should rate herself objectively on the following list of ten traits. (Also get a friend to have several people who know you rate you too—anonymously, so their ratings won't be affected by fear of hurting your feelings.)

Here is the Small Business Administration's list. For each trait, place a check mark beside the description you think most nearly fits you. And no wishful thinking! Being honest about yourself is painful, but for your own good.

RATING SCALE FOR EVALUATING PERSONAL TRAITS
IMPORTANT TO THE PROPRIETOR OF A BUSINESS

Instructions: Check the trait that you think best describes you.

Initiative
Additional tasks sought; highly ingenious
Resourceful; alert to opportunities
Regular work performed without waiting for directions
Routine worker awaiting directions

Attitude toward others
Positive; friendly interest in people
Pleasant, polite
Sometimes difficult to work with
Inclined to be quarrelsome or uncooperative

Leadership
Forceful, inspiring confidence and loyalty
Order giver
Driver
Weak

Responsibility
Responsibility sought and welcomed
Accepted without protest
Unwilling to assume without protest
Avoided whenever possible

Organizing ability
Highly capable of perceiving and arranging fundamentals in logical order

Able organizer
Fairly capable of organizing
Poor organizer

Industry
Industrious; capable of working hard for long hours
Can work hard, but not for too long a period
Fairly industrious
Hard work avoided

Decision
Quick and accurate
Good and careful
Quick, but often unsound
Hesitant and fearful

Sincerity
Courageous, square-shooter
On the level
Fairly sincere
Inclined to lack sincerity

Perseverance
Highly steadfast in purpose; not discouraged by obstacles
Effort steadily maintained
Average determination and persistence
Little or no persistence

Physical energy
Highly energetic at all times
Energetic most of time
Fairly energetic
Below average

Most of your check marks should be near the top of each category. If most of them are near the bottom, you probably don't have what it takes to work on your own, and it's just as well to recognize that now rather than later.

CHOOSING A HOME BUSINESS

Some women who have built up successful home enterprises had no trouble in choosing their area of operation. They saw a business opportunity that was simply too good to pass up, or had a hobby for which the business provided a profitable outlet. But most women who would like to make some money at home have a hard time settling on the way to do it.

WHAT DO YOU HAVE TO OFFER

Your skills. Choosing a field of work is so important a decision that it is worthwhile giving a great deal of thought to it. Sit down with pencil and paper and evaluate yourself again—this time on your specific abilities. First list the things you do best, your special skills or talents. Perhaps you don't think you have any, but if so, you just haven't thought hard enough. All kinds of things can be the basis of a home business. These may include a way with flowers (or pets or children), a flair for food, a typing speed of 70 words per minute, an instinctive ability to size people up, a talent for organization, a knack for restoring furniture, even just a pleasant telephone voice.

Your experience and background. Next, think back to any work experience you have had, paid or volunteer, and analyze how that might be put to work for your own benefit. Have you ever worked on the publicity committee of a charitable organization? Chaired the entertainment committee of a club? Organized a white elephant sale for your church? If so, you already have valuable insights and techniques (to say nothing of contacts) that could be utilized for a home business. The same thing is of course true of any background you may have in the business world.

And don't forget to list any special training you may have had, which you might pass on to others. Perhaps your ambition to become a concert pianist proved impractical long ago, but you may still be qualified to teach piano. Tutoring and language lessons are additional possibilities, but not the only ones in the teaching field. If you've ever had a child by natural childbirth, for example, you might be able to teach the techniques involved. Lessons in figure control or shorthand and typing are other examples of ways to make money from your skills.

General education will help too. Says the Small Business Administration, "While there are usually no educational requirements for starting your own business, the more schooling you have had, the better equipped you should be. For example, in most businesses you must know how to figure interest and discounts, keep simple and adequate records, and conduct necessary correspondence." If you feel yourself deficient in any of these areas, you might want to investigate the evening adult education classes sponsored in many communities by the public school system or the local Y.

Your time and facilities. How much time you are willing

and able to contribute to your own business while still fulfilling your family responsibilities will obviously be a factor in your choice of work. So, as was pointed out at length in Chapter I, will be the location and size of your home or apartment and the facilities that can be made available for your business use.

Your goals. What you want out of a business is also important. If you are content with pin money, that will point you in one direction. If you are out for bigger game (and are willing to put up with the greater effort, and sometimes risks, that go with it) , you will want to head in another.

When you have all this down, try to match up what you would *like* to do with what you know you *can* do, perhaps have already done in some form in the past. The closer these two coincide, the more enthusiasm you will have for your work, and enthusiasm can go a long way toward helping you succeed. It can't go all the way, though. Be wary of undertaking any enterprise for which you have absolutely no background—unless you are willing to undergo a preliminary period of training.

If you do want to invest time and money in acquiring new skills, here are some sources to investigate:

College evening courses and extension classes. For a list of accredited colleges offering night classes, write to the Association of University Evening Courses, University of Oklahoma, 1700 Asp Street, Norman, Oklahoma 73609.

Business schools, the obvious place to acquire secretarial and bookkeeping skills, also offer courses in real estate, insurance, and travel. For information, consult your nearest Better Business Bureau or write to the Accrediting Committee for Business Schools, Suite 724, New Center Building, 7430 Second Avenue, Detroit, Michigan 48202.

Home study may be the logical choice for you, but be sure you select a reputable school. A list of approved college correspondence courses is available from the National University Extension Association, 122 Social Science Building, University of Minnesota, Minneapolis, Minn. 55455. For noncollege courses, a directory is published by the National Home Study Council, 1601 Eighteenth Street, N.W., Washington, D.C. 20009.

IS THERE A MARKET FOR YOUR BUSINESS?

Once you have tentatively chosen a moneymaking project, make sure there is a market for it in your community. To do this, you should know something about the people who will be your potential customers. What is the average age? The average income? How many families have children? Of what ages? What do people spend their money on? How do they dress? Eat? Spend their leisure time? Are their tastes simple or sophisticated?

Some, maybe a lot, of the answers to these questions will be obvious to you simply because you live in the community. You can also talk to your neighbors, question business-oriented groups like the Chamber of Commerce, and study businesses similar to yours (if there are any) .

Another invaluable source of information is the Bureau of the Census, which can provide you with all kinds of data on the people in your area. In addition to its *City and County Data Book* and *Statistical Abstract of the United States,* available in most public libraries, the Bureau publishes a whole set of reports for each state, including data on every county and city in it. The cost for all the reports for your state is from $5 to $10, depending on whether you live in a big state or a small one. You can order the reports directly from the Superintendent of Documents, Washington, D.C. 20402.

Census data will tell you the number of people in your

area by sex, school grade, race, single adults, widows, size of families, education. They will reveal whether their income is increasing or decreasing; what kinds of products and services they buy most; how many own their own homes; or, if they live in apartments, how much rent they pay, what appliances they use, how many automobiles they own, and many other useful facts.

Other sources of population and marketing statistics are *Editor and Publisher Market Guide* and *Rand McNally Commercial Atlas and Marketing Guide.* These are available in many public libraries.

If your research reveals that your immediate neighborhood isn't a particularly good bet for your business, you may be able to aim at another section of the city or at neighboring towns. But in this case you will have to count on additional expenses for advertising to reach these more removed potential customers.

What about competition? If there is none, it *could* mean that there is no market for your service in the area. On the other hand, it could also mean that you are ahead of everyone else with a very good idea. Good market research will suggest which is the right answer.

The chances are, however, that you will have to compete for your customers with established businesses. Consequently, you must offer something special. Above-average quality. Lower prices. A convenience, such as pickup and/or delivery. Better service.

A final thought to keep in mind in researching your market is the importance of keeping up with new developments. This year's fad can turn into next year's bankruptcy for those who ignore the frequent shifts in personal tastes and business trends. You can keep abreast of these by reading the business pages of local newspapers, trade papers and magazines in your field, *Business Week,* and the business sections of *Time* and *Newsweek*. Dip into the *Wall Street Journal,* too. Its usefulness is not limited to corporation executives. Often it carries news of national and regional trends that can be of great interest to small (even very small) businesses.

DO YOU HAVE ANY MONEY TO INVEST?

How much money, if any, you have available for investment is still another factor that may affect your choice of a business. Some of the 101 ways to make money listed in this book require none at all. Among these, to name only a few, are market research, selling subscriptions to magazines, or being a "bird dog" travel agent. Others require very little. But before going into any business, it's wise to make a careful, long-range analysis of exactly what expenses are involved. Some types of work which, at first glance, may seem to involve only pennies can, in reality, require a considerable expenditure before any return can be expected. There are two main points to remember:

1. Any business that calls for equipment, inventory, or raw materials requires a respectable amount of capital. You can start small, pinch pennies, and cut corners, but a shoestring will carry you only so far.

2. Businesses that do require capital investment usually take about a year before they break even or show a profit. If you expect to recoup your investment instantly, you're bound to be disappointed.

Precisely how much capital you'll need depends, naturally, on the business you choose. Here are examples of three different patterns of expenditure.

Ann M. runs a bookkeeping service in a midwestern town, her 16 clients being mainly local merchants and two doctors. As a trained bookkeeper and typist with five years of fairly recent job experience, she spent nothing to brush up her skills. Her total initial investment broke down like this:

Business permit: $2
Adding machine (used) : $49
Business-announcement cards for direct-mail advertising: $20
Postage: $36
Letterheads and envelopes: $34
Office supplies (paper, carbons, file folders, etc.) : $74
   TOTAL: $215

Mercedes W. owns a baby-sitting service in a Washington, D.C. suburb. These were her initial expenditures:
Attorney's fees for incorporation and other legal advice: $100
Stationery and business cards: $25
Office supplies (file cards and filing box) : $5
Advertising: $70
   TOTAL: $200

Polly C. operates a wig shop in the basement of her California home. Because her expenses involved inventory, they ran a bit higher than those for the two service businesses.
Inventory (one of each kind of wig, wiglet, and hairpiece she planned to offer) : $435
Accessories (head forms, clamps, cases, cleaners) : $75
Advertising: $20 (Deceptively low because most of the business came in through word of mouth)
Business permit: $5
   TOTAL: $535

DON'T FORGET ADVERTISING COSTS

In some businesses, your main costs will be for advertising to attract customers. These vary so much with the area and the circumstances that it is impossible to give any average figures. Here, however, are some typical costs for various advertising materials and media.

- *One-sheet mimeographed flyer* (you supply stencil) : On white paper, $7 per thousand; on colored paper, $8. To have stencil prepared for you costs an additional $3 to $5, depending upon the complexity of the copy.
- *One-sheet printed flyer:* On white paper, $12 for the first thousand; $7 for each additional thousand. On colored paper, $15 for the first thousand; $10 for each additional thousand. Inclusion of photographs increases cost.
- *Four-page 8" x 10" circular in black-and-white:* $50 to $60 for the first thousand; $15 to $20 for each additional thousand. Prices assume the use of at least one photograph.
- *Four-page 8" x 10" circular in four-color:* $150 to $200 for the first thousand; $25 to $50 for each additional thousand. Prices assume the use of one photograph; additional photographs increase cost.
- *Printed business cards:* $20 per thousand.
- *Classified ad in local weekly "shopper"* (giveaway newspaper) : $3 for 25 words.
- *Classified ad in local weekly newspaper:* $1.10 per column inch.
- *Classified ad in county-seat daily newspaper:* $2.50 per column inch. Sunday rates run about 20¢ a line higher.
- *Classified ad in big-city daily newspaper:* $1.10 per line daily, $1.50 on Sunday.
- *Listing in classified telephone directory* ("Yellow Pages") : If you have a business phone, you are entitled to one free regular listing of name, phone number, and address.
- *Advertising in classified telephone directory:* This may consist of a regular listing made more prominent by the use of heavy type; a space listing, in sizes from one-half inch to two inches; or a display ad, which may range in

size from a quarter column to a double half column. Each local telephone company sets its own rates, but here are some typical examples (all rates are quoted per month). BIG CITY: Bold-type listing, $5. One-inch space listing, $22.50. One-quarter-column display ad, $40. Double half-column display ad, $240. SMALL CITY: Bold-type listing, $2. One-inch space listing, $7.50. One-quarter-column display ad, $18. Double half-column display ad, $72. SMALL TOWN: Bold-type listing, $1.25. One-inch space listing, $3.60. One-quarter-column display ad, $5.50. Double half-column display ad, $22.

If you are convinced you have a sound idea for a home business, but need more money than you yourself have to invest, you may want to investigate possible sources of credit (see page 33).

WHERE TO GET HELP

You may be convinced that your prospective business has a good chance of success, but before you plunge in, it's wise to get expert advice. Fortunately, a great deal of this is free.

The U.S. Department of Commerce publishes an awesome batch of publications which analyze various businesses. From their business bibliographies, fact sheets and management pamphlets, you may get handy insights into your own project.

The Department also has 42 field offices, located in various cities throughout the country, which will help you with specific problems, either in person or through the mail. Your local Chamber of Commerce can help you locate the field office nearest you. If you write, be sure to spell out exactly what the problem is, and indicate your objectives.

State governments also have commerce departments, some of which offer help for small businesses. Two—New

York and Massachusetts—even have special Women's Programs. These provide free advice (by phone, mail, or personal appointment) on making money from a home product or service; sponsor regular business clinics where experts discuss pricing, marketing, packaging, and what sells and why; and issue a number of helpful publications on home businesses. (State services are limited to the residents of the particular state.)

Another excellent source of advice is the Small Business Administration. You can write to the SBA in Washington, D.C., or take your idea to the nearest of its 73 regional offices (for the location, consult your classified telephone directory or your local Chamber of Commerce). Initially, the SBA will help you determine whether a similar enterprise exists in your locale and, if so, whether there is a need for another one; it will also offer guidance in setting up your business. In addition, the SBA publishes information on almost every conceivable business problem. Its hundreds of pamphlets and booklets (free, or well below a dollar) not only cover subjects such as marketing, loans, insurance, advertising, record-keeping, but even offer advice on how to determine whether you can afford delivery service, or how to use your public library.

Requests for lists of publications issued by the U.S. Department of Commerce and the Small Business Administration should be addressed to the Superintendent of Documents, Government Printing Office, Washington, D.C. 20402.

Aid in marketing home products is offered by cooperative groups known as woman's exchanges. There are 41 of these located throughout the country (for their addresses, see below), and they sell all kinds of handcrafts and food products on consignment. You are paid when your goods are sold, less a commission of from 25 to 50 percent retained by the exchange. Goods left unsold after a reasonable period of time are returned to you. If your product sells well (and you are able to produce it in sufficient quantity), the local exchange may be able to arrange for it to be offered by other exchanges. Woman's exchanges throughout the country are loosely linked in a federation, whose council meets once a year to discuss offering one another's best products.

FEDERATION OF WOMAN'S EXCHANGES

Arizona: Family Arts Exchange, 5807 W. 7th St., Phoenix, Arizona 85014; Woman's Exchange Specialties of Tucson, 4215 N. Campbell, Tucson, Arizona 85717.

Connecticut: Fairfield Woman's Exchange, Inc., 332 Pequot St., Southport, Conn. 06490; Greenwich Exchange for Woman's Work, Inc., 28 Sherwood Place, Greenwich, Conn. 06833; The Woman's Exchange, 993A Farmington Ave., W. Hartford, Conn. 06107; The Stamford Woman's Exchange, 45 Prospect St., Stamford, Conn. 06902; Litchfield Exchange for Woman's Work, Inc., Cobble Court, Litchfield, Conn. 06759.

Florida: Woman's Exchange, 143 St. George St., P.O. Box 501, St. Augustine, Florida 32084.

Georgia: Henry Grady House, Athens Jr. Assembly, Athens, Georgia 30661.

Indiana: The Hen House, Tri-State Woman's Exchange, Inc., 4816 Tippecanoe Dr., Evansville, Ind. 47715.

Maryland: Woman's Industrial Exchange, 333 N. Charles St., Baltimore, Maryland 21201.

Massachusetts: Dedham Woman's Exchange, Inc., 445 Washington St., Dedham, Mass. 02026; The Hay Scales Exchange, Inc., 2 Johnson St., N. Andover Center, Mass. 01845; Old Town Hall Exchange, Lincoln Center, Mass. 01751; Beverly Farms Exchange, 29 West St., Beverly Farms, Mass. 01920.

New Jersey: Newark Exchange for Woman's Work, Inc., 32 Halsey St., Newark, N.J. 07102; Woman's Exchange of Monmouth

County, 32 Church St., Little Silver, N.J. 07739; The Hunterdon Exchange, 155 Main St., Flemington, N.J. 08822; The Depot, 217 First St., Hohokus, N.J. 08074; Community Woman's Exchange, P.O. Box 1022, Plainfield, N.J. 07061.

New York: Woman's Exchange of Brooklyn, Inc., 76 Montague St., Brooklyn, N.Y. 11201; Five Towns Woman's Exchange, 573 Chestnut St., Cedarhurst, L.I., N.Y. 11516; New York Exchange for Woman's Work, Inc., 541 Madison Ave., New York, N.Y. 10022; Scarsdale Woman's Exchange, Inc., 33 Harwood Court, Scarsdale, N.Y. 10583; The Elder Craftsmen's Shop, 850 Lexington Ave., New York, N.Y. 10021; Craftsmen Unlimited, Inc., Bedford Hills, N.Y. 10507.

North Carolina: Sandhills Woman's Exchange, Pinehurst, N.C. 28374; The Country Store, 113 W. Franklin St., Chapel Hill, N.C. 27514; Senc-Crafts, Boys Home Country Store, Lake Waccamaw, N.C. 28450.

Ohio: The Woman's Exchange, 3507 Michigan Ave., Cincinnati, Ohio 45208; The Sassy Cat, 88 N. Main St., Chagrin Falls, Ohio 44022.

Pennsylvania: The Old York Rd. Woman's Exchange, 429 Johnson St., Jenkintown, Pa. 19046; Ladies Depository Assoc. of Philadelphia, 109 S. 18th St., Phila., Pa. 19103; Woman's Industrial Exchange, 541 Penn. Ave., Pittsburgh, Pa. 15222; Woman's Exchange of the Neighborhood League, 185 E. Lancaster Ave., Wayne, Pa., 19087; The Woman's Exchange of West Chester, 10 S. Church St., West Chester, Pa. 19380; The Woman's Exchange of Reading, Inc., 720 Penn. Ave., West Reading, Pa. 19602; The Woman's Exchange of Yardley, 47 West Afton Ave., Yardley, Pa. 19067.

Tennessee: The Woman's Exchange of Memphis, Inc., 88 Racine St., Memphis, Tenn. 38111; Ridgetop Exchange, P.O. Box 282, Ridgetop, Tenn. 37158.

Texas: St. Michael's Woman's Exchange, 5 Highland Park Village, Dallas, Texas 75205.

In some areas there are also other cooperative marketing groups. Check to see whether there is a nonprofit organization in your community.

HOW TO RUN A HOME BUSINESS

You can choose the right business, have everything needed to handle it, find a ready market, and still fall short of success if you are not aware of certain facts of life of the business world. Generally, these break down into seven areas: types of business ownership, rules and regulations, taxes, record keeping, credit, buying, and advertising and publicity. Not all the details under each of these categories will apply to *your* venture, so don't let the length of this chapter scare you. Some of them will, though, so it's best to take a look at everything that is involved.

TYPES OF OWNERSHIP

There are three types of business ownership: individual proprietorship, partnership, and incorporation. Most small businesses are of the first type, at least at the start. But it's well to know the advantages and disadvantages of each, for consideration later if not now.

The pluses of *individual proprietorship* include fewer tax complications, a minimum of government regulation, and flexibility in operation. You sign all contracts in your own

26

name, report all income on your personal tax return. On the other side of the coin, you must take personal responsibility for business debts, you sometimes pay more in taxes than you would if you were liable for a corporate tax, and you may have difficulty in getting loan capital.

A *partnership* may be desirable if you find you need help—financial or otherwise. Partners pool their resources and talents to run the business and share, according to the terms of the partnership, in its profits. Each partner reports on his personal tax form his proportionate share of the income of the partnership. A drawback of this form of organization is the fact that each partner is personally liable for the business debts of both himself *and* his partner (s) .

A *corporation* is a statutory form of organization, a separate entity under law, with ownership represented by shares of stock. The biggest advantage of a corporation is that if your business fails and you can't pay its debts, your personal liability is limited.

Another advantage of a corporation is that it exists as a legal person. It can sell or transfer stock to obtain new capital, sign contracts, bring law suits, and own property. And by electing to report on your personal tax return your share of the corporation's taxable income, you can avoid a corporate tax, if such an arrangement is to your financial benefit.

There are many legal details connected with establishing partnerships and corporations. If you are considering either for your business, you should consult a lawyer.

RULES AND REGULATIONS

Again, these break down into several categories:

1. *Zoning regulations* (see page 11) .

2. *Licenses and permits.* A *license* is a certificate of permission granted by a government agency (usually on the

state level) to conduct a particular business. Only certain businesses (for example, life insurance or real estate) need licenses to operate.

A permit is similar to a license, except that it is granted by a local government. In some communities, a permit is needed to conduct almost any sort of business. In others, the requirement is mainly limited to those who sell food, open a home shop, or sell from door to door.

3. *Safety and sanitation regulations.* These apply to many products and services. Food is particularly subject to controls—local, state, and federal (if you sell across state lines) as embodied in the Food, Drug and Cosmetic Act. The latter regulates the preparation, packaging, and labeling of food products.

Some materials, such as inflammable cloth or synthetic fabrics, also come under special regulations. If you have a business involving sewing, upholstering, weaving, or handcrafts, you may find that some of these regulations affect your operation.

If you plan to hire anyone to help you, you should be familiar with the labor laws, if any, that apply. Write to your state labor department (in your state capital) for information on requirements for unemployment insurance for employees. If you have even one helper, you may be subject to minimum wage regulations. And social security taxes must be paid for *every* full-time employee.

4. *Business names, trade names, and trademarks.* If you use your own name for your business, there's no need to register it. But if you operate under a company (business) name, you must file a certificate with your county clerk and (usually) pay a small fee. Business names should also be recorded (there's no charge) at your post office, so delivery of mail is assured.

Incidentally, it's worth some effort to think up a name

that will intrigue customers into trying your service. Some existing examples: The Children's Atelier (arty play group for preschoolers); Royal Rags, Et Cetera, Tapemeasure (boutiques); Wonderful Weddings (wedding planner); Everything for Everybody (personal services).

Trade names and trademarks are words, symbols, or emblems used to identify a product or service and reserved exclusively, by law, to the owner. The proprietor of a small local business need not be too concerned about protecting its name. But if you deal across state lines, particularly in direct mail, it's wise to register the name with the U.S. Patent Office, Washington, D.C. The fee is $35.

5. *Insurance.* In a few businesses—transporting people for hire, for example (see #44, Kiddie Taxi) —accident liability insurance is required by law. Whether required or not, adequate insurance is vital to the success of a home business. Sit down with your insurance agent and discuss your particular needs. If you produce a product, you may need additional fire and theft coverage. You will probably also need additional public liability coverage, particularly if customers come to your home. This will protect you against lawsuits for injuries sustained on your premises or as a result of your activities. And if your business involves sending employees (baby sitters, for example) into other peoples' homes, you should look into fidelity and surety bonds.

For help in finding out which local, state, and federal regulations may apply to your business, see your town or city clerk.

RECORD KEEPING

According to Dun & Bradstreet, 90 percent of business failures are caused by a lack of managerial skill. Weakness in this area is often the result of failure to keep adequate records. It's impossible to know how to price a product or service properly if you don't know how much it costs you to create it. Adequate records are also needed for tax purposes, for establishing bank credit, and to keep you aware of how well your business is doing.

To start a record system, you must figure out your net worth. The first step is to list what you own (in terms of your business). If you intend to open a mending and alterations service, for example, this might be limited to a sewing machine, some supplies, and $50 you have saved from household money. Next you list what you owe—perhaps a balance on the sewing machine, a carpenter's bill for installing shelves, and a skirt-marking platform. The difference between the two is your equity in the business.

As you actually start to operate, you will need to keep accurate records in order to prepare periodic profit-and-loss statements. This is simply a matter of keeping track of what you spend as against what you take in. For what will seem an unconscionably long time, all your entries will be in the "Loss" column. Include, in your business records, *all* relevant costs—equipment, supplies, advertising, insurance, interest on a bank loan, if any, *and* a proportionate share (for record-keeping pusposes only) of the light, heat, telephone, and mortgage or rent bills. The latter is overhead, and unless you take it into account from the first, you won't be able to build up a reserve that may later enable you to expand your business, if you choose. (You also need these records to claim certain deductions on your income tax—see page 32.)

There are two main ways of keeping records for profit and loss (or P and L) statements. In the *cash* system, commonly used by small, one-person operations, no entries are made for income until cash is actually received; no entries for expenses until bills are actually paid. The *accrual* system

shows expenses incurred and income earned for a given
period, even though you haven't yet paid your creditors and
your customers haven't paid *you*. The cash system is a bit
simpler, the accrual system more accurate (because all income and expenses are recorded in the year in which they
occur). Both are acceptable as a basis for figuring your
income tax returns—the important thing is to make sure you
keep accurate, detailed records.

You can get forms for record-keeping at any stationery
store. If you don't know how to use them, or if the record-
keeping system you set up for yourself doesn't work, pay an
accountant or bookkeeping service a one-time fee to set you
on the right track. Later, if your business prospers, it will be
worth your while to have an expert take over all your bookkeeping for you. In the meantime, to help keep things
straight, open a separate bank account for your business
transactions, keep personal and business income strictly
segregated, and pay for all business purchases by check.

TAXES

Many owners of small businesses do not pay federal business taxes (see "Types of Ownership," page 26). Instead,
they report all business income on their personal tax forms.
Those who work from their homes are eligible for certain
deductions not available to others, and these can add up to a
sizable tax break. The deductions are not automatic, however; you have to qualify for them. There are three criteria
to meet: You must in fact work at or from home; you must
derive profits from your efforts (otherwise the Internal
Revenue Service regards them as a hobby); and you must
be able to identify a specific part of your home or apartment
as your "office" or "workshop."

Say, for example, that you live in a six-room house or

apartment and use a spare bedroom as your office. In this case you might be allowed to deduct one-sixth of all your home maintenance expenses. If you don't have an extra room but must do your work in a corner of the room where you also sleep, the one-sixth allowance would have to be multiplied by the percentage of the time the room is used for your work.

Home maintenance expenses, for deductible purposes, include real estate taxes and mortgage interest (both of which are deductible, in any case, if expenses are itemized), plus depreciation if you own a home, rent if you live in an apartment. Also included are light, heat, insurance, repairs, and domestic help; all these expenses are prorated according to the amount of space your business activities pre-empt. Telephone charges are also deductible on a use-for-business ratio. (If you have a separate telephone line used solely for your work, the total bill can be deducted.)

Another area of deductions not to be overlooked is connected with the equipment you purchase for your business. On major items, such as a typewriter, filing cabinet, desk, you may deduct a depreciation charge. Leased or rented equipment, if used strictly for business, is also deductible.

An additional deduction to investigate, if your at-home work proves to have a long-term future, is that allowed by the Keogh Plan—a retirement plan for the self-employed that permits you to set aside up to 10 percent (or a maximum of $2500) of your earned income for retirement. You can't just put the money in a bank, though; it must be invested under a plan approved by the Internal Revenue Service, and you can't touch it until you reach the age of 59 years and six months. The earnings on the investment are nontaxable income in the year earned; you pay tax only when you receive the accumulated fund.

In addition to federal income tax, you must pay a self-employment tax if the income from your business amounts to $400 or more a year. This tax provides funds for Social Security and Medicare benefits for you.

If you hire someone to help you, you must pay a Social Security tax for the employee (and deduct his portion of the tax, plus withholding his income tax, from his pay).

In states with personal income taxes, the procedures for reporting business income are usually similar to those required by the IRS. In other states, special business taxes are levied. Sales taxes—state and/or local—may also apply to your business; if so, it is up to you to collect them, keep a record of the amounts, and then turn the money over to the proper agency at stated periods.

As you can see, taxes can be a complicated matter. Before you launch your business, make sure you know exactly what will be required of you in this area. For information on federal taxes, consult the nearest Internal Revenue office. Your state tax commission will give you information on state taxes; for local taxes, see your local tax administrator.

CREDIT

For some of the jobs in this book, you'll need money to get started. Not a lot, but some. It's a good idea to supply as much of it as possible from your own savings. Still, you don't want to spend what you have put away for a rainy day. If you need more money than you can comfortably risk, you may want to apply for credit. There are several ways to do so.

Trade credit. Suppliers quite often extend credit to their customers. Suppose, for example, you want to open a wig shop in your family room. If a wig wholesaler believes you're reliable (and that can be a big "if" when you're just starting out), he might agree to supply you with stock and wait for his money—for a consideration, of course. It works like this: Cash discounts are quoted if a bill is paid within 10, 30 or 60 days. For example, a term of sale quoted as "2–10; net, 30 days" means that a cash discount of 2 percent will be granted if the bill is paid within 10 days. If not paid in 10 days, the entire amount is due in 30 days. If you do not take advantage of the cash discount, you are paying 2 percent to use money for 20 days, or 36 percent per year—a very high interest rate.

Bank loans. If you need only a few hundred dollars to tide you over the first few months until customers start paying their bills, you may want to apply to a bank for a short-term personal loan, repayable within a year. Usually no collateral is necessary; current interest rates range from around 10 to 13 percent annually.

For major expenditures, most commercial banks offer special Small Business Loans, with monthly repayment terms ranging from 12 to 60 months and a current annual interest rate of about 11 percent. The catch is that it's hard for someone embarking on a business venture for the first time to convince a bank to part with the money. The bank is interested in your ability to run a business and your ability to repay the loan. Factors taken into consideration will be previous business experience, your reputation in the community, your personal credit rating, the business you want to go into, and the collateral, if any (property, life insurance, stocks and bonds, etc.), you can put up.

Even if you feel your chances of getting a loan initially are slight, visit your bank's loan officer, explain your plans and needs, and ask for his advice. If you don't qualify right now for one of the long-term business loans, he may be able to tell you how you can qualify once your business gets under way.

Still another source of credit is the Small Business Administration, which makes loans for equipment, materials, or working capital. Before it grants a loan, the SBA will want you to show that you have put up some capital of your own and that you have tried to obtain financial assistance from other sources. For specific rules currently in force, and current interest rates, consult your local SBA office.

BUYING

All products and some services require the purchase of materials and equipment; consequently, smart buying is an important factor in the success of a home business. That should be no problem for a homemaker. The secret is comparison shopping. Anyone who is accustomed to wheeling a shopping cart down supermarket aisles qualifies as an expert.

In shopping for a business, however, there are a few additional factors to consider. Should you aim at the savings possible in quantity buying of materials, or stick with small lots? In the case of equipment, should you buy or rent?

Wholesale vs. retail buying. Buying in quantity entitles you to discounts; the bigger the order, the bigger the discount. Sometimes these can add up to considerable savings. Nevertheless, quantity buying is not always the most economical method for a small business. You can tie up so much of your money in supplies that you don't have enough left for day-to-day expenses. Second, some materials deteriorate if kept too long. Third, your customers' tastes may change, leaving you with a big inventory for which you have no market.

Quantity buying *can* be used successfully if you have a good idea of your market and can dispose of the materials you buy in a reasonable length of time.

Buying equipment secondhand. When it comes to equipment, it's often possible to make big savings by scouting thrift, Salvation Army, Goodwill Industries, and other second-hand stores. Some manufacturers also sell reconditioned equipment and fixtures.

Renting or leasing equipment. In the long run, renting or leasing equipment can be expensive. However, when you are starting out, it has two advantages: It gives you a chance to try out the equipment before you buy (and most suppliers will apply rental fees against purchase), and it cuts down the initial investment needed. Further, as mentioned on page 32, rental and leasing fees are deductible from your income tax.

To locate supply sources, look in the classified telephone directory of your community or the nearest big city; also consult trade directories and trade journals in the field you want to enter. In some communities the Chamber of Commerce or local government publishes a directory of manufacturers in the area. Two directories of national supply sources, available in many public libraries, are *Thomas' Register of American Manufactures* and *MacRae's Blue Book*.

ADVERTISING AND PUBLICITY

Shrewd promotion, via paid advertising and free publicity, can mean the difference between life and death for any small business. To assure the good health of yours, you should plot an effective program from the very beginning. Your promotion budget needn't be large—indeed, if you take advantage cf all the free or nearly free opportunities available, it can be modest. But your campaign must be carefully thought out.

The first step is to decide on the image you want to project. Then concentrate on creating it through all the means at your disposal. Here are profiles of two different businesses whose owners used a specific image to build a successful operation.

Image. An exclusive, high-quality service for discriminating patrons.

Circumstances. Jane B. runs her bouquet-of-the-week service like a book- or fruit-of-the-month club. Each week she delivers a different and distinctive bouquet to a list of subscribers—middle- and upper-middle-income—home owners, high-rise apartment dwellers, and a few professional and business people. Her business is popular because (a) she offers the convenience of regular service and (b) her bouquets are unusually handsome. Jane's job grew out of her hobby of growing and arranging flowers. When her idea was still in the planning stage, she took a part-time job with a local florist for a few months to learn something about the business.

The campaign. First came the name: she called herself The Flower Lady, the quaintness of this sobriquet being deliberately designed to appeal to her conservative, solid-citizen audience. Her paid advertising consisted of sending a personally typed letter, with a well-printed brochure, to a mailing list of a thousand likely prospects; she also took a listing in the classified telephone directory. To solicit new subscribers, she delivers free bouquets to a few prospects each week. Around Christmas time, she promotes her service to businessmen as a unique gift to clients.

Since Jane's business was the first such service in her area, the local newspaper ran a feature story about her (relying heavily on material Jane herself supplied). This gave a helpful initial boost to her business, which has since become firmly established.

Image. Something special for the city child.

Circumstances. Abby C. throws birthday parties for kids. She organizes and supervises, does as much or as little as the parents wish. Her background: four years of volunteer teacher's aide experience and two children of her own. Abby lives in a big city in a neighborhood which is mainly middle class, some families struggling to exit for the suburbs as soon as possible, others to stay where they are. In nearly all cases, her young clients live in apartments.

The campaign. Abby's company name is fairly tame, but it gets the message across: Kiddie Parties, Inc. While researching the idea, she talked to principals and teachers in the public and private schools in her area, to play-group directors, and to mothers. This preliminary digging to see if a market for her idea existed paid off in another way: she got word-of-mouth advertising before she even started.

Once under way, she took paid advertising in a local newspaper or "shopper" (a weekly paper distributed free), and in a small weekly magazine. In addition, she got permission to post her gaily designed business card on bulletin boards in schools, libraries, supermarkets, and laundromats throughout the neighborhood. Though her initial attempt to get free publicity for her service in a daily newspaper failed, the women's page editor kept her release on file and eventually used it in a roundup feature of services for children. How much this helped, Abby doesn't know, but after three years, her business is well known to local residents.

Whatever image you decide upon, you might keep in mind a few tips for getting and keeping customers:

1. Local or neighborhood newspapers are better bets than a big-city paper. Classified ads are good (and relatively cheap), but you should use them regularly or not at all. Display ads cost more, but they're worth it to announce your opening. (See page 21.)

2. Don't overlook ads in specialized publications: employee magazines, what's-going-on-in-town giveaways or "shoppers," club newsletters, local theater programs.

3. A listing in the classified telephone directory gives your business an image of permanence and reliability.

4. Mail announcements (mimeographed or typed) to appropriate community organizations who might be interested in hearing of your business. For example: singles clubs, PTA's, Elks, dog clubs, church groups.

5. Post your flyers or business cards on bulletin boards in supermarkets, libraries, laundromats, etc. (Check first whether the owner's permission is required.) Some local merchants may also allow you to display posters in their windows.

6. Notify related businesses that may be in a position to recommend you. A caterer, for example, should make her service known to party planners, wedding consultants, ministers, bakeries, small hotels, and party equipment rental firms.

7. If the circumstances indicate it, don't be timid about calling or visiting prospective clients and making an in-person pitch.

8. Send a publicity release to local papers. The release should be typed, double spaced; be written in a crisp, factual style; and include your name, a description of your business, location, opening data, unique feature, and your telephone number. Address the news release to the managing editor.

9. Investigate local radio and television stations with interview programs. If your business is a little off-beat, they may be interested in having you as a guest. Find out the name of the show's director and write a note about yourself.

10. If a prospective client's first impression of you will be from a letter or business card, it's worthwhile to spend a little extra on stationery.

11. Another wise investment is a separate telephone line for your business, *especially* if customers normally get in touch with you by phone. Otherwise, your wire may be tied up with personal calls when a customer is trying to reach you. Also, a separate line enables you to answer in a professional manner by stating your company name or the telephone number.

12. For many of the jobs in this book, an answering service can be extremely valuable. Not only will the service pick up your calls when you're away, but it can also answer when you *are* home but busy. Average cost is $15 to $20 a month.

For some other advertising costs, see page 21.

HOW TO EXPAND INTO MAIL ORDER

If you choose to build a business around a product, you may find, to your delight, that it has potentials for expansion into mail order. Not right away, of course. You must get your business established first, make sure your product has appeal, and develop a means of producing it in *real* quantity before you can hope to tap the wider market available to you through the mails. Many women won't want to bother to take that next step. This chapter is for those who will—those who have a product such as a mailable food or handcraft item that is a natural for mail order, and who possess the energy and ambition to take on the extra work involved.

Mail order can also be a business all by itself. Instead, that is, of using it to sell products you *make,* you can *buy* items from wholesale manufacturers for the express purpose of offering them through the mail. Both kinds of operations are run essentially the same way.

To make a success of mail order, you must be aware of the many factors involved. The following expert advice is adapted, with the kind permission of the magazine, from a booklet developed by *House Beautiful*, a sister publication of *Good Housekeeping*. (For many years the Window Shopping section of *House Beautiful* has been a major, specialized advertising source for both big and little mail-order companies.)

HOW MUCH MONEY DOES IT TAKE TO START?

If you are interested in starting a direct-mail business, the first question you are likely to ask is: "What's the very least amount of money I need to start?" While there are many successful mail-order businesses today that started on as little as $600, that is the bare minimum and will leave you nervously undercapitalized without any margin for error. A good, round, firm minimum figure would be $2,000. Let's see where the dollars would go.

Merchandise. To begin a mail-order business you must have an *item*. If it is handmade, you must have an inventory of at least three dozen before you place an ad. If you are buying from a wholesaler, the same figure will be your minimum order, with the assurance from your supplier that he can back you up quickly with additional quantity. Let's assume that the item you select, either for making or buying, retails for $7.50. Your cost, either way, would probably be around $3.75 per item. Your initial order would therefore cost you $135.

Advertising. In the beginning, the road to a mail-order business is through advertising in the mail-order section of a national magazine, one that has a proven readership of lively mail-order customers. Several size ads are available to you. Recommended for the beginner is the smallest unit of space, usually one-twelfth page. Such an ad may cost you about $450.

Incidentals. You're not in the mail-order business unless you are equipped to send your items to customers through the U.S. mails. This means wrapping paper, cartons, boxes, sticky tape, mailing labels, stationery, postage, etc. These supplies, including postage, may come to another $300. If you decide to operate under a name other than your own, there may be a small fee for registering it.

So far you have spent under $1,000. But you don't have to be a CPA to figure out that when you have sold every one of your three dozen items of merchandise at $7.50 each, your total income will be only $270. Therefore, you will have to take that money and use it to make or buy six dozen more items at $45 a dozen. When you've sold these at $7.50 each retail, you will have taken in an additional $540—or, with your initial sales of $270, a total of $810. Obviously, you're going to have to buy more supplies or merchandise at cost, sell at retail, and so on until you get in the black.

This is a good place to list a few basic rules for anyone interested in starting a mail-order business.

Rule Number One: Don't start a mail-order business unless you can afford to lose your initial investment. Not every ad will pay its own way. Some will be dismal flops, but there is always the thrilling possibility that "this time you'll hit the jackpot." You have to be a gambler to start a mail-order business on a shoestring because there is always the possibility that your ad won't sell enough merchandise to bail you out.

Once you have taken the first giant step, as outlined above, you will want to work yourself up to being a twelve-time advertiser as quickly as possible. Some months you will just break even; some months you will lose money; and some months you will strike it rich. Remember that you are engaged in the arduous job of building a business, and you don't do it in just a few months.

Rule Number Two: Decide on what kind of business you want—and stick with it. As your mail-order business grows, so do the problems, the competition, and the financial rewards. But the character of your business should remain the same in spite of growth. If you start out as a small company offering a *quality* item or items by mail, tomorrow you should be a much larger company, still offering *quality* items by mail. The temptation to increase your customer list dramatically by advertising inexpensive items that pull hundreds of orders is very great. Indeed, it is good business to do this occasionally, provided the item in question is compatible with the taste level of your normal merchandise.

For example, there are items that attract the so-called carriage trade whether the price is $1 or $100. But the chances are that the $1 items will bring in at least 100 times as many of these customers as the $100 item. Your net profit will be less, because of the cost of servicing so many orders; but the additional customer names on your mailing list, if they are the right kind of customers, are worth the profit difference. Later, we'll talk about why and how your mailing list is so important.

Rule Number Three: Have a solid business reason for everything you do. Unfortunately, many mail-order companies who got off to a good start have fallen by the wayside in their unsound compulsion to get big too fast. Move forward consistently, but let every move be deliberate.

Most of today's big mail-order operators claim that volume is essential to a successful operation—that you have to be big to make it; and by "big" they usually mean a mailing list in the six-figure bracket. We agree with them—if your goal is big business. But if you are content to build a business of your own with a potential of netting you an income in the neighborhood of ten thousand dollars, it need not be predicated on the big mail-order operator's concept of volume.

Rule Number Four: Get yourself an item education. First, and perhaps obviously, give yourself a thorough mail-order-item education by studying very carefully the mail-order sections of magazines. Send for the catalogs from companies whose offerings appeal to you. Make a project of this, and pursue it with zeal. Notice prices, headlines, copy angles, type faces, photography. Read the mail-order columns in magazines and the catalogs with critical awareness. Send away for several items from different firms. Make note of how soon you receive your order; how it is packed; if the company encloses a catalog in your package in order to persuade you to order additional things from them. If, for any reason, there should be a delay in shipping your order, see if you are promptly and courteously advised of this. Should you be dissatisfied with the merchandise and return it for a refund, pay attention to how this aspect of the mail-order business is handled by an experienced company. And note, especially, how your single mail order to a company will assure you of receiving a copy of every catalog they mail during the year. You may have ordered one $2.95 item from the XYZ Company, but if their catalog items appeal to you, before the year is over, you may order 20 times this amount. And all because a single item caught your eye in a magazine shopping column.

When you have educated yourself in this way, you may want to do additional groundwork to the extent of writing to a mail-order firm located near you, and ask if it would be in accordance with their policy for you to pay them a visit in order to seek advice. You may get turned down politely but firmly on this one. On the other hand, some companies remember their own beginnings and are willing to pass on words of wisdom to newcomers. Established mail-order operators realize that this is a field that attracts hundreds of new ventures every year, and the more qualified the newcomer is the better it is for the industry in general. It is the fly-by-night operator that is anathema to the mail-order business, because one irresponsible company can do irreparable harm to all.

After you have done this, and if your enthusiasm has not flagged, your next step might be to set up an appointment with a representative of one of the magazines that features a mail-order section. In most cases you will find them helpful, knowledgeable, and understanding. Some magazines list their representatives in the Table of Contents. Here you will find the names and addresses for the magazine's offices in various cities around the country.

At this point you may be wondering why, since the procedures and, often, even the profits are the same, anyone would bother to produce items for mail-order selling when she could more easily buy them from wholesalers. The reason has to do with the big secret of mail-order success: item selection. Some items sell like hot-cakes; others fall on their faces, and nobody is sure of the reason why. When you buy items for resale, you have no experience in whether they will sell or not; moreover, you are in competition with other mail-order companies for the same merchandise. With a product of your own that has previously proved its appeal, and that is both handmade and unique, you will have a firmer base to build upon.

HOW TO FIND ITEMS

But suppose you *do* want to buy items to sell through the mail, either on their own or to supplement handmade products. Where do you find them? Obviously, the first place to start your search is in the wholesale gift market of a big city. New York, for example, has its "225 Fifth Avenue" building, a gift center made up of hundreds of manufacturers' representatives offering gift items at wholesale to qualified retailers and mail-order buyers. Other cities, such as Chicago, Atlanta, Dallas, Los Angeles, have similar centers. In addition, there are various gift shows scheduled in major cities across the country at specific times. A letter of inquiry to the magazine *The Gift and Decorative Accessories Buyer*, 212 Fifth Avenue, New York, N.Y. 10010, will get you the Gift Show schedule. (Incidentally, this magazine is a good one to subscribe to, It reports on trends as well as new items of interest to the gift trade, tells you where to find them, and the wholesale price.)

Don't place an order on your first go-around. Item-hunting in the wholesale gift centers can be a bewildering experience. You'll see dozens of things that, at first look, will seem to be "it." Carry a notebook with you and write down all the pertinent facts about merchandise that appeals to you. But sleep on it. And when you find something worthy of consideration, be sure to tell the supplier where you plan to feature it. It may be that one of the giant operators already has it scheduled for the magazine in which you are planning to advertise. Look for items that take advantage of basic facts of life today. For example:

• We are nearing the crest of a bridal wave that is scheduled to grow bigger each year. More than three million potential customers of yours will be getting married this year. So give a long, hard look at gifts for engagements, showers, weddings; at presents for bridesmaids and ushers.

• Although the birth rate is slowly dropping, the baby market is still booming. Four million new babies will be born this year. So keep your eye peeled for new and different ways to welcome the crib crowd.

• Increased leisure may be the most influential factor in the way of life of all of us. So look carefully into hobby items, items for automobiles, for gourmet cooking, for gardening, for travel, for self-improvement, for sports. The mail-order industry offers almost every gadget imaginable, for instance, to the golfer. But perhaps you will come across something with exciting potential that is more expensive than the items generally available—a personalized leather album, maybe, with pages for mounting a golfer's score cards; or a golf glove with a new fillip to it; or a putter with a monogrammed sterling silver head. Will they sell? Your guess is as good as ours. As a wise old woman used to say, "Nothin' beats a failure but a try."

Be quick to recognize a trend. With more and more people giving up smoking, for instance, isn't it possible that the women among them might be taking up knitting or needlework to keep busy? Whatever the reason, the sale of products in this field is steadily increasing.

And experts tell us that we can look forward to the return of "The Elegant Look" in home furnishings. Maybe a do-it-yourself kit of wall-to-wall carpeting for the bathroom, even a bathroom chandelier, would rack up an interesting sales performance.

Think of a need and try to fill it. Perhaps a "Filter Buttler" is needed for cigarette butts on summer lawns. (A decorative or amusing bucket filled with sand for patios and gardens.) Or how about a slicked-up version of a prong on the end of a broom handle for picking up butts without bending?

Then there is the almost universal need for extra storage space—for bedding, linens, silver, canned goods, medicine-cabinet overflow, out-of-season clothing, Christmas tree ornaments, household records. Items that fill these needs have sold well, but the need is still there.

And what about the problem of getting white kid gloves cleaned? If you can find a cleaner who will take them, it takes forever and is expensive. Wouldn't a White Kid Glove Cleaning Kit fill a need?

The point is: develop the habit of thinking "items"—either to buy or to make.

Don't be afraid to play hunches. If you have a strong feeling, for instance, that the cut-steel or rhinestone shoe buckles of your grandmother's day are due for a return to fashion, try to gather a collection of old ones, and then sell them by mail. One way to do this might be to buy a small ad in such a publication as *The Antique Trader,* Box 327, Kewanee, Illinois. A display ad costs $4 per column inch; if you use the space to indicate your interest in old shoe buckles, or whatever, the response may surprise you.

Or, if from the same era, your instinct tells you that the *mouche,* or beauty mark, is ready for a revival, make or find a source and promote it.

Or maybe you have a "thing" about San Francisco sour dough bread, can't find it in your area, and have a hunch that lots of people would buy a loaf a week, or every two weeks, if such a service were offered by mail. If you don't know how to make it yourself you might, then, explore the possibility of working something out with a San Francisco baker.

There is really nothing new under the sun, and a new twist for an old item is what it is all about. Do you remember the Surprise Balls of several years ago? They were available from dozens of firms. They consisted of yards and yards of crepe paper wound into a ball and interspersed throughout with miniature toys and favors. As the child unwound it, the surprises were revealed one by one. They sold like hot cakes. We have a hunch that a Surprise Ball for Men would make a good Christmas item.

Watch your timing. February and September are the traditional months to promote housewares in department stores. If you carry this type of merchandise, profit from their experience and follow their lead.

December is, of course, one of the primary gift-giving

months. And don't forget special occasions, such as Valentine's Day, graduations, Bar Mitzvahs, Mother's and Father's Day.

January and August issues, considered by many general advertisers to be slow, are surprisingly productive for mail order.

And remember that Lent is a quiet time when people are filled with good intentions and inclined to stay at home. It might be a good time to offer a workshop project.

Personalize wherever possible. At this point, we would like to remind you of the power of personalization in mail-order items. If you are able to offer an item stamped, or hand-painted, or engraved, or embroidered, or printed with a name or monogram, your sales will increase. Some time ago a friend of ours received from a couple who have a farm, a gift carton of apples, each wrapped in a sheet of tissue-like paper that was imprinted "picked especially for Nancy Miller." What a mail-order item that could be! The same idea could be used for many other items—e.g. a fruit cake "Baked especially for _____," or a sampler "Especially embroidered for _____," and so on.

Search out off-beat markets. We've told you about the obvious hunting grounds for mail-order items. The disadvantage is that many other mail-order people are looking there, too, so your chances of finding reasonably exclusive items are limited. You must, of course, cover the major gift centers. But also conduct your search in markets that are not highly trafficked by mail-order people. Furniture is a good example. In the last year or so, a trend has begun to develop for boutique furniture—the occasional piece with high impulse-buying appeal. It might be a schoolmaster's desk or an eighteenth-century dog bed or a tea cart or a sewing table. The mail-order potential is interesting and the prices are high enough so big volume sales are not necessary.

Another off-beat area to investigate would be a local

woodworking shop, kiln, or printing shop. Here, or course, you yourself would have to come up with the idea for the item and have it made for you.

Lest there be any misunderstanding, let us repeat: starting a mail-order business, even a relatively small one, is hard work. It is hazardous. There is no magic formula to guarantee success. When you pick a "hot item" the mail pours in and the checks flutter out of all those envelopes. Ah! then the sun is shining and life is sweet; your bank account is healthy, and you're a genius. But when you pick a "dud" (and you will!), the lilting tune becomes a dirge. The unwanted items gather dust in your basement; the supplier's bill must still be paid; your bank account deflates like a pricked balloon; and nostalgia sets in for the good old days when you were "just a housewife!"

HOW TO BUILD A MAILING LIST

Since we are trying to help you *start* a mail-order business, we will not dwell on the subjects of mailing lists and catalogs, other than to tell you that herein lies the heartbeat of a mail-order business. You *start* by making or finding an item and placing an ad. Whether you make money, break even, or lose money on it is secondary to the primary purpose of that ad—which is to get names and build a mailing list. The quality of the names you get determines the quality of business you have. This is why it is so important to decide what kind of business you want to establish and then stick to your course. If you start out offering items that appeal to people of taste and higher incomes, your mailing list will be a profile of such a market. Later, when you have accumulated enough names to make it economically feasible to produce a catalog and mail it to this list, the chances are that your mailing list will respond commensurately with its potential only if the merchandise featured in your catalog is similar in character to that featured in your magazine advertising.

WHEN TO PRODUCE A CATALOG

Now, let's assume that you've been in business for a year, have advertised consistently, and have built a customer list of 3,000 names. That is not enough to justify producing a catalog. You should have a minimum of 10,000 to 12,000. In order to get those additional names, you can do one of two things. You can rent them from a list broker at an approximate cost of $20 per thousand. Or you can very carefully select a few other mail-order companies whose mail-order appeal is similar to your own but whose merchandise is not highly competitive, and suggest that you swap names. Let us say you want an additional 9,000 names to add to your own 3,000. Therefore, you would have to swap with three different companies before you would have a total of 12,000. For beginners, we are inclined to favor the second method.

Let us assume that you produce 12,000 Christmas catalogs at a cost of $.15 a catalog in the mail. This figure includes the manufacture of the catalog and the cost of mailing. It does not include the cost of merchandise. Now you are out of pocket $1,800.

What can you expect in returns? If you are *very* smart and *very* lucky, it is possible to realize a 10 percent return from your own mailing list. In other words, 300 of your 3,000 customers could send you an order from your catalog. A more realistic expectation would be 6 percent, or 180 orders. The average order from this group could be $7. This adds up to $2,100 on a 10 percent return, or $1,260 on a 6 percent return. If you are even smarter and luckier with your "swap" list of 9,000 names, it is possible to realize a 5 percent return. This means that 450 customers could send you an order. A more realistic expectation whold be 3 percent or 270 orders. From this group, the order might average $5, bringing you in $2,250 on a 5 percent return, or $1,350 on a 3 percent return. Gross returns from your total mailing would be either $4,350 or $2,610.

From this, deduct $1,800 for the cost of the catalog; deduct about 50 percent of your gross returns for the cost of supplies or merchandise; another $500 to $600 for incidentals and overhead, and you wind up losing anywhere from $125 to $1,000. But you have taken the second giant step toward establishing yourself as a mail-order operator. You have added names to your precious mailing list; you have added immeasurably to your mail-order know-how; and the cost, if any, has been negligible. Your second catalog will probably show a small profit.

You may want to take out a loan to finance your catalog. Most people do. This is sound business practice, provided your new mail-order company has made progress during its first year and continues to show promise. But be sure to include your interest payments in your cost accounting.

When to mail. Like most sound solutions to mail-order problems, this question should be resolved by testing. But when you have only 12,000 names, that may not be practical. One ingenious answer that a mail-order operator decided upon when he was a beginner has always delighted us. He waits until he receives his Sears, Roebuck Christmas catalog, and then immediately gets his own in the mail. He figures that he can do much worse than follow the lead of the giant of all mail-order companies.

A WORD ABOUT SERVICE

Always remember that mail order is primarily a service business, so build your reputation on the quality of your service. If your ads promise "satisfaction guaranteed" or "money back if not satisfied," dedicate yourself to keeping that promise. Answer complaints at once. Make refunds even faster. If you are capable of shipping orders within 24 hours of receiving them, let all your advertising carry a small line so stating. Such a promise will increase your returns. But if you don't make good, you will have done yourself and the entire industry a disservice. In the mail-order business, customers take you on faith. Be sure you keep faith with them.

HOW TO PREPARE A MAGAZINE AD

Let's limit this discussion to the advertising unit of space most popular with mail-order firms—a one-twelfth page.

Let us also state unequivocally that the best way to prepare and place an ad is to put yourself in the knowledgeable hands of a good mail-order advertising agency. Quite apart from putting together a professional ad for you, he can give you priceless guidance. Any representative of the magazine you plan to advertise in will be glad to give you the names of several qualified agents.

However, if for one reason or another, it is not possible for you to work through an agency, you may prepare your ad yourself and place it directly with the magazine. The publication would prefer receiving from you a copper half-tone engraving, usually referred to as a "cut" (an engraving made from the glossy photograph of your item), together with the copy (your description of the item) set in type. But since many small companies cannot do this, the magazine will usually have a halftone engraving made for you from your photograph (the cost is approximately $15), and will have your copy set in type at no charge.

Be sure the photograph you supply is a good clear one. Sometimes the supplier from whom you bought the item will have a glossy print which he will give you. But if he doesn't have one, or if it's not as good as it could be, have your own photograph made. A word of warning: In the long run, it is bad mail-order procedure to have a photograph look better than the item itself. Customers will be disappointed, and disappointed customers won't order from you again. Repeat business is the lifeline of mail order.

You will also have to supply copy. Copy for a mail-order ad consists of three basic elements.

1. *Headline:* This is the most important element. David Ogilvy, in *Confessions of an Advertising Man,* says that five times as many people read it as read the body copy. Its function is to catch the eye of the prospect. If the name of the item has a strong selling name such as "Scrap Trap" or "Decorator Burlap" or "Fortune Telling Cards," use it. If the nature of the item warrants it, let your headline make a strong promise— "At sixty miles an hour, the loudest noise in the new Rolls Royce comes from the electric clock," or "Lose 10 pounds in 2 weeks without feeling hungry." Or if the item has appeal to a special group, flag them down with a headline that is right to the point—"Amazing Relief for Foot Sufferers" or "What Every Bride Should Know."

2. *Body Copy*: Mail-order copy is a very special writing technique. Its purpose is not to win prizes or prove that you are an English major. It has only one reason for being—to sell merchandise. So make every word count. Give the prospect every fact that will push her into buying. Don't be obscure or cute or tricky. This is not the place for fancy, high-flown writing. In writing body copy, pick out an ad of the size you intend to run and count the number of "characters," or letters (also include numbers and spaces) in each line. Then limit your copy to this area for each line. Price will take up another line. This should be easily seen (perhaps set in bold-face type), and should state whether the price is post-paid, whether shipping charges are collect, or

whether the customer should add a specific amount for postage and handling. If you want to include a promise, such as "money back if not satisfied" or "orders shipped within 24 hours," this can be set in italics, either under the price or under your name and address.

3. *Your name and address:* This can be set in any standard type face, or you can have a signature cut made. This is an engraving made from artwork of your hand-lettered name. Some companies include a small illustration in their signature cut. "The Ladybug Shop" might feature a ladybug; "The Carousel" might feature a merry-go-round horse. Keying your ad is axiomatic in mail order. It enables you to tell instantly, when orders are received, how various media are pulling for you. As a beginner, this may seem unnecessary, as you will probably be able to afford only one magazine. But you might as well start with keying because it will be essential as you grow. The simplest system is to make your key a part of your address. Let's say your ad is to run in the September issue of *House Beautiful.* Then your keyed address might be: 18 Elm Street, Dept. HB9, Anytown, U.S.A.

Layout is a technical term for something very simple. A layout is nothing more than a precise plan of what your ad should look like. So if your ad is to be one-twelfth page, draw the outline of the space on a sheet of paper. Trace it accurately from a similar ad in the magazine you plan to advertise in. It can be a vertical shape or a horizontal shape. Allocate approximately half of it for your photograph, and so designate this area with a ruled line. The balance of the space is for copy.

Roughly pencil in your headline; and indicate the body copy by penciled lines. Ditto for your name and address. That's all there is to it!

WHERE TO GET MORE INFORMATION

WOMEN AT WORK

Born Female, Caroline Bird. David McKay Co., Inc., New York, N.Y., 1968. Also paperback.

The Feminine Mystique, Betty Friedan. W. W. Norton & Co., Inc., New York, N.Y., 1963. Also paperback.

Help Wanted: Female, Alice Gore King. Charles Scribner's Sons, New York, N.Y., 1968. Also paperback.

WORKING AT HOME

Checklist for Going into Business (Small Marketers Aids #71), Small Business Administration. Superintendent of Documents, U.S. Government Printing Office, Washington, D.C. 20402. Free booklet.

The Home Office Guide, Leon Henry, Jr. Arco Publishing Co., Inc., New York, N.Y., 1968.

Homework Schemes, National Better Business Bureau, Inc. 230 Park Ave., New York, N.Y. 10017. Free booklet.

How to Run a Small Business, Marketing Research Association. Gallup & Robinson, Inc., Research Park, Princeton, N.J. 08540.

How to Start a Moneymaking Business at Home, Laura Robertson. Frederick Fell, Inc., New York, N.Y., 1969.

The Moonlighter's Manual, Jerry LeBlanc. Nash Publishing Corp., Los Angeles, Calif., 1969.

A Woman's Guide to Earning a Good Living, Elmer Winter. Simon & Schuster, Inc., New York, N.Y., 1961.

RESEARCHING YOUR MARKET

Basic Library Reference Sources (Small Business Bibliography #18), Small Business Administration. Superintendent of Documents, U.S. Government Printing Office, Washington, D.C. 20402. Free booklet.

Discover and Use Your Public Library (Management Aid #202), Small Business Administration, Superintendent of Documents, U.S. Government Printing Office, Washington, D.C. 20402. Free booklet.

Marketing Research Procedures (Small Business Bibliography #9), Small Business Administration. Superintendent of Documents, U.S. Government Printing Office, Washington, D.C. 20402. Free booklet.

The Research Handbook: A Guide to Reference Sources, Adrian A. Paradis. Funk & Wagnalls Co., Inc., New York, N.Y., 1966.

The Small Business Administration, Addison W. Parris. Frederick A. Praeger, Inc., New York, N.Y., 1968.

Small Business Administration. What It Is. What It Does., Small Business Administration. Superintendent of Documents, U.S. Government Printing Office, Washington, D.C. 20402. Free booklet.

Using Census Data in Small Plant Marketing (Management Aid #187), Small Business Administration. Superintendent of Documents, U.S. Government Printing Office, Washington, D.C. 20402. Free booklet.

WHAT FORM OF OWNERSHIP?

Choosing a Legal Structure for Your Firm (Management Aid #80), Small Business Administration. Superintendent of Documents, U.S. Government Printing Office, Washington, D.C. 20402. Free booklet.

Starting and Managing a Small Business of Your Own, Small Business Administration. Superintendent of Documents, U.S. Government Printing Office, Washington, D.C. 20402. Booklet.

Steps in Incorporating a Business (Management Aid #111), Small Business Administration. Superintendent of Documents, U.S. Government Printing Office, Washington, D.C. 20402. Free booklet.

GOVERNMENT REGULATIONS AND INSURANCE

Starting and Managing a Small Business of Your Own, Small Business Administration. Superintendent of Documents, U.S. Government Printing Office, Washington, D.C. 20402. Booklet.

RECORD-KEEPING

Analyze Your Records to Reduce Costs (Small Marketers Aid #130), Small Business Administration. Superintendent of Documents, U.S. Government Printing Office, Washington, D.C. 20402. Free booklet.

Managing the Small Business, Lawrence L. Steinmetz, John B. Kline, and Donald P. Stegall. Richard D. Irwin, Inc., Homewood, Ill., 1968.

MONEY AND CREDIT

The ABC's of Borrowing (Management Aid #170), Small Business Administration. Superintendent of Documents, U.S. Government Printing Office, Washington, D.C. 20402. Free booklet.

Building Strong Relations with Your Bank (Small Marketers Aid #107), Small Business Administration. Superintendent of Documents, U.S. Government Printing Office, Washington, D.C. 20402. Free booklet.

A Handbook of Small Business Finance, Small Business Administration. Superintendent of Documents, U.S. Government Printing Office, Washington, D.C. 20402. Booklet.

SBA Business Loans, Small Business Administration. Superintendent of Documents, U. S. Government Printing Office, Washington, D. C. 20402. Free booklet.

BUYING AND SELLING

Are You Kidding Yourself About Your Profits? (Small Marketers Aid #25), Small Business Administration. Superintendent of Documents. U.S. Government Printing Office, Washington, D.C. 20402. Free booklet.

Pleasing Your Boss, The Customer (Small Marketers Aid #114), Small Business Administration. Superintendent of Documents, U.S. Government Printing Office, Washington, D.C. 20402. Free booklet.

Starting and Succeeding in Your Own Small Business, Louis L. Allen. Grosset & Dunlap, Inc., New York., 1968.

What Is the Best Selling Price? (Management Aid #193), Small Business Administration. Superintendent of Documents, U.S. Government Printing Office, Washington, D.C. 20402. Free booklet.

ADVERTISING AND PUBLICITY

Checklist for Successful Retail Advertising (Small Marketers Aid #96), Small Business Administration. Superintendent of Documents, U.S. Government Printing Office, Washington, D.C. 20402. Free booklet.

Knowing Your Image (Small Marketers Aid #124), Small Business Administration. Superintendent of Documents, U.S. Government Printing Office, Washington, D.C. 20402. Free booklet.

Managing the Small Business, Lawrence L. Steinmetz, John B. Kline, and Donald P. Stegall. Richard D. Irwin, Inc., Homewood, Ill., 1968.

Selected Advertising Media—A Guide for Small Business, Small Business Administration. Superintendent of Documents, U.S. Government Printing Office, Washington, D.C. 20402. Booklet.

TAXES

How to Run a Small Business, J. K. Lasser. McGraw-Hill Book Co., New York, N.Y., 1963.

The Home Office Guide, Leon Henry, Jr. Arco Publishing Co., Inc., New York N.Y., 1968.

MAIL ORDER

How to Start and Operate a Mail-Order Business, J. L. Simon. McGraw-Hill Book Co., New York, N.Y., 1965.

National Mailing-List Houses/ (Small Business Bibliography #29), Small Business Administration. Superintendent of Documents, U.S. Government Printing Office, Washington, D.C. 20402.

Selling by Mail Order (Small Business Bibliography #3), Small Business Administration. Superintendent of Documents, U.S. Government Printing Office, Washington, D.C. 20402.

THE WORLD OF FOOD

Of course you can cook. But so, when you think about it, can most other people. The trick is to make money from cooking, and that takes more than just knowing how. It requires that you also know something about your potential customers—their tastes, their eating habits, and their income level. But most of all it calls for enough experience in the kitchen to turn out a perfect dish every time.

That doesn't mean you have to be an all-round cook with an extensive repertoire. Your steak Béarnaise can be a disaster, so long as your chicken curry evokes oohs and aahs. The prime requirement is the ability to make well a food or foods that many people like. If you enjoy decorating cakes, treasure a special recipe for spaghetti sauce, have creative ideas about sandwiches, or can turn out a mean batch of divinity fudge, read on. There may be a job in this chapter for you.

With all the other sources of prepared foods available today, including frozen and packaged products, why should anyone buy your wares? There are four possible reasons: (1) You have a particularly good product; (2) Your service is a convenience; (3) You offer unusual and appealing gift ideas; (4) You give special personal attention.

Jobs involving the preparation of food naturally differ somewhat with the type of service offered. But since any kind of catering can be demanding work, it is best to start small and concentrate on one type of food. This is particularly true if you are limited in your culinary abilities or preparation facilities.

GENERAL GUIDELINES

• Any kind of food preparation for sale to the public requires a permit from your local health department. That may involve proof of your good health and an inspection of your cooking facilities. In some areas, and for some food products, a separate workroom—not the family kitchen—may be required. Check on this before you start. Also see your town clerk or zoning board for zoning regulations that may apply to your business. If you sell your product across state lines you may be subject to additional state and federal regulations. Your local health department can advise you on these.

• One of the basic requirements for this type of work is a well-organized, fully equipped kitchen with plenty of working space. A wide refrigerator and a freezer are almost essential, since preparing ahead is important for an efficient catering operation. Some extremely helpful extras, depending on the type of food included are: a mixer, a blender, a double oven, a rotisserie.

• Experience requirements are minimal—after all, you've been "catering" for your family for years. But doing it for money does call for certain personal qualifications: interest in, and a flair for, food; organizing ability; tact with people;

and coolness and flexibility in the face of emergencies, both your own and those of your customers.

• In this line of work, your services will often be in most demand when other people are at leisure—in the evenings and on weekends, the party-giving times—so be prepared to adjust your household routines accordingly.

• The financial investment required can be small. If you already have suitable kitchen facilities, you may be able to start on a shoestring. Some women have gone into this business with as little as $25. A more realistic beginning budget, exclusive of major equipment, might be $75 to $100.

• See "A Word about Prices," page 5.

HELPFUL HINTS

• If you are to meet your customers in any way, good grooming is an absolute must. Personal neatness inspires confidence in the wholesomeness of your wares.

• Delivery can be a key part of your service. Encourage customers to pick up their orders, but be prepared to deliver on request. If your community is so widely scattered that delivery would be expensive, a profitable operation may not be possible.

• The packaging and/or display of a food product can make or break you. Pay almost as much attention to this aspect as to the product itself. There are many attractive disposable containers, such as plastic parfait holders and colored-foil pans and cupcake liners.

• Cooking in quantity is different from cooking for smaller numbers. Use recipes especially developed for quantity cooking or develop your own. Practice your specialty until you can make it with your eyes shut.

• As soon as you have some idea of your market, begin buying in quantity—staples such as flour and sugar, large containers of ice cream, cases of number 10 cans of fruits, vegetables, and sauces. There are also many partly prepared frozen gourmet foods, such as chicken Kiev, chicken Cordon Bleu, puff pastry, hors d'oeuvres, available in quantity; these merely need finishing off. Get in touch with a food wholesaler in your area.

• No one is so impatient as a hungry man, or as a woman who has a family or guests to feed. Promptness is not only a virtue in this business; it's a necessity.

HOW TO GET BUSINESS

For some types of food product, you need only find an outlet—a food or health shop, department store, women's exchange, or bakery—that will agree to handle your wares. For others, you will have to rustle up your customers yourself.

If you have enough contacts in your community, through membership in church, clubs, the PTA, and other organizations, or if you have a wide circle of acquaintances and friends, you may be able to build up a business through word-of-mouth alone.

Usually, though, it is also necessary to advertise. There are a number of ways of doing so. (Also see specific suggestions for particular jobs.)

1. Have mimeographed or printed flyers made up and distribute them to a selected list of potential private customers, business firms, fraternal organizations, clubs, church groups, PTA's, party-supply rental services, party consultants, caterers, and any other person or group you think might be interested. Follow the flyers up with visits or telephone calls to particularly good prospects.

2. Write to, or if possible obtain interviews with, the women's page editor of your local newspaper and the women's news editor of the local radio or TV station. Send

or take along samples of your product, and try to interest the editors in a story on your operation.

3. Place a newspaper ad on a regular basis. Happily, for small local businesses, small local newspapers both yield the best returns and have the lowest rates. The preferred position for food ads is the women's page or dining-out section, if any.

4. Place an ad in the classified telephone directory.

5. The very best way to advertise a food product is to have potential customers see and taste it. So occasionally donate samples to church suppers, charity raffles, bake sales or other events where a number of people will be exposed to your product.

PRICES

The mistake many beginning caterers make is to consider only the cost of their ingredients in fixing prices. Because, usually, they work in their own kitchens with existing equipment, it doesn't occur to them to make an allowance for such things as rent, heat, electricity, and depreciation. As a result, they fail to build up a reserve that could later be used to expand their business. Other expenses to consider are insurance, laundry, packaging supplies, and delivery.

Once you have determined your costs, you must put a value on your own time in order to arrive at a reasonable profit. If you find this difficult to do, you can try one of several alternative methods. The New York State Department of Commerce Woman's Program suggests doubling all costs as a simple means of setting prices. The rule-of-thumb favored by the Massachusetts Department of Commerce singles out the cost of ingredients and fuel for delivery and triples that figure. The Department adds in passing, however, that a marketing authority told them the figure of three was no longer realistic; it should be four. By the time you read this, inflation being what it is, the formula may be up to five.

Check whatever result you arrive at against what other local caterers are asking. A price advantage may be helpful in establishing your business, but beware of setting your prices too low, or you will end up working for nothing. Also, in some communities, prices that are too low are looked upon with suspicion, as indicating inferior quality.

1

CANAPÉS AND HORS D'OEUVRES

These are something you pop into your mouth with your left hand, usually while holding a drink in your right. They should, ideally, both look too good to eat and taste too good to resist.

Three good reasons for specializing in these bite-size goodies are: (1) Every party needs them (your best market will probably be the cocktail-party crowd) ; (2) The average hostess is too harassed to find the time to make 200 tiny concoctions that will disappear in about twenty minutes; (3) For the specialist, canapés are relatively simple to produce en masse. (If you are not a specialist, and aren't willing to put in the practice to become one, don't be fooled into thinking that because canapés are small, they are easy. There is quite an art involved in making them as lovely as they are delicious.)

Decide on about ten different hors d'oeuvres, at several cost levels (don't forget to figure in your time) , and learn to turn them out to perfection. In an average order, include four or five varieties; for really big orders (over a thousand pieces), provide all ten. Hot hors d'oeuvres are trickier to make than cold ones, so you may want to stick to the latter for a start. Following are some suggestions for both kinds, classified according to the cost of ingredients:

HOT HORS D'OEUVRES

Expensive
Quiche Lorraine
Fried Shrimp

Moderate
Seafood Puffs
Cocktail Franks (plain or wrapped in pastry)
Fried Chicken Pieces
Barbecued Chicken Wings
Teriyaki (in pieces or on skewers)
Rumaki (chicken livers, water chestnuts, wrapped in bacon)

Moderate to Cheap
Stuffed Mushrooms (seasoned)
Midget Hamburgers or Meat Balls

Cheap
Cheese Puffs
Tiny Potato Pancakes with Applesauce
Cheese Straws
Potato Knishes

COLD HORS D'OEUVRES

Expensive
Cold Smoked Salmon on Toast Triangles
Caviar on Melba Rounds
Shrimp Cocktail
Chicken Liver Paté

Moderate
Crabmeat Biscuits
Shrimp Salad or Tuna Pinwheels
Salmon Pinwheels
Ham and Cheese Triangles

Moderate to Cheap
Deviled Eggs

Cheap
Egg Salad Rounds
Deviled Ham Fingers
Sardine Pasties
Open-Face Cucumber Sandwiches
Pickled Mushrooms
Pickled Carrots
Stuffed Celery
Cheese Balls

Keep in mind that canapé catering is a party service and therefore somewhat seasonal. It really swings in May, June, and during the fall and winter holidays; January to March, and July to September are fairly dead. Remember too that to make a success of this kind of business, you must live in, or have access to, a community where there is a lot going on—home entertaining, community activities, club functions, and business parties. If everyone for miles around rolls up his sidewalks at 8 P.M. and snuggles down with a good TV program, your prospects are bleak.

Utensils. You will need lots of small mixing bowls, narrow spatulas, cookie cutters, a strainer, a colander, an assortment of sharp knives, cutting boards, tube cake decorators, an electric blender or a food grinder, and graters.

Packaging. Use large, shallow cardboard cartons (pizza boxes are just right). For a supplier, look in the classified telephone directory under "Paper" or "Boxes" and order the minimum quantity, usually 200 at around 13¢ per 12" by 12" by 2" box, or 300 at 10¢ per box. This size holds 50 canapés.

Prices. Prices are usually quoted per hundred. A common charge is $10 to $15 per hundred, although this will vary from area to area and from year to year.

Kathleen Gilbert Cipriano of Tonawanda, N.Y. has been

in business for three years. "When I started out, I wrote down the amounts of everything I used and the cost. They differ with each type of hors d'oeuvre. Then I estimated the time spent on the whole job. Add the cost, and an allowance for overhead, and there's the answer." She estimates that to make 200 of her canapés, it costs her $4.30 and takes four hours ("not rushing"). Based on her charge of $10 per hundred, she clears almost $4 an hour. Most of Mrs. Cipriano's customers pick up their orders. For delivery, she charges $1 extra.

WHERE TO GET MORE INFORMATION

Cocktail Parties Made Easy, Mary Dodge Silk. Mountain View House, Whitefield, N.H. 03598.

Counseling Notes on a Catering Service. Small Business Administration, Washington, D.C. 20416. Free leaflet.

The Good Housekeeping Cookbook. Good Housekeeping Books, 250 W. 55th Street, New York, N.Y. 10019, 1963.

Hors d'Oeuvres and Canapés, James Beard. Bantam Books, New York, N.Y., 1967. Paperback.

2

DESSERTS ONLY

Here's another type of specialized catering, this one directed to the sweet tooth that almost everyone has. Despite all the people on diets, you have only to watch how many frozen dessert delicacies are sold at supermarkets to realize the potential market. If you make a rich-tasting torte, baba au rhum, Nesselrode pie, or a positively wicked chocolate mousse, there's no reason you shouldn't share in the loot. None, that is, if you keep certain essentials in mind.

• Don't try to compete with readily available frozen or packaged products that may not be quite as good as your homemade version, but that are lower in price and easy to prepare. (This category includes many baked goods; for exceptions, see jobs #3 and 8.)

• Do specialize in desserts that no commercial version can match or that are exotic enough to have little commercial competition. Among the former might be a spectacular fruit-filled meringue shell or charlotte Russe, or an old-fashioned raisin-and-rice pudding; among the latter, such delicacies as chocolate cheesecake, cold lemon soufflé, frozen chestnut pudding, citrus-rum chiffon cream, Swedish pancakes and lingonberries, or crêpes suzettes (with directions for flaming).

• Children's tastes being what they are (*anything* sweet is good), you probably won't get much family demand for your specialties. So aim at hostesses who entertain often, childless couples and those whose children are grown, bachelors and single working girls, bridge clubs, men's organizations, and other groups much given to socializing.

• Unless you specialize in desserts that freeze well, the highly perishable nature of your product (in appearance and flavor, if not in wholesomeness) may make it difficult to deal on an individual customer basis. Your best bet will probably be to persuade a local gourmet food shop, bakery, or delicatessen to handle your creations, or to concentrate on group functions. You might also want to investigate the possibility of supplying one or more local restaurants.

• One way to handle a direct-to-customer business is to plan a different dessert for each day of the week. Announce the week's schedule on handbills distributed at the beginning of each week, and ask for advance orders. (But always make enough of the daily special to handle a walk-in trade. Desserts are often an impulse item.)

• Desserts should look as luscious as they taste. Take special pains with decoration and presentation. On big orders you deliver yourself, try to oversee the serving of individual portions. This would be especially desirable for spectacular flambé desserts such as cherries jubilee, crêpes suzettes, or café brûlée.

Utensils. An electric mixer is a must, a blender extremely helpful. Depending on your specialties, you will also need molds, springform pans, pie plates, baking dishes, and other equipment. Start out small; add to your stock as your business grows.

Packaging. For individual orders, buy disposable containers and cardboard cartons or paper bags to pack them in. Special group or gift orders you may want to serve in pretty, permanent dishes (customer pays a deposit, to be refunded when the dish is returned). Some customers may supply their own dishes, in order to give their guests the impression the dessert is their own creation.

Prices. Unless you sell to an outlet that will take everything you make, or take only custom orders, don't forget to add to your costs an allowance for your average unsold output. (Even if your family eats it, it's still part of your investment!)

WHERE TO GET MORE INFORMATION:

European Desserts for American Kitchens, Elaine Ross. Hastings House Publishers, Inc., New York, N.Y., 1962.

The Good Housekeeping Cookbook. Good Housekeeping Books, 250 W. 55th Street, New York, N.Y., 1963.

The New York Times Menu Cookbook, Craig Claiborne. Harper & Row, New York, N.Y., 1966.

The Viennese Pastry Cookbook, Lilly Joss Reich. The Macmillan Co., New York, N.Y., 1970.

The Wilton Book of Classic Desserts. Wilton Enterprises, Inc., 833 West 115th Street, Chicago, Ill. 60643, 1970.

3

CAKES FOR SPECIAL OCCASIONS

This is a job for the creative cook who likes to lavish her artistic talents on cake design and decoration. Weddings provide the most lucrative market (and the best chance later to expand your operation to cover all phases of catering for this very special occasion). Other events to aim at are anniversaries, christenings, Bar Mitzvahs, showers, engagement parties, small-fry birthdays, and, of course, holidays of every description.

The first step is to develop a few really tasty recipes that can be adapted for any occasion. Some caterers pride themselves on family recipes handed down from generation to generation. Others operate just as successfully with mixes. A cake for any occasion should obviously taste delicious. But just as important for the special cakes we are talking about, is the way they look. Since you may be competing with the local bakery (and other caterers) a big part of the appeal of your product will be the appropriate uniqueness of your designs, and the deftness with which they are executed.

Here are examples of what other women have created:

• A wedding cake in the shape of a church, with an illuminated (battery-powered) wedding bell shining on the figures of the bride and groom.

• A christening cake shaped like a baby bassinet, complete with baby, and decorated with tiny forget-me-nots.

• A birthday cake for a ten-year-old boy, in the shape of a baseball diamond, with all the plastic players in place.

A fairly elaborate wedding cake takes approximately half a day to bake and another full day to decorate. Birthday cakes require just a few hours. Streamline your operations by working out eight to ten basic icing designs (flowers, leaves, rosettes, lettering styles, etc.) that can be used for almost any occasion.

Utensils. You will need at least two sets of cake pans—one round and one square. (A set includes five pans, graded in size from 6″ to 14″.) Also a standard round angel-food tube pan, springform pan, bundt pan, sheet-cake, jelly-roll, and layer-cake pans. Later you may want to invest in such specialty items as heart-shaped pans, and pans in the shape of musical instruments, or fairy-tale figures (available from mail-order houses) .

You will also need a professional cake decorating set containing 26 or 52 of the most often used tubes (they come specially boxed, with each tube on its own holder for instant design identification) ; frosting base (or make your own) ; decorating jelly or gel; spatulas; flower nails; a decorating comb; unusual birthday candles and candle holders; edible rice-wafer-paper designs; and paper doilies.

Packaging. See the classified telephone directory for sources of cardboard cake boxes; buy them in several sizes. Heavy cardboard cake boards and string will be your only other packaging needs.

How to get business. In addition to the targets mentioned on page 65, zero in on bakeries with no decorated cake service, department-store bridal departments, bridal shops, bridal consultants, florists, jewelers, linen-supply houses, hotels and motels, country clubs, and restaurants. Visit members of the clergy in your community and let them know of your services for weddings and other church functions.

Prices. Prices for wedding cakes are customarily quoted per portion; prices for other cakes are based on size. Check to see what bakeries and other caterers in your area are charging.

Delivery. Although individual customers will often be willing to pick up their orders, the chance of mishap to an elaborate, tiered wedding cake is too great to risk. Deliver it yourself. If it's in sections on pedestals, you may want to assemble it at the site of the reception. In any case, bring a container of extra frosting for touch-ups.

WHERE TO GET MORE INFORMATION

Art of Creative Cake Decorating and Holiday and Party Cakes, Esther Murphy. American Trade Publishing Co., 71 Vanderbilt Ave., New York, N.Y. 10017. Vol. I, 1953; Vol. II, 1958.

Artistic Cake Decorating from A to Z, John J. Zonker. Clissold Publishing Company, 105 West Adams St., Chicago, Ill. 60603.

Decorating Cakes for Fun and Profit, Richard Snyder. Exposition Press, New York, N.Y., 1953.

The Homemaker's Pictorial Encyclopedia of Modern Cake Decorating, 6th ed., McKinley and Norman Wilton. Wilton Enterprises, Inc., 833 W. 115th St., Chicago, Ill. 60643. 1969.

The New Cake Decorating Book, Jean Bowring. Arco Publishing Co., Inc., New York, N.Y., 1970.

There are a number of mail-order houses that specialize in providing supplies and equipment for baking and decorating. One with a very complete line is *Maid of Scandinavia.* For a catalog, send 50 cents to the company at 3245 Raleigh Avenue, Minneapolis, Minnesota 55416.

4

"MEALS ON WHEELS"

This business supplies prepared meals, ready to pop on the table with only a fast reheating, to people who don't have time (or the desire) to cook. Restaurants often make considerable money from this service as a sideline. TV dinners, the frozen version of the idea, are a national institution.

Since you can't compete with the latter in price, your best customers will be people who are willing and able to pay a bit more for good food and who have adventurous palates. You can expect almost no family trade; your customers will be mostly working girls, bachelors, and childless couples, together with an occasional harried hostess faced with unexpected guests. Consequently, this service does best in cities and larger towns.

"Meals on Wheels" constitutes a custom service for which orders are taken on or before the morning of the day the meal is wanted. And, as its name indicates, the service usually includes delivery to the customer's door. Delivery is less onerous, in this case, because it can be limited to two, or at the most three, regularly scheduled trips between the dinner hours of six to eight. Establish a delivery area and charge customers outside it a fee.

The first step in setting up the service is to develop a number of appealing meals, a different one for every day of the week, and learn to prepare them in quantity. What you offer will vary with the type of cuisine preferred in your area and with your own cooking abilities. But your menus should be imaginative, and include enough gourmet (but not wildly exotic) dishes to satisfy a number of culinary tastes. They must also be able to travel well, and withstand reheating without losing flavor. Since few vegetables can meet that last requirement, you will do best with meals that feature a hearty main dish, salad, and dessert, with the occasional addition of a first course and/or a hot bread. Some sample menus:

1. Chicken curry with peach chutney and saffron rice, plus a fresh fruit compote marinated in kirsch.

2. Seafood paella, mixed salad greens with garlic dressing (in a separate container), blueberry tart.

3. An unusual soup (e.g., gazpacho), barbecued spareribs, corn bread, fresh fruit, and a wedge of Brie cheese with crackers.

4. Beef Bourguignon or Stroganoff, buttered noodles, garlic bread, marinated artichokes, and crème de menthe parfait.

Utensils and Packaging. Although, at the start, you may be able to get along with what you have, before long you will probably need to invest in several large kettles, pans, baking dishes, and other equipment large enough for cooking in quantity. You will also need a number of disposable foil, cardboard, or plastic containers, and plastic bags to pack your meals in (each course in a separate container), and cardboard cartons for transporting them. See the classified telephone directory for suitable packaging.

How to get business. At the beginning of each week, distribute typewritten, mimeographed, or printed flyers listing and describing each menu, the price per person, and the day of the week it's available. Try to make your specialties sound as delicious as they are, and specify the ground rules of your service, such as how long in advance orders must be placed and in what areas you deliver free of charge. Concentrate your efforts on business offices, local chambers of commerce, women's and men's clubs, and apartments with many single tenants.

For this business it also pays to place an ad on a continuing basis in a local newspaper, as well as in the classified telephone directory under "Catering." (Sample copy: " 'Meals-on-Wheels' delivered to your doorstep if you are within the delivery area; for a small fee if you live beyond it. A different menu each day. REASONABLE PRICES. Delicious homemade food, cooked to order." Include a few of your specialties, and your address and phone number.) In addition, send a free meal to the women's page or dining-out editor of the local paper and ask her to "review" your cuisine.

Prices. In addition to prices for individual meals, set up quantity prices per quart or gallon of various dishes for those who may want to feed a whole tableful of family or guests.

WHERE TO GET MORE INFORMATION

Cooking for Crowds, Sarah Morgan. The Bethany Press, St. Louis, Mo., 1963.

The Good Housekeeping Cookbook. Good Housekeeping Books, 250 W. 55th Street, New York, N.Y. 10019, 1963.

5

BOX LUNCHES

Depending on your wishes and the area in which you live, this can be a largely seasonal activity or a year-round occupation.

Everybody loves a picnic, and during the summer almost every club and business organization sponsors one. In addition, in resort areas, there is a demand for individual box lunches to be taken on a day's outing. If you intend to confine yourself to this type of service, direct your selling efforts at clubs, fraternal organizations, the officers of business firms, local tourist attractions, camping grounds, motels and hotels.

If you live near a business area, you might want to consider a year-round operation to supply daily lunches to office or factory workers. You can do this in one of two ways: Take telephone orders for delivery, or make up box lunches in advance and sell them from a car or station wagon at office or factory sites. Each has both advantages and disadvantages.

With telephone orders there is less waste, since the lunches are assembled on demand, but delivery is a problem; if you develop any volume at all, you will have to hire one or more delivery boys. You may also be forced into offering a choice of beverages, which will add considerably to the complexity of your operation. Selling box lunches on business premises is easier but requires the permission of the owner, and he may demand a fee or a percentage of your profits for the privilege. In either case, your best form of advertising will be flyers listing selections and prices and distributed widely and frequently in or outside offices and factories.

For either a picnic or a year-round business, concentrate on quality rather than variety. Plan three or four different menus, priced according to contents. Each box should include a sandwich, cookies or cake, and fruit; the price differential comes in the kind of sandwich, cake, fruit, etc. Provide a second sandwich at an additional flat rate within each category. In warm weather, remember the dangers of food poisoning and stay away from such salmonella-prone foods as potato salad or other mayonnaise mixtures, and cream fillings.

If you live in a resort area where there is a demand for it, you might try specializing in haute cuisine picnic baskets, featuring (in thermal containers) such sophisticated choices as an iced summer soup and crabmeat salad, plus a small loaf of French bread and a half bottle of white wine. Charge a deposit fee for the basket and equipment, to be refunded when they are returned.

WHERE TO GET MORE INFORMATION

The Good Housekeeping Cookbook. Good Housekeeping Books, 250 W. 55th Street, New York, N.Y. 10019, 1963.

Modern Sandwich Methods. American Institute of Baking, 400 East Ontario St., Chicago, Ill., 1967. Leaflet on quantity sandwich making.

6

GIFT SPECIALS

Food products that make attractive gifts on holidays or other special occasions, or simply as a friendly token any time, are, under the right circumstances, a good bet for a home business. In this case, the right circumstances are: (1) An ability to make a particularly good specialty product and to package it appealingly; and (2) Success in finding a retail outlet whose customers appreciate something a bit different. In types of products, fruitcakes, cookies, candies, jams and jellies, and special breads are all proven winners; while appropriate outlets include gourmet and gift shops, cheese purveyors, health food stores, fine-grocery departments of department stores, delicatessens, woman's exchanges and roadside markets.

Selling through an outlet is much easier than trying to find your own customers, because of the wider market reached, and may be more profitable as well, despite the commission the store takes. But it also demands that you meet a more rigorous schedule. Once a store agrees to sell your product, it expects regular shipments. You can't take a day off whenever the fancy strikes you or reduce your output at will. So don't be tempted to promise more than you can deliver.

Packaging is an extremely important part of this business and in most cases will represent a significant part of your initial investment. If there is a woman's exchange in your area (see page 24), they may be able to advise you on this aspect of your operation. Later, if your product proves successful, it may be to your advantage to consult a professional package designer, to get the best package for the best price. This becomes a necessity if you carry the gift-special idea to its logical conclusion—mail order (see page 41) .

Some specific ideas for products:

Candies. The most important factors are a good recipe, an accurate candy thermometer, superior ingredients, and the right market. Some varieties that have been successfully produced at home are: caramels, fudge (standard and divinity) , pralines, penuche, nut brittles, candied fruits (apricots, pineapple rings, orange and grapefruit peels) , stuffed fruits (dates, prunes) , mints, lollipops and other hard candies. Forget about chocolates. They're too hard to make, and you'll never beat the competition from a commercial candymaker. Attractive, creative packaging is vitally important. Colorful see-through paper with matching ribbon or elastic is appealing. Unusual containers—brandy snifters, plant holders, sand pails—add to the cost but also to the interest, and may be worth trying.

Jams and Jellies. To compete with the profusion of products on supermarket shelves, you'll need a variety that is rare or slightly exotic—apricot-nut preserves, kumquat or gooseberry jam, herb and wine jellies—or a special recipe for something as common as grape or strawberry jam that makes it taste deliciously different.

With regional specialties using fruits for which your area is known, you can clean up over a summer by selling to the tourist trade at gift shops and roadside markets. Vacationers can't resist sampling the local food, and jellies are one item easily transported back home for gifts.

Your packaging problems are simplified by the inherent attractiveness of the product itself. But work out a distinctive label, and try decorating the jars with bows or rosettes.

Bread. There is something irresistible about a golden,

crusty loaf of home-baked bread. A really good bread sells almost anywhere. The trick is to specialize in a variety that isn't widely available in local stores and one that makes a good gift or special treat. For although you could probably sell as much as you could bake of a good plain everyday loaf, on the small-scale basis on which you will be operating, you couldn't make enough at a reasonable price to make a profit. For that you need a specialty bread for which customers are willing to pay a bit more.

With quick breads you may run into too much competition from mixes and frozen baked products, which—let's admit it—are pretty good. Yeast breads are an open field. Herb, onion, cheese, oatmeal, Swedish Limpa, rye and sticky buns are possible varieties. In New York City, a male librarian whose hobby is baking, spends four nights a week plus Saturday making bread—in an apartment, at that. He makes a honey whole wheat and two varieties of cheese bread ("liberally seasoned with coarsely ground pepper") which retail at a specialty cheese store for 49 cents a loaf, and at last reports couldn't keep up with the demand.

For packaging bread, a clear plastic bag with a colorful tie and tag would suffice to start.

WHERE TO GET MORE INFORMATION

Fleischmann's New Treasury of Yeast Baking. Box 2695, Grand Central Station, New York, N.Y. 10017. Booklet, 25 cents.

The Good Housekeeping Cookbook. Good Housekeeping Books, 250 West 55th Street, New York, N.Y. 10019, 1963.

Jams and Jelly Favorites. General Foods, Box 5016, Kankakee, Ill. 60901. Free booklet.

Making Money in Your Kitchen, Helen Stone Hovey. Wilfred Funk, 1953. (Out of print, but available in many public libraries.)

7

OTHER FOOD SPECIALTIES

Sweets of various kinds are not the only food products that can become the basis of a home business. One item that has proved successful in a sophisticated New Jersey suburb is snails, the delicacy often listed on French menus. Finding that her guests raved over the way she prepared them, one woman froze several batches and persuaded the proprietor of the local gourmet food shop to take them. They sold well, and she extended her market to food shops in neighboring towns. Finally, the demand grew to the point where she was able to move out of her kitchen and into a small plant of her own, where today she has several helpers.

Another New Jersey woman, Sylvia Bedrosian, of Washington Township, got the idea for her product a number of years ago, when she read that the government was having difficulty in disposing of a large wheat surplus. Mrs. Bedrosian, who comes from an Armenian family where pilaf dishes using wheat instead of rice are great favorites, tried to interest several big food companies in producing a wheat pilaf base, but without success. Finally, in 1965, she began experimenting in her own kitchen, combining raw Bulgar wheat with vermicelli noodles and a special dry broth for a product that, when cooked with water and butter, made a delicious pilaf dish. Packaged in simple polyethylene bags, it sells for 39 to 49 cents per 7-oz. bag in local cheese and other gourmet food shops.

Mrs. Bedrosian made her first sale before she even had an order. With the packaged product, she had taken along a small pot of prepared pilaf for the proprietor of a food shop to taste. She was trying to convince him that his customers would like it when one of them entered the store. She agreed to taste it too, and was so enthusiastic that she bought several bags from Mrs. Bedrosian on the spot. That persuaded the food-shop owner, and another successful home business was on its way. It has remained small (Mrs. Bedrosian likes it that way), but it continues to be a steady source of income.

As these two examples indicate, foods that companies may not think it worthwhile to offer (because the market is not big enough for large-scale production) can nevertheless be a profitable home product. It all depends on the tastes of people in your area.

8

HOLIDAY CAKES, COOKIES, AND PIES

Although many people delight in doing their own holiday baking, there are just as many others who don't have the time or the skill to do so and would be happy to buy home-made products rather than the commercial kind.

You may want to limit your business to the most profit-able holidays, Thanksgiving and Christmas. Or you can also take in Easter, Halloween, Valentine's Day, and other festive occasions.

The range of possible products is wide, and includes

fruitcake, rugelach, lepkuchen, steamed puddings, stollen, mincemeat and pumpkin pies, decorated cookies to hang on the tree, gingerbread houses, Norwegian fruit bread, Hungarian coffeecake, or whatever else is your specialty. Again, try to avoid competition by offering things not available elsewhere.

You may want to sell your products through a local woman's exchange or other nonprofit cooperative. If not, the best way to market them is to mail flyers listing your offerings and prices to clubs, churches, PTA's, offices, and individuals you think are particularly likely customers. State how much advance notice you will need for orders, the area in which you deliver, and include an order blank. If you plan a year-round operation, you should make three or four mailings a year. If not, your mailing should go out in late October for Thanksgiving and Christmas. A seasonal ad in local newspapers is a good followup.

WHERE TO GET MORE INFORMATION

Cookie Cookery, John and Hazel Zenker. M. Evans & Co., Inc., New York, N.Y., 1969.

The Good Housekeeping Cookbook. Good Housekeeping Books, 250 West 55th Street, New York, N.Y. 10019, 1963.

Pillsbury's Bake-Off Cookbook. Simon & Schuster, Inc., New York, N.Y., 1970.

Also see sources listed under #3, "Cakes for Special Occasions."

9

PARTY COOK

This specialty is the exception to the rule that you don't have to be an all-round cook to make money in catering. It's for the woman who really knows and likes food, who is constantly trying out new dishes to please her family, whose company dinners have her friends talking about them for weeks afterward.

A party cook must be able to suggest the perfect meal for a special occasion—and then go into the customer's kitchen and prepare it. This calls for imagination, experience, and the ability to cope with whatever situation you find yourself in. You may swear by a gas stove and find your customer's is electric (or vice versa), her working space may be cramped, her refrigeration inadequate. Nevertheless, you must come up with a meal that will make her reputation as a hostess.

On the other hand, this job requires almost no investment on your part. For certain of your culinary specialties you may want to carry along your own equipment if your customer's kitchen can't furnish it. Otherwise, all you supply is your skill.

Obviously, this business requires a fairly affluent community, and one that does a good deal of entertaining. If you have access to such a market, you'll have little trouble in getting requests for your services. Once your first customer's guests have admired your perfect little dinner or imaginative luncheon, your fame will spread by word-of-mouth, and you'll probably get more requests than you care to fill.

To get started, notify party consultants, party-rental agencies, greeting card and party supply stores, clubs, church groups, and other organizations of your service, as well as the women's page editor of the local newspaper. Make clear just what you are prepared to do—cook only, or do the marketing, cooking, *and* serving—and how many guests you will agree to handle. For situations where extra help will be needed, you should be able to suggest available sources.

Your fees should be set on an individual basis, and calculated largely on the amount of your time you estimate will be involved. Before actually accepting a job, you should visit the customer's home and inspect the facilities that will be available to you.

WHERE TO GET MORE INFORMATION

Classic Dishes Made Simple, Marguerite Patten. Nash Publishing Corp., Los Angeles, Calif., 1970.

Great Dinners from Life, Eleanor Graves. Time-Life, Inc., New York, N.Y., 1970.

New York Times Menu Cookbook, Craig Claiborne. Harper & Row, New York, N.Y., 1966.

Splendid Fare, Albert Stockli. Alfred A. Knopf, Inc., New York, N.Y., 1970.

10

SCHOOL LUNCHES

Despite the National School Lunch Program, launched in 1946, which makes federal funds available to school districts that agree to provide their students with nutritious lunches, there are still many schools that do not have lunch rooms.

Some of these are in poor districts, where the unpaid help of all concerned citizens is needed to make a low- or no-cost food service available to the community's children.

Other schools without lunch rooms are in average- or above-average income areas. Here the children either bring a cold lunch, go home to eat, or fill up on food, at local food shops and lunch counters, that is often both low in nutrition and high in cost.

In such an area there is an opportunity for someone who lives near the school to start a lunchroom service for children whose mothers would prefer them to have a wholesome, home-cooked meal, but who can't, for some reason, provide it themselves. Several years ago, Mrs. Joan Ellis, of Chicago, Illinois, set up such a service in her home for a dozen local children. Here's how Mrs. Ellis got started:

A few words to several mothers who can't be home to supervise lunch hours, and my venture was off and winging. I then applied for a foster day-care license from the Illinois State Department of Children and Family Services. One of the department's inspectors came to my home to look over the facilities for the cooking and serving of food. In addition, he talked to me at length in order to determine whether I was a fit person to care for other people's children. Having passed those tests, I took the required medical checkup and received my license. I have a large, finished basement equipped with a picnic table and benches, card tables and chairs. Plenty of room for my "clientele" of twelve. Paper napkins, plastic place mats and sturdy plastic dishes keep my maintenance costs down. I provide a balanced hot meal, with milk or a milk drink.

When Mrs. Ellis started her service in 1968, she charged five dollars per week per child. Inflation has pushed up the cost of food since then; to serve nutritious lunches similar to those the National School Lunch Program provides—and still make some money for yourself—you would have to charge, in most areas, a higher fee now. Before seriously considering a lunchroom service, figure out your costs, and check to see what neighborhood children are now spending for "soda-fountain lunches." If you can provide better food for the same amount or less, the chances for a successful operation are good. The second step is to find out, as Mrs. Ellis did, what health and other regulations apply.

WHERE TO GET MORE INFORMATION

A Menu Planning Guide for Type A School Lunches (PA-719), U.S. Department of Agriculture Consumer and Marketing Service. Superintendent of Documents, U.S. Government Printing Office, Washington, D.C. 20402. Leaflet. Meant for schools participating in the National School Lunch Program, this will also be helpful to anyone planning a good private service.

11

HOME RESTAURANT

Although running a regular restaurant is a major undertaking requiring considerable capital, experience, and managerial skills, there are opportunities in some areas to develop a less demanding mini-business, catering to office workers who want a home-cooked lunch or to people (often single women or men) who prefer to dine out but don't like the atmosphere (or prices) of commercial establishments.

It's an idea to consider, especially if you have an enclosed porch or other area near the kitchen that can be reached by an entrance other than the one the family uses. It should be big enough to hold three or four tables and the necessary number of chairs, plus a cabinet that can be used as a serving station and to hold supplies. You may also need to invest in some pretty tablecloths (or mats), napkins, and some additional silver, glassware, and china. Little cooking equipment beyond that which you already have should be needed.

The nature of your prospective clientele, as well as your own family responsibilities, should determine whether to have a lunch or dinner business (or perhaps both). In any case, if you are to operate without help, you'll have to keep your menus simple and offer only one specialty a day (though there should be a different one for every day of the week). As in "Meals on Wheels" (see page 76), the basic menu might consist of a hearty main dish, salad, dessert, coffee, tea, or milk. For a lunch business, depending on the preferences of your customers, you might offer instead of a main dish, a choice of several sandwiches or salads. The smallness of your operation may enable you to develop regular customers who will agree to take their meals with you every day, or at least to notify you in advance when they plan to eat elsewhere. This will keep waste down to a minimum and let you set prices (perhaps on a weekly basis) that will compare very favorably with those charged by other eating establishments in the area, yet still return you a profit. However, since you can handle only a few customers a day, your total income from a home restaurant won't be great.

How to get business. If you live in a neighborhood suited to this type of operation (and that is something you should determine before you start), word-of-mouth spread by friends and acquaintances should bring you all the business you can handle. Or, if business is slow at the start, try running a few ads in the local newspaper, or distribute flyers in nearby office buildings or business establishments. A sign outside your home, if that is permitted by local zoning laws, may also bring in customers.

WHERE TO GET MORE INFORMATION

How to Be a Success in the Restaurant Business, M. Gray and Vass de lo Padua. Nelson-Hall, Chicago, Ill.

Restaurants and Catering (Small Business Bibliography No. 17), Small Business Administration. Superintendent of Documents, U.S. Government Printing Office, Washington, D.C. 20402. Booklet.

SEWING AND NEEDLECRAFT

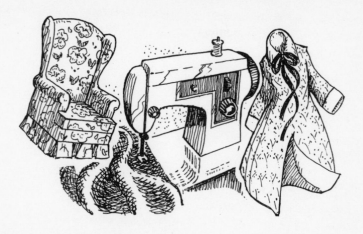

A poor French tailor produced the first sewing machine that worked, and was almost murdered for his trouble by an ignorant mob that looked on it as the work of the devil. Today a greatly improved version of his idea is a boon to the woman who wants to make money at home. Despite the vast outpouring of readymade clothing and household accessories, there are still many things that can be made, or services that can be performed, better or more cheaply by the home sewer than by big business.

GENERAL GUIDELINES

• Experience is the key requirement for making money from any kind of sewing. It takes too much time to be profitable to any but an expert who, through practice, has streamlined her methods.

• There are enough women who don't know how to sew but who want custom sewing services to make these successful almost anywhere. Obviously, the greatest demand will be in cities or in prosperous suburban communities.

• A separate sewing room—perhaps an unused bedroom, enclosed porch or unused garage—is desirable, especially if your customers come to you to be fitted. But it is not absolutely necessary. A fully equipped sewing center can be built into remarkably little space along one wall of a room and closed off out of sight when not in use. (Plans for this "In-a-Wall Sewing Room," designed by Good Housekeeping, are available. Send 35 cents to Good Housekeeping Bulletin Service, 959 Eighth Avenue, New York, N.Y. 10019.)

• In addition, you may need a dressing room or curtained booth for customers and a closet (if you have young children or pets, you should be able to lock it) to store work in progress. A platform for marking hems is a back-saver.

• As an experienced needlewoman, you probably already have most of the equipment needed. Here is a checklist for general sewing; if you specialize in one area, you may not need all these items: sewing machine, dressmaking scissors and shears, needles, thread, pins, thimble, tape measure, rulers, yardstick, tailor's chalk, press cloths, iron and ironing board, sleeve board, tailor's hem, press mitt, wooden clapper, velvet board, dressmaker's carbon paper, tracing wheel, loop turner, small sharp awl, bodkin, ripper, hem gauge, skirt marker, cutting table, full-length mirror, adjustable dress form.

• Other expense can be kept to a minimum. One of the pluses of most types of sewing business is that very little, if anything, need be spent on paid advertising. If you can make money at prices women in your area can afford, you'll find you will soon have to turn business away, not advertise for it.

• You'll pretty much be able to fix your own hours. But whatever hours you decide upon, stick, to them. Or you may elect to see customers by appointment only. One tip: Be sure to allot some evening hours for seeing working women and others who cannot come during the day.

• Packaging needed may be nothing more than plastic garment bags, of the kind cleaners use, or plain cardboard boxes. But if you offer a custom dressmaking service, it may pay you to invest in distinctive boxes with a label identifying your business—e.g., "Colette's Couture Dressmaking."

• Most customers will pick up their orders; if delivery is requested, charge a small fee. (Home furnishings and re-upholstery are exceptions; for the special circumstances that apply, see these specific topics.)

• See "A Word about Prices," page 5.

HELPFUL HINTS

• When applied to food, the word "homemade" implies a superior product. In sewing, on the contrary, professionalism is the image to aim at. Advertise your service as "custom sewing," never "home sewing."

• If you specialize in women's clothing, you'll see all kinds of hopeless shapes and classic figure problems. You'll need tact, sympathy, and a knack for making people feel that you are interested in making them look their very best.

• You should be able to steer a middle course between doing exactly what the customer says she wants, though you know it isn't suitable, and antagonizing her by opposing her views too openly. Both extremes can lose you business, the first because the chances are that the customer herself won't like the piece when it's finished—and will blame *you* for it.

• To keep up on new equipment, time-saving appliances, materials, etc., send for the brochures and catalogues of such companies as Singer, Necchi, and other sewing machine manufacturers; Coates & Clark, and American Thread companies; Dritz-Scoville Company.

• For style trends, read and study high-fashion and women's magazines and leading home decorating magazines; when you go to the movies or watch television, keep your eye out for new styles, colors, and fabrics in clothing and home furnishings.

HOW TO GET BUSINESS

For some kinds of sewing business—alterations, for one—all you may have to do is tell your friends and acquaintances; the word will spread fast. You might also leave your business card with department-store dress departments, specialty shops, and dry-cleaning establishments that do not have such a service. Notify women's clubs too; if you do dress designing, offer to put on a fashion show, featuring some of your creations.

If zoning laws permit, place a sign outside your house or in a window to call attention to your service. These methods will usually be enough to attract customers for basic sewing services; for such specialties as custom home furnishings and reupholstering, you may have to place ads in local papers and in the classified telephone directory, and/or distribute flyers in likely neighborhoods.

12

ALTERATIONS AND MENDING

Time was when every girl learned to sew at her mother's knee. Today many women are all thumbs when it comes to shortening or lengthening a hem, repairing a tear in a delicate fabric, altering a new dress or remodeling an old one.

As a result, an accomplished seamstress who is willing to take on these tasks will find herself in demand almost anywhere.

In most areas you won't have much competition. Department stores and tailoring shops sometimes do alterations as a service to their customers, but their prices are high; even so, they often find that their high overhead makes the practice uneconomical. As for other women who may have the same idea as you, you'll probably find that whatever services exist, there will be plenty of work for you too.

Periods in which a major fashion change is in progress will be particularly good for your business, since many women will prefer to have their present wardrobes altered, if possible, rather than be forced to buy a completely new one. But at any time there are enough women who can't be properly fitted in readymade clothes to keep you busy taking in or letting out seams, shortening sleeves, raising waists, and adjusting hems.

Mrs. Vernice Michalack of Fond du Lac, Wisconsin, who started an alterations business several years ago, did not have to advertise at all. She never left calling cards at shops, never gave a fashion show or any other kind of promotional event. All she did was to tell her friends and acquaintances of her service—she has never lacked for customers since. Mrs. Michalack's investment included $400 for a new sewing machine and $200 for sewing materials and equipment for a sewing room. Her husband's carpentry talents helped defray the cost of building cabinets, clothes racks, and a railed platform for customers having hem adjustments.

Prices. These vary widely from one area to another. Here are the rates (labor only) currently being charged in a nonmanufacturing city of 150,000, as compiled by the New York State Woman's Program:

COATS:	hem	$5.00 to $6.00	
	shorten sleeves	$2.00 to $3.50	
SUITS:	*Skirt*—raise waist	$3.00 to $3.50	
	take in seams ...	$3.00 to $3.50	($1.00 per seam)
	hem	$2.00 to $3.00	
	hem, pleated	$3.50 to $5.00	
	Jacket—shorten	$2.00 to $3.50	
	shorten sleeves .	$2.00 to $3.00	
	raise back	$3.50 to $6.50	
	take in seams ..	$3.00	($1.00 per seam)
	narrow shoulders ...	$2.50 to $3.50	
DRESSES:	hem	$2.00 to $3.50	
	raise waist	$2.50 to $3.50	
	narrow shoulders	$2.50 to $4.00	
	raise back	$3.00 to $5.00	
	take in seams (armhole to waist) ..	$2.00	
	take in seams (armhole to hem) ..	$3.00	
	take in seams (waist to hem)	$2.50	
	shorten sleeves	$1.50 to $3.00	

Rates will be lower in small towns and rural areas, higher in cities and prosperous suburbs. Some big-city department stores are currently charging as much as $5 to alter a dress hemline, $10 for a coat. Whatever rates you charge—and they should of course be competitive with other local services—stick to them for everybody. The New York State Woman's Program advises: "Know your value. Don't undersell or oversell yourself. You can't start low and expect to raise your prices—your clientele won't stay with you. Nor can you afford to have one price for friends and relatives and another for customers. Know what you're worth and demand it."

WHERE TO GET MORE INFORMATION

The sources suggested below are also applicable to #13, #14, #15, #16, #18, and #19.

Good Housekeeping New Complete Book of Needlecraft, Vera Guild. Good Housekeeping Books, 250 West 55th Street, New York, N.Y. 10019, 1971.

Modern Sewing Techniques, Francis F. Mauck. The Macmillan Co., New York, N.Y., 1962.

Sew and Make Money, Drucella Lowrie. Viking Press, New York, N.Y., 1956.

Singer Sewing Book, Gladys Cunningham. Golden Press, New York, N.Y., 1969.

13

CUSTOM-MADE CLOTHING FOR WOMEN AND CHILDREN

Another sewing service that has promising possibilities is dressmaking. Some women have figure problems that make it too expensive to alter readymade clothing to fit them properly. Others are willing to pay more for the luxury of being able to select the styles, fabrics, and colors they like best instead of being limited to what is currently available in the stores. And though, in general, ordinary clothing for children can't be custom made cheaply enough to be worth while (it's outgrown too fast), special occasions sometimes call for specially made outfits.

The one trouble with dressmaking is that the considerable time and labor involved make it necessary to price custom-made clothing higher than the ordinary woman can afford. Consequently, unlike alterations, this business must be located in an area with an above-average income—usually a fairly large city or town or a well-to-do suburb.

Some dressmakers work from commercial patterns; others create their own designs. One woman who has made a success of the latter is Mrs. Thelma Dabney, of Rockville, Virginia, near Richmond, who started out with an alterations service and worked up, with the help of correspondence-school courses in advanced tailoring and dress design, to a full-fledged dressmaking service specializing in wedding costumes.

Gowns for the bride and her attendants are the most profitable area for specialization because your prices can compare favorably with those of readymade gowns. Besides, what girl wouldn't prefer a bridal gown made especially for her? But there are other possibilities. Despite the improvement in recent years, many readymade maternity styles are still stodgy and matronly-looking. In areas where there are a good many fashion-conscious young wives, some seamstresses have made a success of designing and making chic, young maternity outfits—dungarees with a stretch top (to be covered by a loose shirt), for example, or smock dresses in bright, contemporary patterns. Still another specialty for well-to-do areas is girls' clothing for special occasions—first communion, confirmation or graduation dresses, or costumes for holidays or school plays.

You might also consider borrowing a leaf from some big-city semi-custom shops for women that offer a limited number of styles, but will make them up in any color or fabric desired. This kind of standardization will enable you to develop more efficient work techniques and thus speed up your production. Nor, if you choose classic styles, should it cut down the appeal of your service. Most women have a favorite dress style and would be happy to be able to get it in several different versions.

Usually your customers will prefer to furnish their own fabrics, but you should be able to offer suggestions and to let them know of the wide choice available. And if you do your own designing, you will work with particular fabrics in mind. One way to keep up with the market is to subscribe to a fabric service. For an annual fee of a few dollars, these services will supply you, weekly or monthly, with dozens of samples and the sources from which they are available. (Some names and addresses: Fabrics 'Round the World, Inc., 270 W. 38th Street, New York, N.Y. 10018; Designers Fabrics Buy/Mail, 1948 Ridge Avenue, Evanston, Ill. 60204; and the Fashion Fabrics Club, 12 Great Neck Road, Great Neck, New York, N.Y. 11022.) Also, upon request, some fabric manufacturers will send you free samples of their products.

A successful dressmaker must be familiar with the professional techniques that make the difference between a home-made dress and a custom-made one. She must also know how to compensate for a wide variety of figure defects. And if she aspires to create her own designs, she must master the art of pattern-making. If you feel you are deficient in any of these areas, you might want to do as Mrs. Dabney did and take a correspondence-school course or courses. You'll find various schools advertised in sewing and needlework magazines; make sure the one you choose has the advanced courses you need and is accredited by the National Home Study Council.

Prices. Yours should be competitive with other services in your area. At first you may find that you work too slowly to make these profitable, but as, by trial and error, you discover the most efficient work layout and production techniques, your profits should increase. (If not, you don't belong in this business.) Typical dressmakers' rates (exclusive of the fabric) range, depending upon the style and material, from about $10 to $15 for a skirt, $12 to $40 for a dress, $25 to $75 for a suit, and $40 and up (sometimes way up) for a wedding dress. Rates in rural areas will be lower; in high-income, urban areas, higher. In the latter you will also have more competition, either from other dressmakers or from couturier clothing.

WHERE TO GET MORE INFORMATION

Modern Pattern Design, Harriet Pepin. Funk & Wagnalls, New York, N.Y., 1970.

Design Your Own Dress Patterns, Adele P. Margolis. Doubleday & Co., Inc., Garden City, N.Y., 1971.

Also see sources listed under #12, "Alterations and Mending."

14

CUSTOM-MADE SHIRTS FOR MEN

Men too have their figure problems, especially when it comes to that staple of their wardrobes, the dress (i.e., business) shirt. Many is the man who can't get a proper fit at the neck with standard collar sizes, or whose arms are too long or too short for the regulation sleeve lengths. There are men too, who like longer shirttails than those available in readymade shirts or a better fit through the body.

Some men have always had their shirts custom-made by private tailors. Today in some cities there are shops that specialize in custom shirts for both men and women; they attract a devoted clientele able and willing to pay roughly twice the price of a good readymade shirt for one that is a perfect fit. If you have access to customers with an above-average income and can turn out a professionally tailored product, you may be able to build up a thriving business with this one item alone.

Peter Fiduccia, of Carlstadt, New Jersey, did—the success story this time is a man's, but there is no reason a woman couldn't succeed just as easily. Working at first in the basement of his home on his mother's sewing machine, and using techniques he learned from her, Peter turned out shirts for a tailor in the nearby county seat of Hackensack. Eventually, he did so well that he opened his own specialty shirt shop there.

To make a success of this business, you must live in or near a business district; men won't travel any distance to seek you out. Or you can visit your client's home or business by appointment to take his measurements. Once you have these, and have made up and fitted a muslin pattern, you need never see the client again until or unless his measurements change; he will usually order by phone or mail. Or you can work through a tailor, though you make less this way.

Prices. For custom-made shirts (labor plus fabric) the price tag usually begins around $10 and may go as high as $25. Since businessmen, by and large, are conventional in their tastes, a fine-quality white broadcloth will be the fabric of choice in roughly 90 percent of your orders, enabling you to cut costs by buying material in quantity.

Monogramming—both for the shirts you make yourself and for readymade shirts and other items—is another service you might offer. A charge of $2.50 for a three-initial monogram, in any one of a variety of styles, is typical.

WHERE TO GET MORE INFORMATION

See sources listed under #12, "Alterations and Mending," and #13, "Custom-Made Clothes for Women and Children."

15

CUSTOM-MADE FINISHES

A sewing business that might be operated, depending on the demand, either alone or as an adjunct to a dressmaking service or a sewing course (see page 232) , is one that provides professional finishing touches to projects the customer herself has undertaken. These might include bound or handworked buttonholes, covered buttons, French seams, handrolled hems, hand-sewn zippers, decorative trim or other special details. The service might also include expert pattern alteration and the cutting of delicate fabrics or those otherwise difficult to handle, such as plaids or stripes.

Prices should be based on the time involved.

WHERE TO GET MORE INFORMATION

See sources listed under #13, "Custom-Made Clothes for Women and Children."

16

CUSTOM-MADE HOME FURNISHINGS

If you make your own slipcovers and draperies, and do it so expertly that your friends (and even your enemies) think it's a professional job, the chances are good that you can make money sewing the same things for others. But the custom look is essential. Even though you can afford to set your prices considerably lower than the commercial competition (the big reason there is room for you in this field), bargain rates won't compensate for amateurish workmanship.

The prospects for this business are good in almost any middle-income community, particularly one where there is a good deal of moving in and out, and a consequent need for redecorating. A brand-new housing development is an especially good bet—provided the new homeowners haven't so over-extended themselves that they can barely pay the mortgage!

Facilities and equipment needed differ little from those required for other sewing, but you will probably want a bigger cutting table and a sturdy factory-type sewing machine to cope with the heavier fabrics. If you intend to supply the fabrics, you'll have to have a sample case containing good-sized swatches of a number of different types for the customer's choice, plus a bigger display in your workroom for those whom this limited selection doesn't satisfy. The samples themselves are no problem: once you have established your professional status, most fabric manufacturers will provide them free or at cost.

But generally it is better to operate on a system whereby the customer supplies the fabric in the yardage you specify. It will save you the bother of carting samples around and the necessity of tying up money in fabric until you can collect from the customer. You should, however, be able to counsel the customer on her choice. If she picks a fabric that doesn't wear well, or that will fade or shrink after one washing, she is just as likely to blame you as the store from which she bought it. A big part of your service, too, will be interior decorating advice—what colors, fabrics, and styles fit best into the room's decor.

In making slipcovers, some seamstresses are expert enough to work directly from the measurements. It is safer, however, to make a muslin pattern and to return to the customer's home for a final fitting before cutting into the fabric. In making draperies, exact window measurements are vitally important, since you don't have the safety margin a muslin pattern provides.

Because slipcovers or draperies ordered from a department store may take six weeks or more to arrive (local shops sometimes work faster), you have an advantage in being able to provide speedier delivery. Never take on more work than you can handle, and finish one job before you begin the next. In the long run a reputation for fast, dependable service will bring you more customers than if you accept every order that comes your way—and then have to default on promised delivery dates. The personal touch is also important. Always deliver the slipcovers and/or draperies yourself so that you can install them to the client's complete satisfaction.

Prices. Because you won't have the higher overhead, you can afford to undercut big decorating services. But don't set your prices too low; for one thing, you should be putting something aside to pay for possible future expansion. The

New York State Woman's Program advises allowing one-sixth of the total net cost (including the cost of your own labor) for profit. Your selling price—the sum of total cost and profit—should not be higher than one-half the price such items sell for in the stores (the other half of the store's price covers its own selling expenses and profit). Remember, however, that the store's price covers the cost of materials, which yours may not.

WHERE TO GET MORE INFORMATION

Complete Guide to Curtains, Slipcovers and Upholstery, Marguerite Maddox and Miriam M. Paake. Pocket Books, New York, N.Y., 1963. Paperback.

Also see sources listed under #12, "Alterations and Mending."

17

REUPHOLSTERING

Reupholstering is a trade and a demanding one. If you know nothing about it, it is not a very practical possibility for making money at home. There are some women, however, who have learned to overhaul their own furniture—either the hard way, by just pitching in and doing it (with the help of a book on the subject), by taking a course in a local trade school or university extension service, or through a correspondence school. If you have such a skill, or are willing to spend the time and money to acquire it, reupholstering is a potential source of a steady income.

Inflation being what it is, it often makes more sense for a homemaker to reupholster an old but good piece of furniture than to buy a new piece at today's high prices. However, the equally high prices charged by most upholsterers sometimes prevent this from being a practical alternative. In consequence, a good moderately priced service seldom lacks for customers, wherever it is located.

As the financial potential of this business is greater than most other types of sewing services, so is the investment required for equipment. You will definitely need a factory-type sewing machine, a button-covering machine, padded work benches, and such upholsterer's tools as a special hammer, shears, webbing stretcher, ripper, skewer, straight and curved needles, and a stuffing regulator. Springs, filling materials, padding, welt cording and various tacks, screws, dowels, and other supplies are other necessary expenses.

You will need ample space to work in—a garage, basement, or workshed. It is also desirable to have access to a pickup truck and a couple of husky male helpers (like a husband and teenage son) to handle pickup and delivery. Or you can specify that the customer deliver and pick up his own furniture, but in this case you will have to charge markedly lower prices to make this inconvenience worth while. Apart from moving the furniture, nothing about reupholstering requires unusual physical strength; it is a business quite as well suited to a woman's nimble fingers as to a man's.

As in making slipcovers (see page 105), it is easier to require the customer to supply the fabric than to do the buying yourself. You should, however, be able to advise her on her choice, and for this purpose you should have a sample display of the various types of fabric typically used for reupholstering.

Prices. Prices vary with the area and with the style and

condition of the piece of furniture to be reupholstered. Use the same system for determining your prices explained in Custom-Made Home Furnishings, page 106. Another way to make money is to buy junk sofas and chairs, restore them and offer them for sale. If you do a good job, your profit margin can be tremendous.

WHERE TO GET MORE INFORMATION

Essentials of Modern Upholstery, Herbert Bast. The Bruce Publishing Co., Milwaukee, Wis., 1963.

Furniture Upholstery and Repair. Sunset Books, Menlo Park, Calif., 1970. Paperback.

Popular Mechanics All About Upholstering, John Bergen. Hawthorn Books, Inc., New York, N.Y., 1968.

Upholstery, Arthur Bevin. Arco Publishing Co., Inc., New York, N.Y., 1962.

18

DOLL'S CLOTHING

Toy stores are full of things to intrigue a little girl's fancy, from nurses' kits to ballerina costumes. Outselling them all, now as always, are dolls and the clothing to dress them in. In the last ten years, in fact, sparked by the introduction of teenage dolls (who, like their real-life counterparts, apparently require inexhaustible wardrobes) , the sales of doll clothes have reached an all-time high.

For the woman who would like to put her sewing skills to work making doll clothes for sale, this represents both opportunity and formidable competition. Once fairly un-imaginative and confined mostly to dresses and bonnets for baby dolls, commercial clothes for girl dolls now range from bathing suits and tennis costumes to evening dresses and fur stoles, plus a similarly wide choice of clothing for the newly popular male dolls.

Some women who work at home have capitalized on the popularity of teenage dolls by making their own clothing for them and selling it through local toy or gift shops (though of course they cannot use the actual names of the dolls the clothes are meant for—that would be a trademark violation). Others concentrate on clothes for little-girl or baby dolls in popular standard sizes. Still others make a specialty of costume-doll clothing.

This is, however, a limited field, almost entirely depen-dent upon the local situation. Direct-to-customer sales are rare; for any kind of sales volume, retail outlets are needed. Usually these are specialty stores whose customers appreci-ate the out-of-the-ordinary. Even so, because of the neces-sarily low unit price that must be charged for doll clothes, total income from this business is never great. But in the right circumstances, it can be a pleasant way of making some pin money.

WHERE TO GET MORE INFORMATION

Dolls' Dressmaking, Winifred Butler. Van Nostrand Rein-hold Co., New York, N.Y., 1964.

Also see sources listed under #12, "Alterations and Mend-ing."

19

TOGS FOR DOGS

Still another sewing specialty with possibilities for the right area, in this case a big city or a very posh suburb, is—don't laugh—custom-made clothing for overprivileged dogs. If you have never seen a shop that specializes in pet accessories, you may not believe that there actually are people who will buy a needlework collar for a poodle, a chic brocaded outfit for a favorite Peke, or a fur coat for a Great Dane. They do exist, however, and there are even more dog owners, who, while not going to such ludicrous extremes, anxiously bundle their pets up in sweaters, coats, or ponchos at the first sign of bad weather. Typical prices for these range from around $5 to $15.

If there is a pet shop with such a clientele in your area, investigate the possibilities of becoming a fashion designer for dogs. Your friends may laugh at you when you sit down at your sewing machine, but it can bring in a tidy income!

WHERE TO GET MORE INFORMATION

See sources listed under #12, "Alterations and Mending."

FLOWERS AND PLANTS

Ever since Adam and Eve ate the apple and had to take up gardening, there have been opportunities to make a living from it. Each year, florists, nurserymen, supermarkets and dime-store plant departments rake in millions of dollars from people who want a little beauty in their lives or simply feel the primeval urge to grow things. A modest amount of this money can come *your* way if, in addition to a green thumb, you have a realistic idea of what's involved.

GENERAL GUIDELINES

• No matter where you live (unless it's an isolated community), there's a possibility of making money from plants and flowers. In a city you will probably lack the space to grow them—but have lots of potential customers starved for the sight of something in bloom. In that case you might consider a bouquet-of-the-week service (see page 114), based on buying from a wholesaler, as florists do. If you live in the country or the suburbs, your customers will probably have gardens of their own; here you may do well with a service to supply seedlings.

• You must decide whether you want a seasonal business or one that has a year-round potential. While obviously there will be no demand for seedlings in winter, winter and early spring are the best seasons of all for selling flowers and potted plants.

• For a year-round gardening business you must rely on a wholesaler for stock, at least for part of the year. Or you can invest in a greenhouse. These start at about $250 (plus an additional $30 to $40 for the foundation materials), for prefabricated lean-to models. The necessary plumbing and heating are provided by extending the facilities already existing in the house to which the lean-to is attached.

• The nature and extent of your competition will have an important bearing on the type of business you choose and the way you operate it. If the local supermarket offers houseplants, or a nearby nurseryman sells seedlings, a home business of the same kind will thrive only if it can offer a price advantage, a variety (e.g., African violets) not available elsewhere in the neighborhood, or a special service. It would be better still to choose an aspect of the business that would not compete directly with others in the area.

• See "A Word about Prices," page 5.

HELPFUL HINTS

• Although plants are being sold at more and more retail outlets these days, there seem to be fewer and fewer people who know anything about gardening to answer customer's questions. A big part of a business of your own could be your ability and willingness to give advice on gardening problems.

• With every plant or flat of seedlings you sell, try giving the customer a mimeographed or printed sheet with detailed instructions on type of soil preferred, light and watering requirements, the height eventually attained, when and how often to expect flowers, etc. It's a service that bigger operations don't offer, and one that customers love.

• Cut up garden catalogues and paste color pictures of the varieties you offer on the walls of the garage, shed, or stand from which you sell your plants, so novices will know what they're buying (and experienced gardeners can dream that this year their flowers can look like that too).

• Even though you won't really have the time for it, keep active in local garden club affairs, beautify-the-community projects, and flower shows. It will be your best form of advertising.

20

BOUQUET-OF-THE-WEEK SERVICE

Many people who enjoy (and can afford) flowers in their homes don't buy them regularly. They're too busy to go to the florist's, or there's always something else, at the moment, to spend the money for. But they may be good prospects for a service that delivers a distinctive bouquet of fresh-cut blooms to the door weekly, semimonthly, or monthly, and bills them on a regular basis.

Jane Ballard of Old Greenwich, Connecticut, calls herself "The Flower Lady." By spending Fridays and Saturdays in her garage, she's managed to parlay her love of flowers into a business with 130 customers, who get her bouquets on a regular basis. "This is a happy business because you have a product that makes other people happy," she says. "When it's snowing like crazy outside and you arrive with a bouquet of, say, jonquils, it's fun to see the pleasure people get from it."

To make a success of the business, you don't have to live in as prosperous an area as Old Greenwich. But you do have to have access to customers with an above-average income and a taste for gracious living. These are most likely found in a good-sized city or a suburb where the men are at the junior-executive level or above. There too you may find customers for your service in neighborhood businesses and other institutions. For the supply end, you must live in reasonably near proximity to a good wholesale flower dealer.

As for your own qualifications, you should have a love of flowers and a knack for arranging them to the best advantage. But even if you think you know a lot about flowers, it's wise to refresh your memory on how various blooms should be handled. A little research on the subject will remind you that pompons, for example, should be placed in warm water, whereas anemones do better in cold. Woody-stemmed flowers should be cut on the slant, carnations snipped off at a node.

To operate a bouquet-of-the-week business, you'll need a room that can be used as a workshop, specifically one where the temperature can be kept at between 32 and 52 degrees. In temperate zones, a garage or sunporch can be used for most of the year, but in summer it will be necessary to have air-conditioned quarters (or a very cool basement). Little equipment is needed: a ping-pong table or a piece of ply-wood across two sawhorses can serve as a work table. A paper cutter, staples, shears, knives, and florist's paper to wrap the bouquets complete the essentials.

For more elaborate flower arrangements you will need florist's clay, chicken wire, plastic foam, and a variety of attractive containers (since yours will be a regular service, you can cut down on costs by arranging to pick up the previous container when you deliver the next consignment of flowers). To keep the flowers until they are ready to be delivered, wholesale flour or powdered-egg tins make ideal water containers. Ask local bakeries for their throwaways.

Your biggest expense will be the cost of flowers for the first six weeks of operation, the time it takes until your first bills go out and the checks start coming in. You may be able to prevail on a wholesale florist to extend you credit, but don't count on it. Another major expense may be for advertising (see below, "How to get business").

One of the attractions of this business is that it takes only two days' work a week and about eight hours once a month to prepare the bills. Once you get going, your work schedule is simple. Early each Friday morning (before 8 A.M., when you will have the best selection), buy flowers in quantity from a wholesale flower dealer; you will soon learn which ones can be depended upon for fresh, healthy stock at reasonable prices. When you get home, cut the stems and sort the flowers into bunches of a dozen or more, then add greenery such as laurel or huckleberry leaves. Vary the arrangements from week to week. Mrs. Ballard, for example, may offer gladioli with lemon leaves one week, daisies and bachelor's buttons with laurel the next, snapdragons with magnolia greens the third. When the bouquets are ready, wrap them in florist's paper and stand them upright in cans of water.

Deliveries start late Friday afternoon and continue again on Saturday, just in time for weekend entertaining. Since the bouquets must remain in the water cans until they reach their destination, a station wagon is a good vehicle for transporting them. If you have a sizable list of clients, you may not be able to do all the delivering yourself. Mrs. Ballard farms some of hers out to friends, paying them 35 cents for each delivery (the delivery fee she charges her clients).

How to get business. If you have a minimum amount of

money for promotion and advertising, draw up your own list of prospective clients, including not only private individuals but doctors, dentists, lawyers, hotels and motels, hospitals and nursing homes, restaurants, beauty salons, and any other likely business in your area; to these, send out a mimeographed letter announcing your service. Place an ad in local papers (on the women's page if possible) ; spread the word to members of clubs and community organizations you belong to; supply several local merchants with free service, for a limited time, for the privilege of placing posters in their windows.

With more money to invest, you can do as Mrs. Ballard did. She hired a professional mailing service to provide a list of potential prospects and sent to each a printed announcement with a postage-paid reply card. From a 10,000-piece mailing, Mrs. Ballard got a 1 percent return, or 100 customers lined up before she began. The mailing cost her close to $1,000, but once she got going, she began clearing, after expenses, as much as $100 a week.

Fees. A typical charge (customers billed monthly) for a simple bouquet service might be $3.85 once a month, $6.70 twice a month, and $12.35 for weekly service; included in these prices is a 35-cent delivery fee. More elaborate flower arrangements in special containers would call for higher prices. In setting fees, keep your competition in mind; unless you can offer your customers a price bargain, there is no real reason they should patronize you rather than leaving a standing order with the local florist. On the other hand, no business is worthwhile unless you can make enough, after expenses, to compensate you for your time and work.

Here are some helpful tips:

• A good way to attract new business is to give away free bouquets to prospective customers.

• The Christmas season can be your bonanza if you promote your service as a unique gift idea. One bouquet per month for a year would be a wonderful way to please people difficult to buy for, such as invalids, or friends who have everything. Business executives who are looking for unusual gifts for clients are also good prospects. The idea is equally appropriate for birthday gifts.

• If you are located in a suburb, your business will drop off in summer when your customers' gardens are in bloom. However, the price of wholesale flowers is lower then too, enabling you to offer bargains. In a city, the dropoff in business may be less.

WHERE TO GET MORE INFORMATION

Encyclopedia of Flower Arrangements, J. G. Conway. Alfred A. Knopf, Inc., New York, N.Y., 1957.

How to Arrange Flowers for All Occasions, Katherine N. Cutler. Doubleday & Co., Inc., New York, N.Y., 1967.

1001 Questions Answered About Flowers, Norman Taylor. Dodd, Mead & Co., New York, N.Y., 1963.

Retail Florist (Small Business Bibliography #74). Small Business Administration. Superintendent of Documents, U.S. Government Printing Office, Washington, D.C. 20402. Free leaflet.

21

RAISING PLANTS FOR SALE

Today the home gardener who hopes to make money by selling plants faces increased competition, not only from florists and nurseries, but from nongardening outlets ranging from hardware stores to gift shops. Some women have succeeded in this business, however, and you can too, if you are in a good location for it. As for your competition, if you can't beat it, you can perhaps join it—i.e., by arranging to sell to retail outlets on consignment.

Your first step should be to survey your area to see how much potential demand there is for plants, both those meant for transplanting to outdoor gardens, and the patio or houseplant variety. Check with home gardeners, supermarket and dime-store managers, roadside stands, and garden supply stores to find out if there is an opening for you, and if so in what direction it lies. You may find that the best market is for ordinary plants like zinnias or tomatoes. On the other hand, it may be that your area is glutted with suppliers of these, but would welcome exotic specialties such as Venus's-fly traps or orchids. Or you might want to specialize in hanging baskets, or in decorative containers imaginatively planted with such combinations as day lilies and chlorophytum, dracaena and pelargoniums or agapanthuses and dainty nemophilas, or window boxes planned for the various seasons of the year or the aspect (north, south, east, west) in which the box will be placed.

You don't need a lot of space or working capital to start with. You do need an enclosed porch, heated garage, a half basement or any other spare room where light, heat, and humidity can be controlled. Only a modest amount of cash is required for your initial purchases: plants, bulbs, cuttings and seeds, flats, fertilizer, potting soil (usually a mixture of peat moss, sand, and soil) , and a supply of terra-cotta pots in a variety of sizes. If you intend to offer patio and house plants, you'll also need decorative pottery containers to enhance the appearance of your plants and to raise your profits.

Mrs. Angeline Miller of Simms, Montana, runs a seasonal business selling common flower and vegetable plants, which

she raises in a lean-to greenhouse (see page 113). Here is
Mrs. Miller's calendar description of her work:

> In January I begin planting seeds and slipping plants, two tasks
> which will keep me busy through the spring. In February, I con-
> centrate on pansies and petunias. Then in March and April I
> start vegetables (the easiest of all to raise and to sell) and more
> flowers.
>
> March and April are the two busiest months of the year: the
> tiny seedlings are then transplanted into flats and peat pots. As
> they get well started, I transfer them to cold frames and put them
> just outside the greenhouse. There they get their first taste of out-
> door living and become stocky, hardy plants. In the event of a
> cold spell, I cover the frames with canvas and heat them with
> ordinary light bulbs.
>
> May is the most pleasant month of all: the plants are ready for
> sale. June finds my greenhouse empty. Then in September, I begin
> bringing in plants from the garden for my own winter enjoyment.
> All through the cold months, I enjoy the company of geraniums,
> chrysanthemums, carnations, African violets, cacti, ferns.

Mrs. Miller prefers to couple summer profits with winter
pleasure, but other greenhouse gardeners find winter, when
people are longing for a reminder of warmer weather, the
most profitable season of all. They concentrate on houseplants, particularly the flowering kind, and make special
selling efforts at such holidays as Thanksgiving, Christmas
and Easter.

Prices. Prices differ so widely according to what is offered
and how and where that no general figures can be given.
For the home gardener, raising plants for sale is a limited
business and can be expected to produce not much more
than pin money, particularly if it is done on a seasonal basis.
In figuring profits, don't forget to include in expenses the
extra light and heating cost, particularly if you have a
greenhouse. To compete with nurseries, roadside stands,
etc., your prices will have to be at least on a par with theirs.

How to get business. If you live on a well-traveled road (and zoning laws permit you to post a sign on your property) , or if you are well known as a gardener in your community, you may be able to operate a direct-to-customer business—the most profitable, provided you get enough customers. (High visibility and word of mouth will be your best salesmen; also try ads in local papers and a listing in the classified telephone directory.) Otherwise, try selling to local retail outlets (florists, dime stores, supermarkets, garden supply and hardware stores, roadside stands) on a consignment basis, whereby you receive roughly half of the retail selling price.

WHERE TO GET MORE INFORMATION

The Complete Book of Growing Plants from Seeds, Elda Haring. Hawthorn Books, Inc., New York, N.Y., 1967.

Information on Greenhouses and *Greenhouse Flowers and Florists Crops.* Agriculture Research Service Publications, Washington, D.C. 20250. Both leaflets free.

The Nursery Business (Small Business Bibliography #14) , Small Business Administration. Superintendent of Documents, U.S. Government Printing Office, Washington, D.C. 20402. Free Booklet.

The Nursery Manual, L. H. Bailey. The Macmillan Co., New York, N.Y., 1948.

22

GROWING HERBS

The burgeoning interest in gourmet cookery in recent years has led to a greatly increased demand for herbs, a demand food companies have been quick to answer. On a much smaller scale, some home gardeners have also made money from these seasoning agents.

Mrs. Helen Miller of Angola, New York, is one. Mrs. Miller got into the herb-growing business almost by accident—when a woman in Virginia, where she was on vacation, gave her a slip of thyme from her garden. When Mrs. Miller got home, she planted it in her own garden, and, intrigued by the idea, grew other herbs from seed. Her first small crop sold out at the local Farmer's Market. Flushed with success, Mrs. Miller next produced a host of different herbs, but of this crop she managed to sell only a fraction. Trying to recoup the time and labor she had already spent, she dried the remaining herbs and offered them in cellophane packets. But still they did not sell.

On the advice of a friend, she took her problem to the counselors of the Woman's Program conducted by the New York State Department of Commerce (Massachusetts has a similar program), who advised her to spend a little money to repackage her herbs in attractive bottles with printed labels and to put together kitchen kits complete with helpful suggestions on how to use herbs. That got her business off to a good start; it has prospered to the extent that her herbs are now sold by local markets, through mail order, and from the log cabin her husband built her (it sits in front of their home) to serve as a showroom and shop. Profits also enabled her to buy a greenhouse to make her business a year-round one.

There are several ways to market herbs:

1. *You can sell them fresh.* If you yourself have ever tried to buy them, you know how difficult it is to find a source of supply. In a community where gourmet foods sell well, the local grocery or supermarket might well agree to stock your product. Gourmet cooks know that dried herbs simply aren't as flavorful as fresh ones.

2. *You can freeze them.* Frozen herbs are nearly as good as fresh in flavor and color. The following freeze satisfactorily: tarragon, sweet marjoram, thyme, lovage, sage, winter and summer savory, mint, dill, and lemon balm.

To freeze herbs, select plants that are just budding. Snip off sprigs about four inches long and blanch them (one variety at a time) in boiling water for about 40 seconds. Transfer to a pan of ice water, dry on paper towels, and drop into a polyethylene bag. Heat-seal the bag or close tightly with a rubber band, and freeze. Just before delivery to the retailer, slip into colorful paper bags or envelopes labeled with the name of the herb contained.

3. *You can dry them.* This approach has the greatest profit possibilities because it has mail-order potential, as many bigger businesses than Mrs. Miller's have proved. It is also where the greatest competition lies, since dried herbs in utilitarian packages are available in every supermarket, fancily packaged ones line the shelves of gourmet food and gift shops and department stores. You will have to package yours attractively too, at a competitive price, and perhaps have a special gimmick, such as Mrs. Miller's kitchen kits.

How to get business. Herbs are so special a product that at first, anyway, you will almost have to sell through a retailer. Later, if your business proves successful, you may be able to branch out with a shop of your own and a mail-order operation.

How to Grow Herbs for Gourmet Cooking, Frederick O. Anderson. Meredith Press, New York, N.Y., 1967.

23

PLANT AND GARDEN SITTER

When it comes to taking a vacation, the true gardener (whether the indoor or the outdoor variety), like the true pet lover, is in a quandary. While she (it is usually she; women have tenderer hearts) is out enjoying herself, who will take care of her most prized possessions?

Difficult as it is to arrange, she can usually find someone to cut the grass while the family is away. And an accommodating neighbor may come over to turn on the sprinkler so the lawn won't turn completely brown. But who will cultivate her prize rosebeds, spray at the proper times, cut off the dead heads? Who will stake up the gladioli, disbud the chrysanthemums, feed the dahlias? Without such tender care, a garden that would have won a blue ribbon at any flower show at the end of June or July can be a wasteland several weeks or a month later when its owners return from vacation.

A lesser problem, which is nevertheless still a problem, confronts the possessor of indoor greenery. If that consists of only a few small houseplants, the owner can buy a self-watering device for each, or cover them with polyethylene bags and place them in larger containers, filling the space between with moist peat. But that will not do for large imposing palms, trees in tubs, delicate plants with strict watering schedules, or apartment windowbox or terrace gardens.

If you live in a community with a sufficient number of devoted gardeners, indoor or outdoor, you can make spending money during the summer months (and possibly at some other times of the year) by caring for their plants while they are away. You need not have an expert knowledge of gardening (though it helps) so long as you receive a detailed schedule for watering and other tasks from your client.

How to get business. Since your target is vacationers, try to publicize your service through local travel bureaus, gas stations, automobile club offices, luggage shops; post mimeographed notices, if you can get the owners' permission, in plant nurseries and garden supply stores. In late May, start running ads in local newspapers and gardening news sheets. Inform the garden club of your service, and do your best to spread the word through friends, neighbors, and acquaintances. Since "plant sitting," and sometimes garden care too, involves entering someone's home while he is away, your prospective clients will want to be sure of your personal integrity, and will therefore give far more weight to a personal recommendation than to an ad.

Fees. For "plant sitting," the fees are necessarily small—perhaps $2 a week—but so are the duties. Garden care usually involves considerably more work, and should be billed by the hour, at the rates generally prevailing in your area for landscape services. You need have little fear of competition; in most suburban areas it does not pay such services, with their large overhead and lack of skilled help, to perform any but the most rudimentary tasks, such as cutting the grass, trimming, and hedging.

WHERE TO GET MORE INFORMATION

Encyclopedia of Gardening, ed. Norman Taylor. Houghton Mifflin, Boston, Mass., 1961.

Making Things Grow, Thalassa Cruso. Alfred A. Knopf, Inc., New York, N.Y., 1968.

24

LANDSCAPE CONSULTANT

The typical new homeowner in the typical housing development is a person in need of help. Usually one of the reasons for his move from the city has been his urge to possess some land of his own. But now that he has it, what is he to do with it? The builder has departed, leaving some scrawny foundation plantings and an underfed lawn soon destined to become wall-to-wall crabgrass. Beset on all sides by nurserymen pushing "bargains," and neighbors—as new to the land as he is—offering conflicting advice, many a new homeowner might welcome a moderately priced service to help him plan his grounds-improvement program and steer him to reliable sources of supply.

That is where you, if you are an experienced gardener, can come in. People formally trained for the job are called landscape architects, but these usually take on much bigger (and more expensive) projects than any you will be called upon to handle. Your role is simply to use your knowledge

of the area; your familiarity with local soil and weather con-
ditions; your experience with various plants, their rates of
growth, flowering times, the care needed, and so forth, to
steer the homeowner through what for him is a bewildering
new experience, and to keep him from making expensive
mistakes on "exterior" (as opposed to interior) decoration.

Like an interior designer, you too will draw up a detailed
plan for your client. Instead of room color schemes and
furniture placement, you will show him what trees are best
to plant in his yard and where, where flower beds should go
and what they might contain, which plantings will screen
the patio to provide some needed privacy, what kinds of
ground cover to plant to cut down maintenance. Since few
new homeowners can afford to spend a great deal on the
outside at first, the scheme should be planned to be carried
out in stages over a five-to-ten year period, with successive
sketches to show the client what his grounds will look like as
each stage is completed. You can limit your service to this
consultation stage, or go shopping with the client to help
him pick out the most promising young saplings, shrubs,
plants, etc. to fulfill your plan. You do not, however, do any
of the actual planting.

The best location for this business is a middle-income
suburb where the newcomers are eager to emulate the life
style of longer-established residents, with their well-tended
lawns, bright flower beds, and artfully designed terrace or
patio plantings. Needless to say, your own garden and
grounds must be a showplace (though not on a grand
scale), if you hope to make money by advising others on
theirs. A community with a number of nurserymen and
garden supply stores is also needed, because much of your
income will come from commissions earned by steering
customers to a particular source of supply.

How to get business. Since the greater part of the business that comes to you will be through word-of-mouth advertising, make sure that every friend, neighbor, and acquaintance is aware of your service. Notify too any contacts you've made in the landscaping and nursery business, as well as local builders and real estate salesmen. Advertise in the gardening pages of local papers and take a listing in the classified telephone directory. In addition, whenever you learn of new families moving into the area, write or call them to ask for an appointment to explain your service. If you are granted an interview, take along color pictures of your own garden or of any others you have designed, plus color sketches of plans readily adaptable to the typical architecture and yard layouts of the area. Don't be too discouraged if you don't get new homeowners' business right away. The first year they're usually too busy with other matters, such as installing storm windows and buying carpeting. The important thing is to encourage them to come to you when they *are* ready.

Fees. For a consulting service only, it is usual to charge by the hour. Landscape architects get as much as $25 to $50 an hour, but in most communities a nonprofessional consultant will not be able to charge more than $5 to $10 an hour. If the client is willing to buy his supplies through you, it is often more profitable to work on a retail basis. Here, like the interior designer who works on the same plan, you buy at wholesale but charge the client the retail cost, taking as your fee the difference between the two. Or the nurseryman may pay you a straight commission for any sales you bring in.

WHERE TO GET MORE INFORMATION

America's Garden Book, rev., James and Louise Bush-Brown. Charles Scribner's Sons, New York, N.Y., 1968.

Gardening and Home Landscaping Guide, Jack Kramer. Arco Publishing Company, New York, N.Y., 1968.

Landscape Planning for Small Gardens, Frances Hutchison. Soccer Associates, New Rochelle, N.Y., 1969.

The New York Times Book of Home Landscaping, Joan Lee Faust. Alfred A. Knopf, New York, N.Y., 1968.

Patios, Terraces, Decks and Roof Gardens, Alice Upham Smith. Hawthorn Books, Inc., New York, N.Y., 1969.

BUSINESS SERVICES

For women who have had business experience in an office, there are a number of ways to use their skills in making money at home. Typing, taking dictation, bookkeeping, accounting, and answering the telephone are only some of the services that are in demand on a free-lance as well as a nine-to-five basis.

GENERAL GUIDELINES

• If you simply prepare paperwork in your home for mailing or delivery elsewhere, you may not be affected by zoning regulations. But it's always wise to check. Identifying your home, through a sign or an advertisement, as a place of business, or permitting clients to come to it, is definitely subject to such regulations.

• The nature of the community in which you live is important. Obviously, business services are required mainly by commercial firms, universities, and other institutions, so you must live in an area where there are a number of these reasonably nearby. Paradoxically, a city often offers slim pickings, because of the competition from full-time workers and temporary secretarial services. A smaller community, where there is a shortage of skilled clerical workers or where there are a number of businesses too small to employ full-time help, may offer more lucrative possibilities.

• Ideally, you should be able to set off a separate room for your home office. But if this isn't possible, you can make do with a desk, chair, and filing cabinet or other storage place that can be locked.

• The equipment needed is in most cases minimal, but always includes a standard typewriter (preferably electric) in tiptop condition. If you don't already own one, it may pay you to rent a machine by the month at the start. Not only is the fee tax-deductible, but renting allows you to experiment with various brands and types of machines until you know which one best suits your needs. For example, if you do a lot of multiple-copy work, you will need a machine with a sensitive variable pressure control. If you find that your work requires a variety of type styles, a machine with changeable type cylinders is indicated.

• An additional financial investment ($100 is probably a minimum) is needed for stationery and other supplies and advertising (see below, "How to get business").

• See "A Word about Prices," page 5.

HELPFUL HINTS

• Your manner toward your clients should be friendly and helpful but businesslike, your dress and grooming neat and conservative.

• If your skills are rusty, put in a period of intensive practice before you look for customers. Or take a brush-up course either at a local business school or by mail.

• Punctuality is a must. If you have promised a job for a certain date, make sure it is ready, even if you have to stay up the night before to complete it. The corollary of this is never to take on more work than you are sure you can handle.

HOW TO GET BUSINESS

Since what you are offering is a business service, it is important that you have a professional-looking business card. Have cards printed, on good stock, with your name and the name, if any, of your business, your address and telephone number, and the type of service you offer. Distribute them personally (and ask for an interview with potential clients, whenever possible) at business offices, clubs, fraternal organizations, colleges, and schools.

You may also want to run an ad in local newspapers (under Personals or Situations Wanted) and in the classified telephone directory. If you live in or near a college town, make sure your ad appears in the student newspaper and in faculty journals, and make every effort to get permission to advertise your services on bulletin boards in dormitories and study halls.

If these methods fail to bring in enough business, send out individual sales letters (typing, spelling, and grammar should be impeccable) to particularly good prospects, such as doctors, dentists, lawyers, personnel managers, deans of students, professors, small retail stores, and new businesses. (Ask your present clients' permission to use their names in the letter.) Postage fees make this a costly means of promotion if carried out on a large or regular scale, but it can be worth the money.

25

SECRETARIAL SERVICE

Secretarial jobs are frequently considered—by those who hold them, anyway—as a kind of way station leading to something better. (Like a flossier position where *you* get to have a secretary or a permanent position as a wife.) It may come as a mild surprise to you now that those underrated typing and steno skills can put you into business for yourself.

A home secretarial service requires clerical experience plus. Perhaps the plus is as important as the skills. To bosses harried from coping with incompetent help, to small businessmen too small to afford even that, to students frantic to have a term paper typed, your calm, professional air and courteous competence can make you seem a treasure. To obtain such a reputation, however, requires a high level of organization and reliability. Before starting an office service, the Woman's Program of the New York State Department of Commerce suggests you ask yourself a few questions:

1. Will you be able to deliver assignments when promised?

2. Can you make space to work (and store work) away from other family papers and out of reach of children's curious hands?

3. Will you be able to spare enough uninterrupted hours at home to do a proper job?

4. Will you be able to leave home to pick up and deliver work? (It's not usual for clients to come to your home.)

If you can answer Yes to these questions, this may be a business for you.

When you first start out, you'll probably want to take whatever kind of secretarial work that is offered to you, from typing up students' notes to sending out doctors' bills. You may find that, to make ends meet, you will also have to offer additional services, such as bookkeeping or operating a telephone answering service (see following pages). Eventually, however, it may be possible for you to specialize in the type of work you like best, such as typing manuscripts or business reports. If you live in an area where there is a demand for typists specializing in legal, medical or scientific work, take the trouble necessary to learn the special vocabulary involved. The rates for such work are higher.

Fees. Fees for free-lance secretarial services vary a great deal, depending on the area and the type of work. Normally, large metropolitan areas and university towns have the highest rates. Check to see what other secretarial services and/or public stenographers in your area charge. Don't forget delivery costs.

Here are rates currently quoted as typical by the New York State Woman's Program:

• *Typing letters (original and one carbon)* : 65 to 80 cents per page.

• *Typing legal documents or manuscripts:* 65 cents per page (double-spaced) , $1 per page (single spaced) .

• *Dictation and transcription:* $3 per hour for ordinary correspondence, $5 per hour for technical, legal or intricate material.

It's a good idea to buy some work order forms with blanks for the type of job, the promised delivery date, and the payment rate (with extra charge, if any was agreed upon, for a rush job) . You keep a copy and send a copy to the client.

WHERE TO GET MORE INFORMATION

Standard Handbook for Secretaries, Lois Hutchinson. Mc-Graw Hill Book Co., New York, N.Y., 1967.

The Successful Secretary's Handbook, Esther R. Becker and Evelyn Anders. Harper & Row, New York, N.Y., 1971.

26

NOTARY PUBLIC

A notary is a public official who acts as witness for persons signing certain legal documents. The income produced by this service is ordinarily quite small, but so is the amount of effort required. It can be considered simply as a source of occasional pin money, or adopted as a sideline to a home secretarial service, where it is an added attraction for clients whose papers need notarizing. One of its attractions for *you* can be that you need not step outside your door; your customers will come to you.

Notarial services are needed everywhere, but obviously if you live in a strictly residential community where occasions for signing notarized documents are few, you won't get much business. Proximity to a business district with little or no notarial service holds much more promise.

Almost anybody can be a notary. The basic requirements: You must be twenty-one, a United States citizen, and a resident of the state in which you intend to practice. Oh, yes—anyone convicted of a felony isn't eligible.

Your main duty as a notary is to verify with your signature that a paper was signed in your presence. You may also be called upon to witness signatures on affidavits and acknowledgments, administer oaths, and take written testimony of witnesses unable to appear at legal proceedings. In some states, a notary may act as a justice of the peace, and in Florida he or she is even allowed to solemnize marriages. In almost all states, a notary is expected to maintain records of his or her official acts.

While some of these tasks may sound awesomely legal, it's not necessary to understand legal documents or know much about the law. In fact, no notary, unless he or she is also an attorney, is permitted to practice law or share fees with an attorney.

Each state sets its own requirements and fees for notaries. In some states you must pass an examination to receive a license; in others, payment of a fee is sufficient. Fees range from $1 to $25; in addition you must pay for an official stamp and seal. This cost varies, but is usually nominal.

Further, in some states you must post a bond. The amount varies considerably among states and sometimes among different counties. Some states have no fixed amount, some set it at $500, and some have been known to charge as much as $10,000. This requirement is easily taken care of through a bonding company. Fees usually range from $2 to $3 per thousand dollars.

To become a notary, write to the Secretary of State in your state capital and ask for an application and instructions. The examination, where required, is simple; the state helps you prepare with a detailed instruction booklet. The number of notaries in a state is usually not limited; all applicants who qualify are accepted. Your appointment is valid for a period of from two to ten years (depending on the state). Renewal simply requires another application and fee.

Hours. No specific times are specified; some notaries keep hours from sunrise to midnight, others operate by appointment only. Naturally, it's best to be as available as possible. That doesn't mean you can't ever go out, but when you do, hang a cardboard clock sign on your door that reads: "Notary will be back at _____."

Fees. These are regulated by the state in which you live. Usually they range from 25 cents to $1 for each paper you witness.

How to get business. This isn't the kind of business you have to sell or promote. When somebody needs you, he needs you and that's it. However, you do have to let the public know you're there. Some common methods include a listing in the classified telephone directory, a sign outside your house, and an occasional ad in your local paper. Also it's a good idea to distribute your business card to real estate agents and other firms which frequently need a notary.

27

BOOKKEEPING AND ACCOUNTING

This business is not for everyone. Only a woman with a sound knowledge of the theory and practice of bookkeeping and at least two to three years' experience with a bookkeeping firm, or the record-keeping department of a retail or industrial firm, or as full- or part-time bookkeeper for a small business firm, should even consider it. But if you do have that kind of specialized background, there are many opportunities for you to develop a home business.

Essentially, what you do is provide good business records for small businessmen who cannot afford full-time bookkeepers. Not only is there a great demand for such services at the present time, but the Small Business Administration points out that future needs will be even greater owing to increasingly complicated tax laws and the growing awareness that good records are crucial to good management.

A free-lance or "public" bookkeeper may offer one or more of these services to her clients: Straight bookkeeping, designing and installing a record-keeping system, and, if she is expert enough, preparing tax forms. The greatest demand is for bookkeeping, which involves making journal and ledger entries from the client's daily reports, preparing a monthly trial balance and, for some businesses, drawing up a monthly financial statement.

Sometimes it will make sense for you to visit the client at his place of business, especially if it involves only two or three hours of work each week or month. Much of the time, however, the client's transactions will be entered in books that you keep in your office. Daily sales reports will be mailed to you weekly or you can arrange to pick them up. Once a month it will be necessary for you to examine the clients' checkbook stubs, cancelled checks, bank statements and other original records.

Tax work involves more specialized knowledge in order to give the client the best possible benefit, and makes you subject to certain state and federal laws.

Another thing you should think about before you start is the nature of your community. Are there enough small businesses in the vicinity? Is there a need for a public bookkeeping service (or, if one already exists, for another one)? Have you lived in the community long enough to be well known there? Is the town growing or just holding its own? The answers to these and similar questions will provide some indication of how successful you can expect your service to be.

Fees. Setting fees is a bit tricky, and it will probably take you a few months before you can arrive at an equitable arrangement both for your clients and yourself. There are two methods of setting fees.

1. Hourly rates. Here you estimate what your time is worth, and add an allowance for overhead. For help in putting a value on your time, check local want ads for accounting jobs, or write to the Bureau of Labor Statistics of the United States Department of Labor for information on wage levels in your area. (If you have recently worked for a bookkeeping firm, you will already have an idea of the going rate.)

2. Flat fee. Many small business people prefer to have a monthly fee quoted in advance, so they can know just how much the service is going to cost them. This requires you to estimate how much time will be needed to service a particular account. That can be difficult to do before you have had experience with it.

With both methods, you must also take into account your client's ability and willingness to pay. Small businessmen who have never previously had a bookkeeping service may be skeptical of its value.

Usually it's best, at the start, to take clients on a trial basis, with the understanding that at the end of a two- or three-month period, your rates may be adjusted, by mutual agreement, either upward or downward as experience has proved wise.

How to get business. Let's face it: As a woman, you may have a harder time convincing businessmen to trust you with money matters than a man might—even though in bookkeeping firms headed by men, women do most of the actual book work. Your most likely prospects are local businessmen whom you know and who know you—the neighborhood druggist, the grocer, an auto repair shop, a restaurant. Often you will have personal knowledge of their inadequacies as record keepers from your dealings with them as a customer. Approach these people first and show them how you can make their life easier and more profitable.

Also send announcements to any other business in the area that you think might be interested in your services. Detail your experience and background in the field, and give professional and personal references. In a small town where there is no existing bookkeeping service, you might be able to get the backing of the local chamber of commerce or local banks. It will also pay you to participate actively in your community's civic, social, and professional affairs, since the more widely you are known and trusted, the more business will come your way.

You should, of course, maintain a listing in the classified telephone directory. And if you offer tax services, ads in local newspapers at the various tax reporting times of the year may bring in business.

WHERE TO GET MORE INFORMATION

Starting and Managing a Small Bookkeeping Service, Small Business Administration. Superintendent of Documents, U.S. Government Printing Office, Washington, D.C. 20402. Booklet.

28

MIMEOGRAPHING AND COPYING

Even in this age of sophisticated reproduction methods, the mimeograph machine manages to hold its own. Offset printing is better-looking, photocopying is quicker. But reproduction by mimeograph is cheaper than either, and therein lies its charm for many users. Therein too lies the chance for you to build up a little business of your own.

This business does best in a medium-size town or suburban area which has a fair number of small companies, stores, churches, civic groups, and clubs that frequently send out announcements of their various activities. Unless you live right on Main Street, you won't get much, if any, walk-in trade. And though some customers will be willing to pick up their orders, you will have to be prepared to deliver to others. This means you can't operate in too wide an area or your delivery costs will eat up your profits.

Another thing to check before you start is the nature of your competition. If there are several duplicating shops in the area, offering a wide range of services at modest prices, or if some of your prime prospects turn out to have mimeograph or photocopying machines of their own, there probably isn't any room for you.

In many areas, though, a copying service can carve out a respectable niche for itself if it is reliable, reasonably priced, and willing to take minimum orders not accepted by larger shops with expensive equipment. What kind of business could you expect? Church programs, restaurant menus, club bulletins, price lists, news letters, office forms, school newspapers, and flyers announcing sales are only some of the possibilities.

In addition to a good typewriter (preferably an electric one), you will, of course, need a mimeograph machine. At the start it's best to rent one, both in order to try out various models, and to make sure you have a going business before investing too much money in equipment. Rental fees for an electric machine (a wise choice in terms of the savings in man hours) range from $45 to $60 per month, and usually the first three months' payments may be applied to the purchase of a new machine (cost: $500 to $600). A secondhand electric mimeograph machine may cost from

$225 to $450. You will also need at least $100 for supplies—stencils, ribbons, ink, a stapler, and paper.

Fees. For this type of work, the Small Business Administration advises using a three-to-one ratio in setting fees—that is, to charge the client three times the labor cost of the job. Since, at the start anyway, the only labor involved will be yours, it may be difficult to decide what your own time is worth. While warning that prices vary from area to area, the New York State Woman's Program quotes as typical a charge of $1 per stencil, plus $1.50 per 100 sheets (you furnish both stencil and paper). Since a good typist can type a stencil in about 15 minutes and run off a hundred copies in a few minutes more, your earnings could be respectable—*if* (a big if, admittedly) you can get enough business. Some of your customers may also want you to address and stuff envelopes and mail out the work you do for them; for this service your charge should be in the same proportion, based on the time involved, plus the postage. (Also check what other duplicating services in the area charge.)

How to get business. Personal contact will probably bring in the most business. Do a little market research in your town to ferret out your most likely prospects—businesses or institutions whose present reproduction work is being done poorly, or that are passing up a chance to spread their message because of the high cost of new sophisticated duplication methods. Call on these potential clients with samples, impeccably produced, of the many kinds of mimeographs you are prepared to handle. Also include samples in the sales letters you send out. (See page 132.) And in placing ads in local newspapers, don't forget high school or college papers. Usually schools do have mimeograph machines of their own, but students, who, especially today, have a lot on their minds they want to share with others, don't always have access to them. (Speaking of that, be careful about duplicating material that could be considered libelous. You as well as your customer could be held responsible. Don't duplicate copyright material either—books, articles, certain legal documents, even a professor's notes—unless you have the permission of the copyright owner.)

WHERE TO GET MORE INFORMATION

Starting and Managing a Small Duplicating and Mailing Service, Small Business Administration. Superintendent of Documents, U.S. Government Printing Office, Washington, D.C. 20402. Booklet.

29

ADDRESSING SERVICE

Under certain circumstances, this is a possible way of making money at home. Unfortunately, its obvious appeal—anyone can address envelopes, and all you need is a typewriter—has led to its use as a favorite bait by unscrupulous promoters out to fleece the unwary. Beware of ads promising money for addressing envelopes if you are required to buy something—a mailing list, supplies, anything—to get the work. Those are come-ons; their purpose is to make money *from* you, not *for* you. (See page 4.)

In spite of the fact that most companies with sizeable mailing lists now have automatic addressing machines (or employ direct-mail specialists to do their mailings for them), there *is* an occasional need for typists who work from their homes. The occasion may be a special one—a political campaign or a charity drive, or it may result from an overflow of work that a firm cannot handle internally. Sometimes you can find such at-home work by watching the Help Wanted ads, especially if you live in a busy industrial area. But much more often, you will have to ferret out customers on your own. Call on addressing services, local retail stores that send out advertising mailers, nonprofit organizations, clubs, churches, mail-order firms, and leave your name and telephone number. This kind of work, when available at all, is usually only occasional, so don't expect too much from it. But it can provide unexpected pin money. A fairly common fee is $15 per thousand (typed) envelopes.

30

TELEPHONE ANSWERING SERVICE

This is a demanding job, and one that usually requires more initial investment than some other home secretarial services. On the other hand, if you happen to live in the right area, a telephone answering service can be a steady source of income.

The right area, in this case, is a community with a reasonable number of doctors, salesmen, electricians, plumbers, and other people on the move who need someone to take their calls while they're away—an area too where no other service exists to fill this need, or where existing services are overburdened, discourteous or inefficient. Your clients must live fairly near you because, in addition to the area charge, most telephone companies levy a mileage charge if the phone is to be answered from either the client's phone or yours.

It is best too, for this kind of service, if you own your own home. Special electrical equipment must be installed, which means breaking through floors and walls to accommodate the wiring. You'll need room for a switchboard and line-terminating equipment. The latter is heavy, requiring a strong floor beneath it. It's also not very decorative, which is why it's often located in a closet. If you live in an apartment, the permission of the landlord will be required, both for the structural changes necessary, and for permission to operate a business on your premises. And, of course, there are also the local zoning laws to consider.

To make a success of this business, you should have some previous experience in operating a switchboard. You should also be able to take messages accurately. That sounds simple, but you'd be surprised at the number of telephone services that fail this simple test. Remember too that different types of clients (and their customers) use vocabularies peculiar to the business involved. The messages left for a plumber will sound different from those for an electrician. To help in keeping things straight, discuss the meaning of terms you don't understand with your client.

Next to muddled message-taking, the second biggest complaint about answering services is rudeness. No service is deliberately rude. You'll find, however, that when you are trying to juggle three or four calls at once, it takes real control to sound pleasant and unharassed to each in turn. It's of prime importance that you have the ability to think quickly and keep a cool head. If you number doctors or psychiatrists among your clients, you may be faced with medical or emotional emergencies, for which you will need to summon help at once.

Finally, the job is demanding in the sense that, for whatever period you undertake to operate your service, you will be tied to your home, unless you can get someone to stand in for you. That means you can't even work in your garden, if you would thereby be out of hearing of the telephone bell. Some telephone services operate only during business hours, five days a week; others specialize in the night time and weekend hours; still others are always on call, 24 hours a day, seven days a week. Whichever plan you adopt (and that will largely depend on what kinds of clients you get), be prepared to stick to it, through thick and thin.

Investment needed. This varies from place to place, and with the number of clients you start with. In some states a telephone service is required to have a minimum of ten; but starting with 25 clients gives more assurance of success, since a few will drop out before your business really gets going. The Small Business Administration estimates that equipment needed for a small service (about 12 clients) with no plans to expand can be installed for about $25. However, that figure is a rock-bottom minimum. At the other extreme, to start a 100-client service in a large city might cost you over $1000: about $150 for installation; a $200 deposit to cover possible damage to the equipment; another deposit, this time around $700, for a year's phone bill in advance. In addition, rent for the 100-line switchboard might amount to $90 a month. You should also have enough additional cash on hand to make sure you can cover the first few months' expenses (inevitably you will have some clients who are slow in paying their bills), and your initial advertising costs (see "How to get business," below).

Fees. Depending on the type and extent of the service offered, typical monthly payments to an answering service range from $10 to $30 a month per line. The base rate covers a specified number of messages (usually a hundred); an extra charge is made for each additional call taken. Wake-up calls and other special services (such as calling the client to give him his messages, rather than his calling you) are also extra. The average monthly bill per client is usually about $15 to $17.50. Check these national figures with what local services (if there are any) charge.

How to get business. Almost everyone could use an answering service, but to the self-employed it's almost a necessity. Consequently, aim your sales pitch at salesmen, doctors, dentists, electricians, TV repairmen, plumbers, lawyers, actors, models, writers, gardeners, or any other working man or woman in your town who doesn't have access to a secretary's services. Private individuals with a busy social life are other potential customers.

Initially, the best way to attract clients is to mail a printed card announcing your service to a selected list of prospects. Follow-up telephone calls will act as a reminder and give prospective clients an idea of your telephone personality. An ad (or at least a listing) in the classified telephone directory is a must, of course; and in fact, many services report that this is their best source of new clients. Occasionally, newspaper ads will also attract clients. While at the beginning you will probably want to accept just about anybody who applies, you might eventually investigate the possibilities of specializing in a single profession, such as doctors or musicians.

One word of warning: Clients you definitely *don't* want are those on the wrong side of the law, such as bookmakers or streetwalkers. If you have any suspicions about applicants, check with the local Chamber of Commerce or with the police. And don't be surprised if you yourself are investigated by the police when you start your service; in some areas, this is routine for anyone who rents telephone answering equipment.

WHERE TO GET MORE INFORMATION

Counseling Notes on a Telephone Answering Service, Small Business Administration. Superintendent of Documents,

U.S. Government Printing Office, Washington, D.C. 20402. Free leaflet.

Fundamentals of Telephone Answering Service, The Bell Telephone System. Ask your local phone company representative for a copy.

TRADE ASSOCIATIONS:

Associated Telephone Answering Exchanges, Inc., 777 14th Street N.W., Washington, D.C. 20005

Association of Telephone Answering Services, 485 Lexington Ave., New York, N.Y. 10017

31

PUBLIC RELATIONS

According to the Public Relations Society of America, there are an estimated 100,000 PR agents in this country (not counting those in government), of which about 60 percent work on the staffs of business firms and another 10 percent are full-time employees of nonprofit organizations. That leaves 30 percent who are with independent publicity firms. Some of these are huge outfits, others are one-man or -woman operations. If you have the right experience and contacts, you might consider launching your own service.

You must, of course, live in an area where there is public relations work to be done. This might be in a big city, where, though in the teeth of fierce competition few people succeed in starting new agencies of their own, there are opportunities for free-lance assignments from existing firms.

A more promising location might be a smaller city or suburban area where there is considerable social, civic, and business activity but a dearth of professional PR knowhow.

Even though you think you're a pretty good writer and/or publicist, you can't start a PR business cold—or at least it's highly unlikely. Usually you must have had previous experience in the field, on a newspaper, or in advertising, a PR firm, marketing research, or radio or television. Unpaid work counts too. Two California housewives, long out of college and the business world, found they were constantly being assigned to the publicity committees of the various organizations they worked for. After a few years of this, they decided to charge for their services and opened a PR firm of their own, specializing in fund-raising and civic affairs.

In Ohio, a woman working in the PR department of a bank occasionally got outside publicity assignments. Quitting her job, she mailed out an announcement of her free-lance services to local PR firms, who began to throw a job or two her way. Within a few months she felt confident enough to approach clients directly.

A young Chicagoan who had recently married and moved to the suburbs was first amused and then alerted to the business possibilities of free-lance PR work when she saw how pleased local celebrities were when their names appeared in the papers. Drawing on her previous experience with a PR firm and the contacts she had made then, she began to arrange for greater public exposure for a few prominent clubwomen. In addition to this kind of work, the husbands of some of her clients occasionally gave her assignments to write speeches and reports, and she planned the publicity campaign for the annual community chest drive. Although her income from this on-again, off-again kind of activity wasn't much, it did help tide her and her husband over the first hard years of starting a family and meeting the mortgage payments.

Fees. There are no standards; you'll have to feel your way. When you're first starting, you'll probably have to let the client set the prices at least for the first job; if you then find they're too low to make the work worth your while, you will have to say so. When you take on the job of promoting a business or an individual, you may even have to work for nothing for a while until you prove you can get results. Then it's customary to charge a retainer fee based on the amount of time you spend on the client.

How to get business. This is exclusively a personal-contact affair; ads or promotional handouts will get you nowhere. Make a list of potential clients, then telephone or write for an appointment. You will, of course, take your portfolio of press clippings, press releases, brochures, etc., along with you to show. (If you don't have such a portfolio, the fruit of previous experience, your chances of getting PR assignments are slim.) Later on, business may come to you by way of personal recommendations and word-of-mouth.

WHERE TO GET MORE INFORMATION

The Public Relations Handbook, Philip Lesly. Prentice-Hall, Inc., Englewood Cliffs, N.J., 1967.

TRADE JOURNALS:

PR Journal, 845 Third Ave., New York, N.Y. 10022.

Public Relations News, 127 E. 80th St., New York, N.Y. 10021.

32

CLIPPING SERVICE

If your name has ever appeared in print, you have probably clipped and saved the reference just for the fun of it. People whose livelihood depends on their staying in the public eye, and businesses concerned about their public image and about news that directly affects them, collect clippings for a more serious purpose. Therein lies an opportunity for an at-home business that requires no special experience.

There are two ways to make money at home by clipping:

1. If there is already a clipping service in your area, you can apply to it for piecework, which some firms still farm out. (The practice used to be much more common than it is today.) To find clipping bureaus, check the classified telephone directory, or inquire of your local Chamber of Commerce. Be wary, though, of ads for at-home jobs with a bureau. Often these are simply ruses to sell you something.

The advantage of working for an existing bureau is that it requires no investment. The disadvantage is that the payment is very small—usually a few cents per clipping. You would have to do a great deal of reading and clipping to make any money.

2. For an initial minimum investment of $160 to $200, you can start your own clipping service. Whether this has a chance of success will depend on how much competition you face in your area. In view of the large existing national and regional bureaus, you might think that no small venture could survive, but that is not necessarily so. Mrs. Ruth Halberstadt, who since 1959 has run a service in her home

in Hyde Park, New York, says, "A well-run local and regional clipping service stands a good chance of succeeding because it can often give the kind of personalized service that a large national bureau cannot always furnish. I know from my own experience that this is the case because some of my clients use both a national and a regional service."

To make a success of a clipping service, you yourself must have certain qualifications—good eyesight, an ability to scan and to read quickly, good comprehension, and a good memory. You must also be able to stick to a task that demands close attention to detail. Equipment and supplies needed include a large table or desk for clipping, a small photocopier (to reproduce items that appear back to back in a paper or that apply to more than one client), stationery and office supplies, cutting blades for clipping, and shelf space for publications. In estimating expenses, don't forget to allow for postage, telephone expenses, and, of course, the cost of subscribing to publications, which will probably run from about $3 to $7 per year for each weekly newspaper, $35 to $50 per year for each daily.

The first step in starting a service is to determine whether or not your area has a need for one. That will depend partly on the existing competition, partly on the number of prospective clients. These might include businesses of all kinds, government agencies, public relations firms, advertising agencies, politicians, authors, entertainers, local celebrities, clubs. According to the Small Business Administration, a not too populous area covered by three or four daily newspapers and a half dozen weeklies might yield a clientele of 30 or so to a clipping service.

Fees. These will vary, depending on the area and the scope of the service offered. There is usually a flat monthly service fee, plus a charge for each clipping. Rates for local and state service have risen in recent years from the $5 to

$15 a month plus 12¢ per clipping quoted by the Small Business Administration, to a high, in some areas, of $20 or $25 a month plus 15¢ to 18¢ per clipping. A contract should be signed with each client, specifying the date you will start reading; how often (daily, weekly, monthly) clippings should be sent; the geographical area to be covered; specific facts desired; how many copies of each clipping are needed; and how long coverage is desired.

When Mrs. Halberstadt started her service in 1959, it took her four months to make a modest profit of $150. Today she employs several helpers (neighboring house-wives, whom she hires at hourly rates) ; together, they read and clip over 250 papers a week.

How to get business. Once you are convinced a market exists for your service, invest in short-term subscriptions to a number of newspapers in your area and start collecting clippings concerning people and businesses you have pin-pointed as potential clients. Mount them neatly for each client, and start making personal calls on these prospects. Or reach them by a direct-mail campaign, with an individually typed or a printed sales letter or brochure describing your service and enclosing samples of clippings that relate to the particular prospect. Or you can mount a "teaser" campaign by sending out, at intervals, a series of postcards, each of which contains a clipping relating to the potential client—or simply the name of the paper and the date on which such a story appeared plus a notice of your service. (Send local stories, not syndicated or wire service items which appear in many papers throughout the country. It's the material that appears only in your area that companies have difficulty in getting.)

A listing in the classified telephone directory of the area you're aiming at is a must. You may also want to place ads for your service in various trade publications.

Counseling Notes on Clipping Service, Small Business Administration. Superintendent of Documents, U.S. Government Printing Office, Washington, D.C. 20402. Free leaflet.

33

MARKET RESEARCH

Every year, some 2,000 companies and organizations spend a half billion dollars simply to find out what the public thinks, what people read and watch on TV, what products they buy and why, how they vote, and what they like and dislike. On this information rest many of the decisions made by big business, advertising agencies, government and universities.

To gather the information, those in need of it turn to what are called field services, at least one of which exists in every big city and in some smaller communities as well. In the country's major cities there are usually many. (The Marketing Research Association, a national organization, includes 261 field services—many of them, incidentally, headed by women—in its total membership of 467 companies.) These services, in turn, hire interviewers to do the actual work. The majority of the interviewers are housewives, one reason being that much of the research is about products that women use—food, household appliances, and the like. Another reason: the independent working methods are convenient for women who work at or from home.

You don't have to have any particular experience for

these assignments, but basic intelligence and a good education help. The survey companies emphasize that they look for people who have inquiring minds and the ability to follow instructions exactly, listen carefully, and accurately record what is told them. You may be asked to gain information by means of check-off questions, open-end questions, or unstructured interviews, in stores, on the street, door to door, or via telephone. Your investment is nil—any expenses you incur, such as for gasoline, carfare, or telephone calls are reimbursed by your employer.

For beginning survey work, a company may ask you to come in to its local office for a briefing session; or you may be sent instructions through the mail. More complicated and better-paid assignments, like in-depth interviews, result from proving yourself on the job. For these you usually receive further training.

This is part-time, occasional work (though some interviewers in big cities work up to 35 hours a week). When you receive an assignment, it could be for two hours, two days or two months; the average survey lasts ten days to two weeks. Some assignments require you to interview during a specific period of the day or evening; with others you can arrange your hours as you choose, so long as you complete the assignment by the date specified.

Fees. Hourly rates for simple, general interviewing range from $1.50 to $2 an hour (portal to portal) for day work, and from $2.25 to $2.50 for night assignments. Extensive, in-depth interviews may bring as much as $5 to $12 an hour, or $15 per "case."

How to get business. To find market research assignments, first check the want ads in your local paper. If your city is big enough, you may find a few leads in this way. Also look in the classified telephone directory under "Market Research" for local field services. Employment agencies that specialize in supplying temporary help, sometimes handle survey assignments also.

However, you aren't confined to what is available locally. In your local public library consult *Bradford's Directory of Marketing Research Agencies,* and write to a number of the companies listed there. Your letter should include your educational background, business experience, if any (previous interviewing, teaching, or selling, though not necessary, may count in your favor) ; special interests and talents (such as the ability to speak a foreign language) , what time you have available, and whether you have access to a car.

WHERE TO GET MORE INFORMATION

Asking Questions, Marketing Research Association. Gallup & Robinson, Inc., Research Park, Princeton, N.J. 08540.

34

TRANSLATION

If you can read and write a foreign language and if you live in an area where there is a need for your skills, you may be able to put them to use to make money at home. Businesses and industries that deal with foreign clients often need freelance linguists to translate correspondence, advertising copy, sales information and publications; students and professors at universities will sometimes pay for translations of articles and passages from books when these are not available in English.

For this work, a proficient knowledge of the language in question is needed. Needless to say, two years of high-school

French won't do. Moreover, since business translation frequently involves specialized subjects (commercial transactions, legal regulations, electronics, engineering, etc.), you must possess, or have the ability to acquire, the appropriate special vocabulary. The languages most in demand are French, German, Spanish, and Russian; however, other languages are sometimes needed, and in certain areas, because of less competition, may give those who know them a special advantage.

For this work you must be located in a metropolitan area where there is commerce and industry with international dealings or in a university community. Big cities on the East and West coasts and other important ports offer the most opportunities—but also the most competition, since they frequently contain large numbers of native speakers of many languages.

If you have a language skill but no previous experience as a translator, you might check with local language schools or universities to see whether they offer instruction in translation techniques. Literary translation is a specialized skill with a limited market; it is not included in this discussion.

How to get business. It's a good idea to join the American Translators Association, a professional society whose publications and services will be helpful. While ATA is not an employment agency, it does keep members informed of employment opportunities and supplies contacts between employers and people looking for work. The ATA Professional Services Directory lists members available for assignments and is used by translation agencies and other companies. Beginners, as you will be, are eligible to become associate members; the annual dues are $15. Associate members are not listed in the directory, but upon proof of competence may become active members. The dues are the same.

Your best bet is to apply for free-lance work at commercial translation bureaus. You should also register your name and credentials at the foreign language department concerned of local colleges and universities, and at foreign consulates and chambers of commerce; for government work, register (by mail if you like) with the Language Services Division of the U.S. State Department, Washington 25, D.C. You might also write to several local companies that do business abroad—banks, advertising agencies, law firms, shipping companies, importers, and others.

Fees. These will depend upon a number of factors: (1) The language involved. Fees are higher for Japanese or Swahili, for example, than for French or Spanish. (2) The technical level of the material. Obviously, a specialized medical paper will bring higher rates than an ordinary business letter. (3) Whether the translation is submitted in draft or final form. (4) Whether it has to be checked by someone else. Depending upon all these factors, current fees range from 1½ to 4 cents a word, with translations from English into another language bringing higher rates than the reverse.

WHERE TO GET MORE INFORMATION

Handbook of Foreign Language Occupations, June L. Sherif. Regents Publishing Co., New York, N.Y., 1966.

Opportunities in Foreign Language Careers, Theodore Huchener. Universal Publishing and Distributing Corp., New York, N.Y., 1964.

TRADE ASSOCIATION:

American Translators Association, P.O. Box 489, Madison Square Station, New York, N.Y. 10010.

CHILD CARE AND AMUSEMENT

Once upon a time, children were seen and not heard, ate what was good for them, and minded their p's and q's. Some attention was paid to the importance of the early years in intellectual and emotional development, but not much.

Today, all that is changed. Every year billions of dollars are spent on kids: on books for them, toys, sports equipment, TV programs, live entertainment, special educational advantages. As a result, they have become consumers—luxury consumers, in fact.

To capitalize on this market, you should know what children like and/or what their parents want for them. Here are ten jobs in one or both of those categories, involving small-fry care, transportation, and entertainment.

GENERAL GUIDELINES

• There are more state and local regulations affecting businesses that involve children than almost any other kind. So check with your city clerk well in advance on which ones, if any, may apply to yours.

- Also discuss your plans with your insurance agent. He can advise you on what additional coverage you will need.
- Naturally, you must live in a child-oriented community if you plan a business catering to children. But also important is the age distribution. Make your own census—birth registers and school-class sizes are the tipoff—before deciding which type of business to try.
- The nature of the community will affect your choice too. While a baby-sitting bureau will do well almost anywhere, an all-day child-care service will prosper only in an area where many mothers work outside the home. Average income level is another factor to consider.
- Before you undertake any business that involves dealing directly with children, take a good, honest look at your feelings about them. Do you really like children? Respect them? Can you be as heedful of other children as you would be of your own? If not, you'd better go into some other business. Children, like animals, have an uncanny ability to sense when people dislike or fear them, and they react accordingly.
- See "A Word about Prices," page 5.

HELPFUL HINTS

- If you take children into your own home, plan it to cause as little disruption to your family's life as possible. Set off special areas for your charges; all others should be off limits to them.
- If you haven't recently cared for small children, you may have forgotten how much endurance, patience, and stamina it calls for. Take a refresher course, courtesy of a neighbor's children, before you commit yourself.
- When parents leave their children with you, make sure you know where the parents can be reached in the event of an emergency. You should also have the telephone number

of a pediatrician and of the nearest Poison Control Center. In working with children you should be prepared for everything; if contemplation of possible crises makes you nervous, you really shouldn't be in this business.

• For many of the businesses suggested in this chapter, you might consider taking on a partner—a neighbor who could spell you when you are sick, tired, or just want to get away from it all (hard to do when children—and their parents—are dependent upon you).

35

CHILDREN'S BIRTHDAY PARTIES

If you are a mother yourself, you know that children's parties can be hectic affairs. The trick is to have a battle plan. That demands careful preparation, even more than is necessary for an adult party.

As a result, the mere thought of a party often panics the coolest of mothers. That's where you come in. Running a party service means that *you* organize and supervise the celebration, and, what's more, do it with efficiency and flair. Your job is to make sure there is a minimum of tears, tantrums, and jangled nerves, a maximum of fun.

For this business, you'll need a community that is chockfull of kids, preferably from three to ten years old, when birthday-party fever runs high. The suburbs are particularly lucrative, but the party business works equally well in a city.

Talk to your friends to see whether they would be interested in a party service. Find out if you're bucking competition—one party service in any area is generally enough. If there *was* such a service at one time but it went out of business, find out why. A previous failure doesn't necessarily mean you should abandon your plans, but you should take care to profit by a predecessor's mistakes.

Ideally, you'll be using your home as an office only, so it doesn't matter how much space you have. All you really need is an appointment book, a few files, and a closet to store party supplies. However, if you do happen to live in a house with a roomy recreation room and a big backyard, you may want to give parents the option of having the party at your home. (In this case, you might charge a bit more for the convenience.) Be sure your room is big enough for a crowd. In summer you can hold your parties outdoors, but you still need indoor facilities in case of rain.

To run a successful service, you should be aware of how children of different ages act in a party situation. Most two-year-olds have no concept of what a party is or what to do there. It's best to discourage parents who want to start their children's social life this early. Three-year-olds can be chancy too, but they're not impossible to work with. Since they're not ready for much in the way of group activity, keep the party short and the activities informal. Four-year-olds enjoy party giving and going. From this age on, until adolescence looms and they wouldn't be caught dead at an adult-organized party, children are prime targets for your service. Up to the age of nine, children enjoy coed parties. After that, for a period of about four years, single-sex parties go over better.

Your work schedule for a party of four-year-olds might shape up something like this:

Bake and decorate the cake the night before. Arrive at the client's house with at least half an hour to spare. Decorate the birthday table and set up the room to look like a nursery school. Provide enough toys for everyone and remove anything breakable.

When the guests arrive, give each one a toy to keep him occupied. Then ask the host to start opening the gifts.

Next, serve the food—traditional simple fare like cake, ice cream, and chocolate milk. Follow this with an informal play period. At this point, bring out the balloons—and brace yourself. Four-year-olds tire easily, so after an hour of play the party should break up. Present each departing guest with a wrapped favor.

That's the basic format for any party, but each age requires a different approach. Nine- and ten-year-olds, for example, like organized games to test their skills. If you don't channel their energies, they'll get out of hand or sit around and act bored.

You can keep your initial investment below $100 if you buy candles, paper plates, decorations, and other supplies through a wholesale party supplier. Favors (crayons, toy cars, or whistles for younger children; ballpoint pens, marbles, kaleidoscopes for older ones) can also be bought in quantity.

Additional expenses involve food. If you plan to bake the cakes for your parties yourself, buy cake mixes in quantity, plus a tube cake decorator for writing the birthday child's name in icing. If you prefer to buy the cakes, try to get a discount from a local bakery. (Unless the party is being held in your own home, other refreshments should be the responsibility of your client.) And buy a balloon pump. You'll never regret it!

How to get business. Certain groups provide a fertile field for this business: schools (especially nurseries and kindergartens), PTAs, women's clubs, church groups, baby-sitting services, and children's activity groups such as Little League teams. Make contact with these groups either by 'phone or letter. If you can wangle lists of names and birth dates from primary or Sunday schools, send out an individual letter offering your service to the parents of the birthday-child-to-be a few weeks before the date.

Send an announcement to your local paper, or better still, try to interest the paper in doing a story about you and your service.

Fees. These can vary considerably from one place to another, but for a one- or two-hour party, the minimum is about $3 per child; for three hours, $5. If you take photos, charge the client extra for film and flashbulbs.

WHERE TO GET MORE INFORMATION

The Gesell Institute Party Book, Frances L. Ilg. Harper & Bros., New York, N.Y., 1959. Also paperback.

Guiding Your Child from Two to Five, Molly Mason Jones. Harcourt, Brace & World, Inc., New York, N.Y., 1967. (Includes section on parties.)

Parties for Children, Marguerite Kohl and Frederica Young. Cornerstone Library, Inc., New York, N.Y., 1968. Paperback.

Planning Parties for Young People. Science Research Associates, 259 East Erie Street, Chicago, Ill. Booklet.

36

ENTERTAINMENT BUREAU

There are more ways than one to make money from children's parties. Another method is to leave the organizing to others and simply supply the entertainment. The critical word is "supply." You need do none of the entertaining yourself (though two enterprising Phoenix, Arizona, housewives, dressed as teddy bears, make money putting on their own act at children's parties) . Rather, you line up a variety of acts: ventriloquists, trained dogs, bears, chimps, horses, magicians, jugglers, puppeteers, guitarists and other instrumental acts, folk singers, clowns, storytellers, maybe even a children's theater group or a local TV or radio celebrity.

As a talent scout and booking agent, you won't be involved in planning the parties or even attending them. Your role is to tell parents what you have available, engage the performer they select, and collect your commissions.

Obviously, you won't do well with this service in a community where "Pin the Tail on the Donkey" is still popular. What you need is an affluent city or suburban neighborhood where parents are willing to pay for something different for their children's birthday celebrations. As far as your own qualifications are concerned, you should know what children like in the way of entertainment, be able to judge the quality of various acts, and have a businesslike gift for organization.

Most of your time will be spent becoming familiar with local talent, either through auditions or attending actual performances. Talk to amateur theater and musical groups; make your needs known to placement bureaus of nearby colleges; for animal acts, seek leads from local kennel clubs, the ASPCA, training schools, and grooming salons.

Don't be shy about approaching professional talent as well; your enterprise will represent a new market for their services, and one, because it is daytime only, that will probably not conflict with other engagements. For this reason, performers may be willing to reduce their usual rates. If you can't round up enough prospects by simple legwork, run a classified ad ("Help Wanted: Entertainers for Children's Parties") . A word of warning, though: You'll be deluged with would-be, amateur, semi-professional, and professional applicants—more, probably, than you'll ever need.

How to get business. Have simple printed brochures made up that contain the following information:

1. Description of the acts available
2. How long each lasts (45 minutes to an hour is usual)
3. How much notice you require to book an act (at least a week)
4. A guide to age preferences (e.g., five- and six-year-olds love clowns; for subteens, clowns are kid stuff. Ventriloquists and magicians are popular with the older groups)
5. Prices

Send the brochure to clubs, church groups, and civic organizations, thereby hitting two birds with one stone—individual parents, and members of organizations that may themselves be frequent givers of children's parties. Personally visit caterers, party-supply stores, and professional party planners who might be in a position to recommend you. Hand out flyers outside toy stores and supermarkets. Of course you'll tell all your friends and acquaintances and ask them to spread the word; you may also have to run ads in local papers. Also, try to wangle some free publicity by inviting the society or entertainment editor to cover a party whose entertainment you have arranged. Your service should definitely be listed in the classified telephone directory.

Fees. What you can charge will depend on the area, the nature of the act, the number of performers involved, and on whether the party is given by an individual or an organization. (For the latter your fee can be much higher.) Here are some typical price ranges to use as guides (you may have to adjust them upward or downward) :

Clown or magician: $20–$75

Folk singer: $20–$40

Performing dog or chimp: $40–$75 and up
Performing horse: $75–$100 and up
Your fee as booking agent will be from 10 to 15 percent of
the amount charged the client.

37

MOVIE GO-ROUND

An alternative to an Entertainment Bureau, should there
not be enough live talent in your locality to make it possible, is a service that supplies appropriate movies for children's parties. Despite the fact that—or perhaps because—
they see so many old movies and cartoons on television,
children from the ages of three to twelve seem to have an
unquenchable appetite for them.

Almost every movie and cartoon that was ever made re-
poses in some film library, and most libraries rent as well as
sell copies. The rental fee, above a basic minimum, varies
with the size of the audience and the revenue to be derived
from the showing. At first, while you feel out the extent of
your market and its tastes, you can rent films, but soon it
may be wise to put together your own inventory of 8 mm.
silent shorts and cartoons and 16 mm. sound movies. The
same thing applies to the screen (it should be a good-sized
one) and the 8 mm. and 16 mm. projectors needed.

Your film programs should be carefully researched, and
choices made according to the ages of the children to whom
the films are to be shown. Three-year-olds, for example,
prefer fairy tales and cartoons (not too scary ones), with
lots of funny animals. *Our Gang* comedies are big with six-

to eight-year-olds; the eleven- and twelve-year-old group likes old Chaplin movies. Keep an eye on current TV listings as you plan, and stay away from films that have been run there recently. Plan the show to last about an hour, although single films may possibly run a little longer. You should arrive at least ten minutes beforehand, to set up the projector and screen.

You might also look into the possibilities of showing movies to adults—either to clubs or other groups, or as an entertainment at parties. People who would love to see favorite old films again, on a large screen and without the constant interruption of commercials, are often unaware that they are available for rental to anyone. The premium fee such people pay you will be for your services in getting a group together and handling all the rental and other arrangements. (These might include finding a suitable projection place, checking on fire laws, handling payment of the taxes involved, and other details.)

Fees. For children's parties, put together a show that can be priced at the same level as the less expensive live acts (see page 166), and still make you some money above expenses. You can charge higher prices for adult groups, and you will have to—the average cost of renting a full-length feature film for a single showing is around $25 and may be more, depending on the popularity of the film and its current status in theater houses.

WHERE TO GET MORE INFORMATION

With few exceptions, film libraries are situated in big cities (see the classified telephone directory under "Motion Picture Film Libraries"), but they also do business by mail. On request, all will send catalogues. Names and addresses of some of the biggest are:

Brandon Films, Inc., 830 Third Avenue, New York, N.Y. 10022

Associated Films, Inc., 600 Grand Avenue, Ridgefield, N.J.

Universal Sixteen, 221 Park Avenue S., New York, N.Y.

Willoughby Peerless Film Library, 115 West 31st St., New York, N.Y.

38

EMERGENCY PLAY KITS

Emergency play kits are designed to answer the familiar wail—"But there's nothing to *do!*"—that every mother dreads. For a child who is sick in bed or confined to the house on a rainy day, even TV palls after a while. And the price of keeping children occupied on a long automobile trip is joining in with them in interminable games—thus missing most of the scenery (and traffic signs as well).

Some clever, foresighted mothers keep sanity-saving-supplies on hand for just such emergencies. Many others don't, but might welcome the chance to buy them readymade. And therein lies an opportunity for you.

The play-kit business requires some initial investment, but not much, since the materials used can be quite inexpensive. Most of your money will go for advertising, and even this expenditure can be avoided if you market your kits through others—though this way you will receive less return. One woman started a business of this kind for less than $100.

Emergency play kits consist of inexpensive toys, odds and ends, "found" objects, craft materials, anything and everything that will keep a child interested and out of mischief for a while. Obviously the contents differ according to sex and age level, but here are some general ideas:

colored pipe cleaners
mirror to catch sunlight and flash it around the room
crayon and paper
bits of ribbon, lace, velvet
magnet
magnifying glass
beads, spools, buttons or macaroni for stringing
old greeting and/or playing cards
toy soldiers
paper dolls
"magic" slate
smooth stones for decorating

wooden clothespins
small animals, houses, trees, for a bedspread village
pictures of cars (or babies, dogs, etc.) from old magazines
kaleidoscope
balloons
clay
wallpaper scraps for cutting and pasting
tissue-paper-covered comb for playing
paper bags to make masks (include a sample to copy)

If you have children of your own, use them as guinea pigs to see which combinations of things seem most appealing. Ask your friends (and their children) for suggestions too, and talk to local nursery-school and elementary-school teachers and to nurses in the children's ward of the local hospital. Visit toy stores and pore over toy catalogues, both for inexpensive articles to buy for your kits, and for ideas you can adapt for do-it-yourself items.

In making up your kits, keep in mind the purpose for which they will be used. There are three basic types:

Sick-in-bed kits. Sick children usually tire easily and have less ability to concentrate. In selecting playthings, regard the child as a year or two younger than the actual age aimed at. Don't include any games that require a partner, or more than one item with many small pieces. (These tend to get lost in the bedclothes.) No blocks—they're for playing on the floor and are too great a temptation, and no candy, gum, or food of any kind.

Rainy-day kits. In addition to any of the articles already suggested, consider a costume for dressing up, funny hat, harmonica, ball, jump rope, jacks, marbles.

Travel kits. Keep in mind the desirability of persuading the child to sit still in his seat. Among many other items designed to achieve that end, you might include a magnetized board game, book, miniature car or dolls, coin wrapped in tissue paper for spending along the way.

Once you have planned your kits (there should be several different ones) and decided on the contents for each, make sure you can put them together at reasonable cost (see "Prices," below) . To assemble them, you'll need space (in a basement, garage, or attic) for a large table, plus shelves for storing materials and finished kits.

Packaging should be sturdy, since emergency kits are meant to be used, stored, and used again and again as the occasion arises. A sturdy cardboard box such as a shoe box, a plastic shopping bag, or a cloth drawstring bag that can be hung in a closet are all possible containers. While your business is small you can hand-letter or stencil these with your trade name (it should be a catchy one) . Later, if your business grows, you will want to have special packaging designed. Whatever container you choose, keep the various items separated and orderly by means of plastic bags, paper clips, twine, ribbon, and cardboard dividers; otherwise the contents will simply look like junk.

Prices. The aim, of course, is to cover your costs plus a reasonable return for your labor. Using that as a rough guide, you'll have to feel your way, since what you can charge for your kits will depend on the area, the contents of the kits and how they are marketed. (See page 252, under "Handcrafts," for further pricing hints.)

How to get business. This depends on whether you want to sell the kits yourself. Since your return will be greater if you succeed, you might try this first, by placing small ads in local papers. If this proves too expensive, try to interest local stores—department, toy, hobby, children's wear, hospital gift shops, even supermarkets—in taking your kits, with roughly half the selling price going to them, half to you. Play kits also lend themselves to selling by mail order, but this requires considerable initial investment. It is, however, something you will want to consider if your business really catches on. (See "How to Expand into Mail Order," page 41.)

WHERE TO GET MORE INFORMATION

The Complete Book of Children's Play, Ruth E. Martley and Robert M. Goldenson. Thomas Y. Crowell Co., New York, N.Y., 1963.

838 Ways to Amuse a Child, June Johnson. Collier Books, New York, N.Y., 1970. Paperback.

A Parent's Guide to Children's Play and Recreation, Alvin Schwartz. Collier Books, New York, N.Y., 1963. Paperback.

The Rainy Day Book, Alvin Schwartz. Trident Press, New York, N.Y., 1968.

What to Do When "There's Nothing to Do." Boston Children's Medical Center, Delacorte Press, New York, N.Y., 1968. Also paperback.

39

BABY-SITTING BUREAU

Almost the only communities that don't need baby-sitters are retirement villages. So unless you live in one of those, you might well consider setting up a service that matches people who need sitters with people who want to sit. You do no sitting yourself, so you don't even have to like children! What you do need is a talent for organization and an intuitive ability to judge people. Your initial financial expenditures will be limited to advertising costs, a few office supplies, and insurance coverage. Later, if your business grows, you may want to consider a telephone answering service.

Baby-sitting is usually considered an unskilled job. *You* must take a different attitude. Your clients will be entrusting your sitters (and through them, you) with their most valuable possessions—their children. Therefore, the value of your service, and its strongest selling point, will be that you provide not just a body to sit but a qualified, trustworthy person who is able and willing to do everything necessary for the safety and comfort of her charges. This might include preparing the children's evening meal, bathing and putting them to bed, and dealing with minor illnesses according to instructions from the parents or doctor.

You can track down qualified applicants through college placement offices, Y's, hospitals, nursing schools, family service organizations, senior citizens clubs, churches, and residential homes. Screen the sitters you accept for maturity, tact, cleanliness, interest in children, and a general air of competence. Ask for three character references, and *always check them out.* Also insist on a note from a doctor stating that the sitter is in good health.

Usually, your applicants will fall into two major groups—young college students and older women, often widows. Retired teachers make particularly good sitters; so do nurses and nursing students. Use the latter two groups for jobs involving babies and very young children; the parents will feel reassured and you can charge a higher fee for the sitter's special training. Generally, it's better not to accept high-school sitters unless they are exceptionally mature. Besides, students at any level are often not available during vacation periods or over holidays, when the calls for your service may be at their peak.

After you have a list of at least 20 qualified sitters, you are ready to start your service. You will need an appointment book, a detailed map of the area and perhaps a transportation directory (so you can give traveling directions to sitters), and two card indexes. One is for sitters and the hours they wish to work; the other, for customers, will gradually fill up with cards noting name and address, telephone number, number of children, pediatrician's telephone number, names of sitters, and dates they are sent to the client. Also prepare a mimeographed sheet detailing rules for sitter behavior in such matters as use of the telephone, raiding the refrigerator, playing client-owned entertainment equipment, and so on. Make sure that both clients and sitters receive copies.

How to get business. Develop a brochure (at the start, it too could be mimeographed) that describes your agency and details rates per hour, minimum number of hours per call, and any special services you offer, such as overnight, 24-hour, and all-weekend sitting. Send the announcement to PTAs, church groups, women's clubs, hotels and motels. Distribute flyers outside supermarkets and department

stores, and take a listing in the classified telephone directory. This, plus word-of-mouth as your initial customers tell
others, will probably bring you all the business you can
handle, if your service is a good one.

Fees. Baby-sitting rates vary from one area to another, but
are fairly standard in any one locality. In some communities, 75 cents to a dollar an hour is typical, but in some big
cities hourly fees can zoom as high as $2. Charge extra for
any of the following: working after midnight, cooking dinner and washing dishes, giving baths, taking care of babies
under six months. On special occasions like New Year's Eve,
it's customary to charge a flat rate ($7.50 to $12 or more)
for the evening. The cost of the sitter's transportation is the
responsibility of the client.

There are several methods of collecting your commission.
Either you can get it all from the sitter, charging a flat fee
($1 to $1.50) or a percentage (usually 10 percent) for each
job. Or you can collect an hourly commission (say, 35
cents) , of which parent and sitter each pay half.

In New York City, actress Diana Sands, her mother, and a
friend run a service that has 40 sitters on call. Rates vary
depending on the number of children involved: $2 an hour
(with a four-hour minimum) for one or two children, and
$2.50 an hour for three or more, or for care including an
infant under 6 months. The Sands service also offers a
"Freedom Book," a booklet of baby-sitting gift certificates
"for the woman who has everything but freedom." Depending on the number of hours of service covered, the booklets
range from $12 to $52.

WHERE TO GET MORE INFORMATION

A Manual for Babysitters, Marion Lowndes. Little, Brown
and Co., New York, N.Y., 1961.

40

ALL-DAY CHILD CARE

If the Women's Liberation Movement has its way, there will one day be free government- or industry-sponsored day-care centers where working women or others who have responsibilities outside the home can leave their children. But that day is not yet here. Consequently, if you have the room (and the temperament), there is an opportunity for you to earn money by offering the working mothers in your community all-day care for their children.

For this business you should be particularly careful to check out local regulations in advance. Before even considering the idea, make sure your home conforms to the relevant health, safety, and fire rules, or can be easily made acceptable.

This idea naturally works best in an area where there are many opportunities for women workers—usually a city or town with many businesses and industries. Another possibility is a college town where there are many married students. You will need a house with a back yard, or a big apartment within walking distance of a park or playground.

As for your own qualifications, you should have recent experience with small children and affection for them, infinite patience, and a sense of humor. It goes without saying that you must be in good physical health and prepared to stick with your charges through thick and thin. Your working mothers will depend on your being at home and ready to assume responsibility *every* working day. Since emergencies do happen, it is wise to line up a few possible stand-ins—friends or relatives whom you could call upon to take over on such occasions.

Working alone, you probably won't be able to handle more than four or five children, particularly if you have a toddler or two of your own. With a partner, you might increase your quota to 12 to 15. You'll need some equipment, but what you don't already have you can probably borrow or buy secondhand—cribs or cots for naps, a playpen or two, a couple of high chairs, a small table and chairs, a sandbox, and an assortment of outdoor and indoor toys. What the latter consist of will depend upon the ages of your clients. Your major expenditures (besides food for lunches and snacks) will be for renewing supplies such as crayons, paints, clay, construction paper, and other nursery-school staples.

This is a full-time job and a confining one. The children may begin arriving from 7 A.M. on, to stay until 4, 5 or 6 P.M., depending on the mother's schedule. You will not be expected to serve them breakfast or dinner, but you *will* have to provide a hot lunch and mid-morning and mid-afternoon snacks. The rest of your job consists of keeping your charges reasonably contented and out of trouble. You cannot offer the specialized services of a nursery school or a professional day-care center, and you should not imply that you do.

How to get business. Since you can take only a few children, spreading the word to friends and acquaintances may get you all the applicants you can handle. If not, call or write the personnel managers of large companies in your vicinity, and send a notice to their employee newspapers or house organs. If this still doesn't bring in enough clients, run an ad in your local newspaper under "Situations Wanted," e.g.: "All-day baby sitting. Mother wants to care for young children, all ages up to six, in her own home."

Fees. You will have to gauge how much you can charge by estimating the incomes of the mothers. Your fees can't take too big a chunk out of their take-home pay, or it won't be worth their while to work. On the other hand, your rates must be high enough to cover your expenses (you will have to spend at least $1 a day per child for food) and to compensate you for what—as the mothers themselves well know —is a very demanding job. Aim for $25 to $30 a week (five days only) per child.

Here are some helpful hints to keep in mind:
• Make it a rule that if a child is ill on arrival, you can't accept him.
• It is up to the mothers of children who still need them to provide you with disposable diapers and baby formulas.
• By keeping to a small, informal type of operation with a few clients—and a few is all you will be able to handle alone—you can avoid most of the legal requirements for nursery schools. But check with your city clerk anyway.

WHERE TO GET MORE INFORMATION

Counseling Notes on Children's Day Nurseries, Small Business Administration. Superintendent of Documents, Washington 25, D.C. 20402. Free pamphlet.

Child Care and Working Mothers, Florence A. Ruderman. Child Welfare League of America, 44 East 23rd Street, New York, N.Y. 10010.

Day Care for Other People's Children in Your Home (Children's Bureau Publication No. 412-1964) . U.S. Department of Health, Education and Welfare, Washington, D.C. Leaflet.

The New Encyclopedia of Child Care and Guidance, rev. ed., Sidonie Gruenberg. Doubleday & Co., Inc., New York, N.Y., 1968.

The Playgroup Book, Marie Winn and Mary Ann Precher. Penguin Books, Inc., New York, N.Y., 1969. Paperback.

Your Preschool Child: Making the Most of the Years from Two to Seven, Dorothy Kirk Burnett. Holt, Rinehart & Winston, Inc., New York, N.Y., 1961.

41

AFTER-SCHOOL CHILD CARE

A less demanding version of the child-care idea is an after-school service for children from around 6 to 12 or 13. (After that age, a child, wisely or not, is usually deemed old enough to take care of himself when no one is at home.) To run a service like this, you must live near an elementary or junior high school in a community where paid or volunteer work, or popular social activities like bowling or bridge clubs, make it difficult for many women to be home when their children arrive from school.

Ideally, you should have a house with a yard where the children can play outdoors when the weather is good (it will help if it contains equipment such as a swing, slide, and jungle gym), and with enough indoor space to enable you to set off two separate areas for your charges. One of these should be a place (possibly the family room) to play games or watch television; ideally, it should have an adjoining bathroom and easy access to the outdoors. The other area needed is a quiet room, equipped with a table and chairs, for doing homework. Make it clear that all other areas of your home are off limits, unless a child has your permission to enter.

Unless you live within walking distance of the school, or are on the school bus route, you will have to pick the children up; it is, therefore, impractical to draw customers from more than one school. It should be the responsibility of the children's parents to come for them later. Be very definite about the cut-off hour for your service. If children are left with you beyond it, charge time and a half for any overtime.

As soon as the children reach your home, prepare some refreshments—milk and cookies, juice and crackers, or a piece of fruit. After spending all day in the classroom, they are keyed up and will need to let off steam, so allow for a lot of running, jumping, and shouting. Later on, when they've simmered down a bit, you might have a story-telling (or story-reading) hour.

Basically, though, your responsibilities are limited to keeping order, helping out with homework when you can, and listening to what happened in school that day. While it's important that you let the kids know you're in charge, you shouldn't try to discipline them. Report any behavior problem to the parents and let them deal with it; if it recurs, warn them you may have to drop their child unless he behaves.

How to get business. Before you even consider this service, you should discuss it with neighbors, teachers, and local PTA and women's club members. If its chances of success are good, the very people you consult will probably be able to suggest prospective client-families. Also ask permission to post a notice on church, club, and school bulletin boards, and run occasional ads in small local newspapers. If you have school-age children of your own, they too can spread the message.

Fees. Check local baby-sitting rates and set yours accordingly. (Take into account, however, the fact that the child is accepted into your own home and provided with a hearty snack each day.) This entitles you to charge premium rates, as does your pickup service (if provided).

Helpful hints. These ideas may prove useful:

• Clear out a handy closet (or buy a portable cardboard one) in which to keep the children's boots, coats, hats, books, etc., separate from the family's possessions.

• Devise a reasonable set of rules (including permitted hours for watching television and a system for taking turns in choosing programs) and enforce them. Make sure that all the children *and* their parents receive copies.

• For rainy days, when everyone stays indoors, keep emergency supplies (games, books) on hand, and be prepared with ideas for activities—charades, craft projects, word games.

• Make it the parents' responsibility to inform you if a child is not to attend an after-school session. If they fail to do so, make a nominal charge for the afternoon anyway.

• Limit the number of children you agree to take so that you can handle them comfortably. Depending on the size of your home and the ages of the children, this usually works out to about five to ten.

42

CHECK-A-CHILD SERVICE

The two previous child-care jobs suggested (see #40 and #41) are pretty much limited to children from the neighborhood. But if you live in a suburb, in the vicinity of a shopping center, you might adapt an idea that has been used successfully by some far-sighted merchants—a "check-a-child" service for any mother who wants to shop unencumbered by her little one.

The idea is that on her way to the stores, she drops her child (or children) off at your house and receives a slip stating the time of arrival. When she returns to pick the child up, she presents the slip and is charged for the elapsed time according to a fixed schedule (based on local babysitting rates), but with the same proviso used by car parks—any time over the hour, up to a half hour, calls for an additional half-hourly payment; any time beyond a half hour is charged at the full hourly rate.

To operate this service (which is usually summer-only), you need a fenced-in play area with a slide, swings, a sandbox or two, and some toys. You must also be prepared to take the children inside in bad weather; and of course you must have toilet facilities for them. A cot or two for those who feel like napping is also advisable. Serving meals—even snacks—is *not* part of your function, and you should make this clear to mothers who plan to leave their children for several hours. Basically, your job is simply to supervise the play area.

How to get business. The best way to get business is to sell the idea of your service to local merchants. Since women buy more when they don't have to worry about fretful children, there is a good chance that nearby stores will let you post notices on their premises, and will themselves promote your service at every opportunity they get. This source alone will probably bring you all the business you want, and perhaps more. In the latter case, you may have to limit your service to customers of a single store, which pays you a fee for the privilege.

Fees. These should be roughly equivalent to local babysitting rates.

43

ACTIVITY GROUPS

Activity groups are a bright new idea in services for children. Also sometimes called play groups, they offer a regular schedule of activities designed to keep 5- to 12-year-olds entertained and, often, physically active. For a monthly fee, the child is picked up at his or her door after school or on Saturday, and whisked away with other children for two or three hours of swimming, bowling, skating, skiing, or horseback riding. Or the group is taken to the circus, the movies, a baseball game, an amusement park, or on a tour of a museum, police headquarters, an ocean liner, an airport—any interesting locality they might enjoy visiting. The range of activities can be as wide as your imagination and energy. The emphasis should be on things the child can't do in his own neighborhood.

What qualifications do *you* need? If you have had some experience with children *en masse,* either as a teacher or camp counselor, you will be ahead of the game. But merely having escorted your own brood on similar outings qualifies you too. If you plan athletic activities—swimming, skiing—you should of course be limber enough to join in yourself. And before you take your group to some place of interest, bone up on the subject of the visit so you will be able to answer their incessant questions.

Activity groups are popular anywhere there are parents who can afford, and are willing to pay for, things they themselves could do for their children but rarely get around to. Reasonably well-off apartment dwellers in big cities are good targets, but so are suburban parents who feel guilty because they don't spend enough time with their kids.

Shelley Weiner is a 30-year-old director of Shelley's All Stars, a well known New York City activity group he started, for Saturdays only, while he was in college. Now he is the head of a six-day-a-week operation that has 25 adult counselors and 400 children clients, plus a waiting list. It's not necessary, or usually possible, to go that far, though. You can limit your program to one weekly or monthly outing, or offer it only during certain periods of the year. Each outing takes approximately four or five hours, including the time spent to pick up and return the children to their homes.

To start this kind of service, you first plan a schedule of three or four outings you think will appeal to children of an age group that is plentiful in your community. (Eight to ten is ideal; children younger than this are hard to handle, older children tend to be blasé and boisterous.) Include an alternate for each outing, should your first choice prove unavailable or the weather cancel it out. Then get in touch with the managers or proprietors of the facilities you plan to use or visit, ask about group rates, and make tentative arrangements (but no firm commitments) for a group for the dates you have scheduled.

The next step is to round up members for your group. Talk to parents and children you know; send a letter to PTA, church and club groups, and ask permission to post a notice on bulletin boards in schools and Y's. If this doesn't suffice, try ads in your local newspaper. At first, just to get started, you may want to accept children for individual outings, but it will be better if you can sign their parents up for a group of at least four. As soon as you have enough children to make the venture worthwhile (ask for a deposit, returnable only for good cause), make your arrangements definite and buy any tickets needed. One person can handle about 15 children, absolute maximum. If the group goes above that number, you will have to hire someone to help you.

Transportation is your next problem. If your community has good public facilities, you're in luck. Otherwise, if the group is large, you may have to charter a bus, which will add considerably to your expenses. If you plan to drive your own car or station wagon, check with your city clerk to see whether you need a special license or permit to transport children on excursions that involve payment.

Fees. These will vary with the community, but might range from $3 to $5 per child per outing, including transportation, but not any admission fees involved. Ice cream, soda, or other snacks consumed along the way, and souvenirs, are also extra. Parents who sign their children up for a series of outings are eligible for a reduction.

WHERE TO GET MORE INFORMATION

The Book of Outdoor Winter Activities, Gunnar A. Peterson and Harry D. Edgren. Association Press, New York, N.Y., 1962.

Enjoying the Outdoors with Children, Lucille E. Hein. Association Press, New York, N.Y., 1966.

A Parent's Guide to Children's Play and Recreation, Alvin Schwartz. Collier Books, New York, N.Y., 1963. Paperback. (See Chapter 3, "Short and Long Trips.")

Trips. Play Schools Association, 120 West 57th St., New York, N.Y. 10019.

44

KIDDIE TAXI

How many times have you felt that you might as well get your chauffeur's license or join the taxi driver's union? Driving children to and from school or to club meetings, lessons, the dentist, parties, and other essential and non-essential trips can be very time-consuming. That's precisely why a kiddie taxi service might be successful in *your* town. Mothers who would never think of calling a regular taxi to take their children somewhere might pay another mother for this service.

You have to live in or near a suburb, and a pretty well-heeled one at that, to consider this idea. The best source of a steady income is a job driving children to and from a local private school. It's rare that a school doesn't already have one or more semiofficial drivers (paid, however, not by the school but by the parents), but there may be enough work for you too. It's a common parent complaint that their children must leave for school very early and get home late because the school driver makes only one trip.

Next best is an arrangement to drive children to regularly scheduled appointments, such as weekly lessons or Little League practice. You can also make yourself generally available for trips between certain hours—say 3 P.M. to 7 P.M., or 9 A.M. to 5 P.M. Saturdays. But unless you have a telephone answering service (and at first that may not be worth your while), you will have to count on missing some calls while you are out.

Before going to the trouble of getting the chauffeur's

license you will need to operate any drive-for-hire service, scout the chances of its success by talking to the headmaster of the local private school; music teachers; dancing schools and other "lesson" proprietors; local professional people; and members of the PTA and women's clubs. If there seems to be a need for such a service, check with your city clerk on what regulations apply (many cities and states have special provisions concerning the transportation of children) and make arrangements to meet the necessary requirements.

How to get business. Your best form of advertising will be personal letters to the parents of private-school students (you can get their names and addresses by checking the school yearbook against the local telephone directory). Even though they may have made other arrangements for transporting their children to and from school, they may want to use your service for other occasions. (Ask them to make appointments in advance, when they can.) An ad in the school paper and a listing in the classified telephone directory may also be helpful.

Fees. They must cover your costs, plus an adequate compensation for your time. In the former, don't forget to include depreciation on your car, special license fees, and insurance premiums for the increased coverage you will need. Check the rates you arrive at against those charged by local taxi and limousine services.

DOGS AND OTHER BEASTS

According to various estimates, over 25 million dogs and 10 million cats live in this country. Typically, their owners regard them as people and lavish all kinds of goods and services on them, from pink hair tints for poodles to psychological counseling for neurotic cats. In this outpouring of love (and money), there is ample opportunity for a woman who has affection for animals and a knowledge of their needs to create a business of her own.

GENERAL GUIDELINES

• A few of the jobs that follow—dog walking, for instance —can be operated from an apartment. But most require that you own your own home and can set aside a special area for the accommodation of your nonhuman clients.
• Before considering any business in which you bring animals into your home, check local zoning, licensing, and health laws well in advance. You may save yourself a lot of grief.
• Well-heeled urban and suburban communities are obvi-

ously the best bets for the flossier pet services. But don't neglect the possibilities of even modest-income areas for other businesses. Not-so-rich people love their pets just as much as rich ones do, and often have less time to tend to them themselves.

• Your ace in the hole will be your ability to inspire confidence in pet owners that their pets will receive the same kind of personal attention and affection from you that they get at home.

• See "A Word about Prices," page 5.

HOW TO GET BUSINESS

As in other ventures, the important thing is to zero in on your special market. If you concentrate on services for dogs, that's easy; you can get the names of owners from local dog-license bureaus; local kennels and kennel clubs are also good sources of information. With your target so clearly defined, printed or mimeographed flyers announcing the services you offer, either mailed or delivered by hand, will probably be the best method of getting business. If this doesn't bring in enough clients, try classified ads in local papers or dog-club newsletters. Once you get underway, a listing in the classified telephone directory and word-of-mouth publicity should keep you in business.

For special services for dogs, or for locating owners of less common pets, see the specific suggestions under the individual listings.

45

GROOMING SALON

Most dog owners like their pets to be bathed and barbered at regular intervals, but many of them don't have the time or inclination to do it themselves. If you live in an area where this service isn't being offered, or where there's room for one more, you might consider starting a "beauty" salon for dogs.

No one should consider this business unless she has had some experience in grooming dogs. Even if you have, you will probably need additional coaching on the techniques used with various breeds. You can get much of this information from books, but the best way to learn is to take a course at a dog-grooming school.

Most big cities and some smaller ones have grooming schools; check the classified telephone directory. The average duration of the courses offered is from 75 to 100 hours, the cost and tuition fees $500 and up. The instruction covers standard breed clips, the art of brushing, bathing, and trimming, and such specialties as hair tinting, manicuring, and even "mustache" coiffing. Some groomers prefer to specialize in poodles, both because poodles are a popular breed and because they are docile and well-behaved. But you will probably have to take what you can get in the beginning.

You will need to set aside a separate area in your home for your salon, probably an unused garage or part of the basement. An ample laundry tub or two with a connecting hose can serve as the washing area; you will also need barbering space and a "waiting room" where you can park your clients (on their leashes) when you're not working on them or until their masters call for them.

Getting started will cost you about $100 for equipment: brushes, nail files and clippers, ear and nose trimmers, hair thinning shears, hair trimming scissors and combs, and an electric hair dryer (floor, table, or cage model). In addition, you may want to spend another $50 or so for a professional grooming table, which is fitted with a post to which you can tie the dog being worked on. The cost of advertising (see page 20) to bring in business must also be considered in estimating your initial budget.

Grooming salons are run on an appointment schedule, just as human beauty salons are. Working full time, one person can usually groom five or six dogs a day. The amount of time spent on each depends on the size, complexity of hair style, and orneriness of the dog.

Fees. As in human beauty salons, these vary widely depending on the area, the neighborhood, the "cachet" of the salon, and the services performed. In big-city salons, grooming fees sometimes *start* at $10 to $15. In most areas, however, rates are considerably lower. Check to see what other salons and veterinary grooming services in your area charge and use them as a guide in setting your fees.

Pickup and delivery. Try to avoid this if you can; it will add to your costs and cut down on the number of clients you can handle. But if your competition offers it, you may have to too. Just make sure you can charge enough to make the whole venture worth your time.

WHERE TO GET MORE INFORMATION

The Complete Dog Book, American Kennel Club. Doubleday & Co., Inc., Garden City, N.Y., 1968.

Groom Your Dog, Leon F. Whitney. Crown Publishers, Inc., New York, N.Y., 1962.

The New Dog Encyclopedia. Stackpole Books, Harrisburg, Pa., 1970.

46

DOG WALKING

To be healthy and happy, all dogs need outdoor exercise, but those who live in cities and other built-up areas with strict leash laws seldom get enough of it. Fortunately (both for the dogs and for you), some owners have a conscience *and* the money to pay someone else to exercise their pets for them. Most of these people live in big cities, by far the most promising locale for dog-walking services.

For this business, you must be in excellent physical condition, since walking at a brisk double-time pace—not ambling, not strolling—is the crux of the job. But brute strength is definitely *not* called for; it wouldn't do you any good anyway, with 200 or 300 pounds of dogs in tow. Control is what you need, a control that comes from having been around various breeds of dogs enough to have a feel for handling them and the ability to command their respect. It's absolutely vital that both they and you know who's boss, or you may find yourself being pulled along like the caboose behind a powerful locomotive.

To make it worth your while, you should walk from four to six dogs at a time, and your clients should all live in the same neighborhood so that you don't waste too much time collecting and delivering them. As it is, you may find yourself covering 10 to 15 miles a day. Remember too that, like the postman, you'll be expected to show up in hail, snow, sleet, 100° heat, and other fiendish weather variations. Generally, you will walk your clients two hours each day, split into morning and afternoon periods. (For you, however, each romp will be longer than an hour, because you first have to pick the dogs up, one by one, and return them one by one.)

Fees. In most cities, weekly fees for dog walking run from $10 to $18 per dog. Since (unless you take on double shifts) you can't handle more than six dogs at a time, dog walking will never make you rich, nor is it a business that can grow. It can provide a respectable extra income, with a few expense deductions for such items as a brace to let you handle a number of leashes at once, and new shoes to replace the ones you wear out. Expect a dropoff in your business in summer; many city people go away for vacation and either take their dogs with them or board them in kennels during their absence.

How to get business. Sometimes a few phone calls to likely prospects in your neighborhood or one nearby will get you enough clients to start your service. Also notify any local veterinarians or pet shops; since dog walking is not in competition with any of the goods or services they offer, they may be willing to recommend you to their customers. If these methods fail to produce results, try those suggested on page 189.

If you live in the right area for this business, advertising will be the least of your problems. Once word of your service spreads, you will probably find that you will receive more requests than you can fill.

WHERE TO GET MORE INFORMATION

The Complete Dog Book, The American Kennel Club. Doubleday and Co., Inc., Garden City, N.Y., 1968.

The New Dog Encyclopedia. Stackpole Books, Harrisburg, Pa., 1970.

47

ANIMAL SITTING

When dog owners go away for a few weeks' vacation, they ordinarily deposit their pets at a boarding kennel. Most cats, however, vehemently object to being removed from their home turf, nor are there kennels for birds, fish, hamsters, or more exotic pets.

The term "sitter" is a little misleading. You don't sit at all; rather you call at the animal's home to prepare its food, clean its cage or litter, and offer whatever comfort or companionship the pet desires and you are prepared to give. (Alternatively, you can take the animal into your own home for the duration, but this is not always feasible—in the case of a large aquarium, for example—or may be undesirable for some other reason.)

In New York City, Maggie Baran (known professionally as "the Cat Lady") makes as many as 30 cat-sitting calls a day, sometimes starting at 5 A.M. While you may not be that energetic, or have as wide a clientele to draw from, even a modest service can bring in a little extra income. Animal sitting, by the way, is a business that does best in cities, for the simple reason that in smaller, less impersonal communities, people are more neighborly and often take on such tasks for one another without charge.

You don't have to have any particular experience for this job, but you should like animals, and keep a cool head in emergencies (such as a bird's refusing to go back into its nice clean cage, and flying around the room just out of reach, or a hamster's giving you the slip to play hide and seek in the furniture). Ask your client's master or mistress to put feeding and other instructions in writing, and get the name of a vet you can turn to if real trouble develops. Most of your business will be in the summer or over holiday weekends, but in some areas you may get calls at other times of the year from pet owners who travel a lot, for business or pleasure. Animal sitting is not a difficult job, but it can be demanding in the sense that, once you accept a sitting assignment, you must usually make a call every single day, including Sundays, until the pet owner returns.

Fees. These might range from $1 to $3 per day, depending on the distance you must travel to reach the job and the income level of your client. Kennels, for example, charge up to $3.50 per day for cats (those that can be persuaded to go). Food for the pet, if not supplied, is of course an extra charge.

How to get business. Advertise in the classified sections of community newspapers and in local animal-club newsletters. It's also worthwhile to tell pet-shop owners about your service, but a waste of time to approach vets because they are in the dog-boarding business themselves and often board other animals as well. Ask all your friends and neighbors to spread the word too. Since animal sitting involves entering someone's home while he is away, personal recommendations from people who can vouch for your integrity will be the most effective way of getting business. Also try to get a personal interview with the women's page editor of the local paper. In some areas an animal-sitting service is unique enough to rate a newspaper story.

48

DOG TRAINING

A dog owner whose pet has not learned to obey such basic commands as heel, sit-and-stay, and hey-not-on-the-rug, is a person in need of help—for which he is often willing to pay. And then there are owners who want their dogs to have an advanced education. If you have the qualifications, you can make money from one or more of these three branches of dog lore: (1) elementary obedience classes; (2) advanced training for show dogs; (3) problem correction (biting, barking, chasing cars, chewing furniture, jumping on people, and so on) .

Probably the owners most desperate to see their dogs trained are city residents who have to worry about leash laws, health department pleas to "curb your dog," and anti-dog neighbors who react to friendly barking by calling the local police precinct. However, the demand for dog training exists to some degree in almost all communities.

You can't, of course, start from scratch with this business. Previous job experience with a kennel, training school or breeder, or experience in training and showing your own dogs, is necessary. And if you want to work from your home, you probably will have to own a spacious yard, since an obedience class, the service most in demand, might consist of 15 to 25 owners with their dogs. Show-dog training also requires a lot of room. Many dog trainers, especially those who work in cities, prefer to rent space in armories, parks, commercial garages, or dance studios, or to arrange to offer their classes through such community organizations as the local Y or the extension program of the neighborhood high school.

Problem training deals with individual dogs; if you specialize in this, space will not be a dilemma. However, some trainers feel that it is pointless to try to break a dog of bad habits in a place strange to him, where he doesn't connect the teaching with his behavior at home. Only when the problem is that of housebreaking a puppy do they take the dog into their own homes; otherwise they visit the client at *his* home and do the training there.

Before you think seriously of going into this business, check on the competition existing in your area. In some communities, Y's, dog clubs, or the local A.S.P.C.A. may offer dog training, or there may even be free classes sponsored by the city or county government. A simple way to find out what classes are given in your area is to write to the American Kennel Club, 51 Madison Avenue, New York, N.Y. 10010, or Gaines Dog Food Company, 250 North Street, White Plains, N.Y. 10602.

Fees. While rates vary throughout the country, a typical charge for a ten-lesson group obedience course is around $25 per dog owner. Private lessons range from about $10 to $25 per lesson. As always, find out what the going rate in your community is as a guide to setting your fees.

Little or no investment is needed for equipment for this business. But, in addition to the usual overhead expenses, if you plan to rent space for your classes, you will of course have to have enough cash on hand to cover this expense for several months. And you will have to set aside an allowance for advertising (see below).

How to get business. For basic obedience classes, an announcement sent to local papers and dog clubs may bring you enough business. For special and advanced training, continuous classified advertising will probably be necessary.

You should also notify kennels, pet shops, veterinarians, and grooming salons of your service.

WHERE TO GET MORE INFORMATION

Dog Psychology: The Basis of Dog Training, Leon F. Whitney. C. C. Thomas, Publisher, Springfield, Ill.

Expert Obedience Training for Dogs, Winefred Gibson Strickland. The Macmillan Co., New York, N.Y., 1969.

The Koehler Method of Dog Training, W. R. Koehler. Howell Book House, New York, N.Y., 1962.

Training You to Train Your Dog, rev. ed., Blanche Saunders. Doubleday & Co., Inc., Garden City, N.Y., 1965.

49

BREEDING PEDIGREED PUPPIES

Unlike such exotic occupations as mink breeding, which is better left to specialists, breeding pedigreed dogs can be a practical business for a relative amateur—provided you have a solid knowledge of the breed you plan to raise, perhaps from owning and breeding your own dogs. Another essential requirement is the infinite patience to act as midwife, mother, and maid to your aristocratic boarders. (Incidentally, they *must* be aristocrats—i.e., pedigreed. You can't make any money from selling the garden variety of dog; there's too much competition from dog pounds, some pet shops, the local A.S.P.C.A., and people who give away unwanted litters.)

Breeding pedigreed dogs can bring you a comfortable

income over the long haul—but it will be a long haul, a fact you must face before you even consider entering the business. Count on several years of reinvesting most of your initial earnings before seeing a profit. Even to start the business in the smallest way possible—by acquiring a single pedigreed bitch—will cost you $200 to $2000 (depending on the blood lines of the dog you select), plus stud and veterinarian fees, as well as the usual (and some not so usual) overhead costs.

But before you spend a penny, investigate local and state zoning, health, and licensing laws. To begin with, an annual license fee is probably required. Then, some laws restrict kennels to rural areas and insist that the operator own a minimum number of acres. The actual kennel building may have to be situated a certain number of feet from the operator's own house and from adjoining property. (Even if you want—and are permitted—to start your business in your own basement and a fenced off area of your yard, the possibilities of future expansion may be limited by local regulations, so check into these well in advance.) Public health laws usually require that your dogs be given shots for rabies, distemper, hepatitis, and other infectious diseases.

Before you buy a pure-bred bitch, registered with the American Kennel Club, to start your business, you'll want to do careful research. The AKC *Stud Book,* available from the American Kennel Club, 51 Madison Avenue, New York, N.Y. 10010, lists the ancestry of every dog registered with the club since 1884. The AKC *Stud Book Register* is the monthly supplement to this book; it publishes in each issue the registration details of dogs and bitches currently being used for breeding. Attend as many dog shows as you can and study the prize winners in the breed you intend to specialize in.

Once you have a bitch, the procedure is to take her, at the

appropriate time, to a first-class kennel to be put to stud with a pedigreed male. When she produces a litter, you sell the males and retain the females for further breeding—at least until you reach the maximum number you feel capable of handling. (Remember that puppies take a lot of attention. They must be bathed, groomed, kept in good health, and at least partially housebroken; kennels must be cleaned twice a day.) Or you can keep particularly noteworthy males for use as studs; some kennels estimate that stud fees account for 25 to 35 percent of their total income.

How to get business. At first you will probably have to advertise fairly regularly in the classified section of area newspapers and in dog-club newsletters; it will also pay you to make friends with local veterinarians, owners of grooming salons, and noncompetitive pet shops. You should also take a listing in the classified telephone directory. Later you may find business coming to you, especially if you train and show your dogs.

Fees. These depend on the ancestry of the dogs you breed. If you deal in top bloodlines, each puppy you sell may bring you $250 or more. Stud fees similarly depend on bloodlines and may range from $75 to $200 or more, with $125 representing the average fee. Or you may prefer to take, in lieu of a fee, first choice of the new litter.

WHERE TO GET MORE INFORMATION

Dog Breeding, Sydney A. Asdell. Little, Brown and Co., Boston, Mass., 1966.

How to Breed Dogs, Leon F. Whitney. Howell Book House, New York, N.Y., 1971.

Raising Puppies for Pleasure and Profit, E. Schuler. The Macmillan Co., New York, N.Y., 1970.

50

ANIMAL TALENT AGENCY

This is a business whose chances of success are almost entirely limited to big cities, preferably those where a good many advertising agencies and public relations firms are located. An animal talent agency works just like a human one, except that most of the clients registered with it walk on four feet. They may be used in television commercials and talent shows, in print ads, in product promotion stunts, at conventions and trade shows, in stage productions, and nightclub acts. Another market is provided by children's parties, both private and organization-sponsored affairs.

Your role is to seek out talented animals, get their owners' permission to represent them, and then convince the agencies, TV stations, anxious mothers, and others that your clients can bring a little sunshine into people's lives, including sponsors' and rambunctious children's. Your reward is a healthy cut of the fees paid (through you) to the pets' owners.

Obviously, this business won't even occur to you unless you have an affection for animals and some experience in handling them. Talented dogs are the clients most in demand and the easiest to find, so start with them; as word of your activities gets around, you'll be surprised at how many people have talking birds or performing mice or some other wonder of the animal world that they want you to represent. If you don't know any talented dogs, try asking dog trainers, veterinarians, owners of kennels and pet shops; also (like scouts for human talent agencies), keep your eye out wherever you go. Remember that an animal doesn't have to be Lassie to qualify; so long as it has an appealing personality and is well trained, it may have a future in the talent business. (Remember too that *you* don't have to be an animal trainer; if the animal won't perform for you, you can usually arrange to take its owner along to act as handler.)

How to get business. Once you have lined up some potential clients to represent, you have to go after bookings for them, and that is a little harder. For commercial bookings, write (on business stationery) or call advertising and public relations agencies, TV production companies, commercial photographers; describe your service and ask for an appointment. Ads in trade papers and a listing in the classified telephone directory will help. For the birthday-party business, write to clubs, PTA's, fraternal organizations, party-supply services, caterers, and a selected list of private clients (the parents of your children's classmates might be a good place to start). Place ads in school, church, and local newspapers, and club newsletters.

Since you pay your clients' owners nothing until the animals are actually used on a job, the investment needed for starting an agency is limited mostly to advertising, stationery, and insurance to protect you both against injury to your clients and the possibility that they, in a moment of excitement, might nip or otherwise injure others.

Fees. Like fees for human models, these vary so widely, depending on a number of factors, that no typical figure can be given; you'll have to check the going rate in your community. You may be pleasantly surprised; it is not unusual in some cities for agencies to pay $30 to $50 an hour for animal talent. From this, you deduct a commission of from 15 to 30 percent before passing the balance along to the animal's owner.

Fees for animal talent at private children's parties are naturally quite a bit lower; you'll have to find out what mothers in your area will pay. (Also see pages 166–167.) Organization-sponsored parties pay more, but also expect more in the way of a professionally presented animal act.

A SHOP OF YOUR OWN

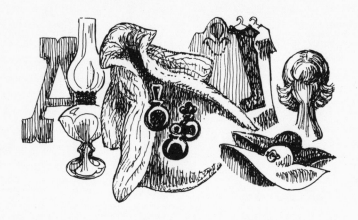

Many a woman with a selling background or with natural selling talent has dreamed of having a little boutique of her own, one that would produce extra income, yet still let her fulfill her primary responsibilities as a wife and mother. Some women have actually achieved their objective. Basically there are two ways to do so: (1) By opening a shop in your own home. This is possible only if zoning laws permit and if you live in a sufficiently central location to draw upon a number of potential customers; or (2) by running, at another location, a part-time or seasonal operation during periods you are free from household responsibilities.

Each method has both advantages and disadvantages. By operating from your own home, you don't have to put out extra cash for such overhead expenses as rent, light, heat, etc. (though you should charge a proper proportion of these to your business in figuring taxes, prices, and profits). Nor are you tied to the shop during its hours of operation, but can go about your household business until summoned by the tinkle of the shop's doorbell. On the other hand, family life is inevitably somewhat disrupted by opening your home to customers.

When your shop is at another, possibly more advantageous location than your home, the potentially greater profits are offset not only by the overhead incurred, but by the limited time of operation.

Because running a business of this kind varies with the kind of shop involved, no general guidelines can be given. Each business must be considered separately, as is done in the following examples of types of home shops that have succeeded. Yardsticks used by organizations such as the Small Business Administration or Dun & Bradstreet, Inc., are not much help, since they envision shopkeeping as a six-day-a-week, year-round affair, conducted on rented premises. Dun & Bradstreet, for example, estimates that to make an income of $45 a week, a gift-shop proprietor would have to have sales of $10,000 a year. Few home shops achieve that kind of volume—but neither do they have the commercial proprietor's expenses.

It is inescapably true, however, that a shop of your own requires a fairly large initial investment. Unless you have handiwork of your own to sell (in which case you would probably be better off to spend your full time producing it and leave the selling to others), you will have to buy your stock outright. A good credit rating may reduce the amount of cash you actually have to spend. It will not reduce the amount you must have in reserve to cover purchases of items that do not sell well, or sales to customers who fail to pay promptly. Usually too you must spend something—if only for paint, cabinets, or lumber for shelves—to fix up the area you plan to use as your shop.

Because of this commitment of cash, it is even more important in this type of business than in others to keep adequate records. If a service or business offering a product that is the result of your own skill fails, the greatest loss is usually for your uncompensated time and work. But a shop that fails can wipe out a large financial investment as well—

perhaps even leave you in debt. Consequently, you must devise an efficient system to tell you at a glance what stock you have on hand, what items sell best, which need reordering, which were a mistake and should *not* be reordered, and so on. In addition, careful records should be kept of your assets and liabilities, current purchases of merchandise, sales, and operating expenses. If you have no head for details like these—and no money to pay someone else to attend to them—shopkeeping, even on a limited scale, is not for you. See "A Word about Prices," page 5.

HELPFUL HINTS

Selling products in your own home involves problems of access, display, and space. Some tips:

• A home shop should have a separate entrance from that used by the family, with a bell which is actuated by the door's opening and which can be heard throughout the house.

• The display area should be located right off the entrance, if possible.

• You will also need space for storing records and inventory. Ideally, this might be a closet near the shop, but it could also be a corner in the basement or attic.

• Unless you live in a city, close to public transportation, you will have to provide parking space for customers. Be careful not to intrude on your neighbor's rights, or you'll be asking for trouble.

• If zoning laws forbid the posting of a prominent sign on your property, try to distinguish your house in some way—perhaps by painting it a color different from that of any other on the block.

• If you live on a road or highway, it may be worth your while to pay owners of the adjoining property for permission to post one or more signs on the approach to your shop.

• To make the most of a convenient location, use an identifying sign as prominent as local zoning laws will allow. And (if the law allows) , display your wares so they can be easily seen from the street. Dressed with care, a home picture window or playroom window wall can be as effective a showcase as a store window on Main Street.

HOW TO GET BUSINESS

Most of the business enjoyed by home shops comes to them either through word-of-mouth advertising or as a result of their convenient location. To put the first of these to work to the best advantage, make sure all your friends, acquaintances, and members of any clubs or community organizations you belong to know of your venture. Write to other groups inviting them to visit your shop and listing its specialties; you might also contribute prizes for raffles and contests sponsored by local fund-raising drives. An opening-day or opening-week event, during which every customer is given a small door prize, is also a good publicity stunt, especially if you can persuade the local paper to announce it. At the start, you might also want to take a few small display ads in the appropriate section of the paper, or hand out mimeographed or printed flyers on the main street of the neighborhood.

51

THRIFT SHOP

Call them cast-offs, trash-and-treasures, white elephants or whatever you like, there's gold in the attics, basements, or garages of your town. And when its owners find out that not only are you willing to take unwanted items off their hands, but that you will do your best to sell them—in which case *they* will receive most of the proceeds—you will have eager suppliers (who themselves may be potential customers for other people's cast-offs) hammering on your door. Some junkyard dealers have grown into tycoons by reclaiming the things people throw out. *You* should certainly be able to make a little money selling the possessions your neighbors save as too good to junk.

A thrift shop can be operated full-time at home, using a basement or an empty garage or barn as the selling area, or on a seasonal basis in rented premises. In Nashville, Tennessee, Mrs. Norma Condra and three of her friends founded The Bargain Spot as a twice-a-year clean-out (of local junk) and cleanup (to the tune of several hundred dollars apiece) for themselves.

> It all began when four of us found ourselves in the same predicament. Deep in the throes of fall housecleaning, we were surrounded by clothing, toys, furniture and household and sports equipment, some of it outgrown, some of it abandoned for other reasons, and all too good to throw away. Each year a lot of the same things were dragged out of closets, and then put back again to go through the same process the next time a thorough house

cleaning came around. We decided to try to sell them, plus other people's "junk," which we'd take on consignment, collecting a tidy 25 percent for the service.

Because none of us has the time or inclination to keep a full-time business going, we limit ourselves to a seasonal operation, opening for a month in the spring and a month in the fall; each of us contribute just a few hours' work a day. After renting a shop in the business area for $100 (we keep total expenses, including water, electricity and phone service under $200), we make up a mailing list from PTA and church memberships and from club yearbooks. Then we mimeograph announcements of the sale and mail them about a month before the opening.

For clothes racks, every available stepladder is pressed into service with iron pipes run between them. We borrow an adding machine, make a divided box for money, and buy some corded tags. Ten days before the opening, people with wares to sell start coming with their offerings; we give them receipts bearing post-sale dates to return for their checks and/or unsold merchandise. We accept only clean clothes; other objects must be in reasonably good repair. Many of our "suppliers," knowing the sales price will depend on the condition of the goods, often go to considerable pains to mend, paint or otherwise enhance their offerings.

Three or four days before the sale, we start sizing the clothes and arranging and pricing our wares. The opening day is always astounding—half of Nashville greets us at the door! But within the week, things settle down and it takes only two to tend shop. At the end of the month, we store the equipment in our basements, divide the profits, and happily return to being "just housewives!"

"Junketeers" (as Mrs. Condra and her friends call themselves) who live in less populous areas than Nashville can't expect so massive a response. Also, a year-round thrift shop will naturally receive less attention than an intensively promoted once- or twice-a-year event. Still, the relatively tiny investment needed for this kind of venture, and its built-in appeal for people (which includes most of us) who enjoy poring over other people's possessions, have made it a moneymaker—at least on a pin-money scale—for many women who have tried it.

Prices. Pricing thrift-shop treasures is a highly developed art, acquired only with experience. Prices even a shade too high will take away the thrill of bargain hunting, which is the main impetus for thrift-shop sales. Price your goods too low and the whole venture won't be worth your while. Unfortunately, there are no standards to check against; you'll just have to learn through trial and error. Depending on your locale, the type of merchandise, and the price, your commission should run from 20 to 40 percent of the latter.

WHERE TO GET MORE INFORMATION

Starting and Managing a Swap Shop or Consignment Sale Shop, Small Business Administration. Superintendent of Documents, U.S. Government Printing Office, Washington, D.C. 20402. Booklet.

52

CHILDREN'S RESALE SHOP

This specialized version of a thrift shop concentrates on clothes, toys, sports equipment, and furniture for infants and children. A children's resale shop is also usually operated on a consignment basis. Mothers whose kids have outgrown these items supply the merchandise, and mothers with children of the right age buy it. Unlike some of the other shops mentioned in this chapter, this one is definitely *not* for well-to-do communities, most of whose residents are unused to buying anything secondhand. On the other hand,

it's ideal for large housing developments or other neighborhoods where there are lots of struggling young families with
kids all about the same age (meaning the swap system won't
work).

The idea is to seek out items—particularly clothing and
infants' furniture—that are quickly outgrown and for which
parents are therefore reluctant to spend too much money.
Think of all the things a child uses and then no longer
needs: cribs, playpens, high chairs, carriages, car seats,
walkers, strollers, bathinettes, wagons, wading pools—the list
is endless. Many of these are handed down from child to
child, of course, or borrowed from friends and neighbors.
Still, these sources are often not available.

Also in demand are expensive toys and sports equipment,
such as electric train sets and bicycles. (Less expensive toys
will be of little use to you: the kids prefer, and the parents
can afford, new ones.) Everything should be reconditioned,
by the seller, before you accept it: clothes cleaned; furniture
repaired or refinished and sterilized, if necessary (most state
laws require this for a number of children's items offered for
rent or resale; check with your local health department);
toys put into working condition and painted to look like
new.

A children's resale shop may be operated on a seasonal
basis or opened once a week, perhaps on Saturday so neighborhood mothers can bring their school-age children to be
fitted. Want ads in local papers, and "garage" sales, are the
best means of finding items to offer; allow 3 to 6 months to
build up sufficient stock to open shop. Notifying schools,
clubs, and PTAs, and handing out flyers in front of supermarkets and in housing projects should get you your first
customers. After that, word of mouth may keep the business
going.

Prices. In buying for resale, the whole point is to make a profit after all costs, including those for reconditioning, are accounted for. Yet your prices must be considerably below those charged for similar new merchandise, even though the latter may be of lesser quality. Your profits will depend on how well you learn to walk the tightrope between these two demands.

WHERE TO GET MORE INFORMATION

See sources listed under #51, "Thrift Shop."

53

CHRISTMAS BOUTIQUE

If you live near a big city where a trade mart is located, or where gift shows are put on once or twice a year by wholesale firms, there is an opportunity for you to have a seasonal business operating a Christmas boutique. Such a business would not have much chance of success in the city itself, where there would be too much competition from department-store boutiques and specialty shops selling out-of-the-ordinary Christmas gifts and decorations. But in a smaller community or a suburb, the uniqueness of your selections and the convenience of the service offered may enable you to make enough money at least to cover your own Christmas shopping, with perhaps some to spare.

The special advantage of a Christmas boutique is that you do not have to carry the actual merchandise to be sold, but only samples, which you use to get orders. Consequently, a home shop in a family room or enclosed, heated porch is perfectly feasible. Your work begins in July or August (the time most of the Christmas trade shows are held) , when you visit the big city to choose the merchandise you will offer to customers. To gain access to these shows, you will have to prove you are actually in business and not just a private shopper. This can be done by providing details of your operation to Little Brothers Shows, Inc., 220 Fifth Avenue, New York, N.Y. 10010. They will put your name on their buyer list, keep you informed about future shows, and, if you register for these, send you the necessary admittance badges. (For a list of trade marts and shows around the country, see the Small Business Administration leaflet, "Gift and Art Shops," listed below.)

If you have an excellent credit rating, you may be able to get your sample merchandise without laying out much, if any, cash, but don't count on it, at least the first year. Choosing the samples is the most crucial part of the whole enterprise, for you must be able to offer a high proportion of things that are not available elsewhere in your community, but which will appeal to community tastes.

In other words, you must outsmart the professional buyers in your area. If that sounds impossible, it really isn't. In the first place, you have a more intimate knowledge of the people (mostly your neighbors) who will be your customers than professional buyers do. And in the second, since you can operate on much lower profit margins than they, you can make a success of items they would have to price too high for sales appeal.

Early in the fall, perhaps even before local merchants have started their Christmas promotions, open your boutique for business. This early-bird operation is vital, since you must allow enough time for collecting orders (so that you can obtain quantity discounts) and then for the ordered merchandise to be shipped. To your customers, emphasize the advantages, both in wider choice and lower prices, of shopping early, and establish a cutoff date beyond which no orders can be accepted. It's far better to turn a customer down than to have to renege on a promised delivery date.

Since you collect the full purchase price from the customer in advance, you won't have to lay out any of your own money for the orders you collect. But if you find that certain items sell especially well, you may want to take a chance on ordering additional stock on these, to sell after the cutoff date for orders has passed.

Why, since your business is essentially a mail-order one, should anyone patronize you rather than ordering directly from one of the heavily illustrated mail-order gift catalogues available at Christmas time? The big reason is that no picture can equal the satisfaction of being able to see and handle the actual object itself. The other lies in the personal service you can give in advising on the choice of gifts and decorations, and in taking care of all the details.

Prices. The formula is the same for any business: you must set prices low enough to attract customers, high enough to make a profit. Talking specifically of operating a retail business such as a shop, the Small Business Administration says: "A good formula is to divide each dollar of expected sales into three parts: one-third for cost of merchandise, one-third for operating costs including selling expense, and one-third for wages and profit for the owner. For example, if an item costs $.50 from the supplier, the sales price should be $1.50." However, on some items—Christmas cards, for one—the manufacturers preset the retail price and pay you a standard commission of 30 to 50 percent.

WHERE TO GET MORE INFORMATION

Gift and Art Shops, Small Business Administration. Superintendent of Documents, U.S. Printing Office, Washington, D.C. 20402. Free leaflet.

54

WIG BOUTIQUE

Once upon a time, wigs were only for old ladies who had lost all their own hair. No one ever admitted to wearing one, although it was obvious when anyone *did*. Today wigs are big business, with almost every woman owning at least one—or wishing she did.

Some women have several, in widely different shades and styles, and switch them about as they do other costume accessories. In addition, there's a big business in wiglets, falls, braids, curls and other partial hairpieces. What has made this possible is the development, in the last few years, of synthetic fibers that closely resemble human hair but cost only a fraction as much, thus bringing the price of wigs down to a level almost every woman can afford.

Despite the competition from retail stores of many kinds, who have been quick to get in on the boom, some women have been successful with home shops that specialize in wigs. One of them is Mrs. Pat Van Wyk, who built up a thriving business located in the basement of her home in Pella, Iowa. By the end of her third year in business, Mrs. Van Wyk was making a net profit of $1,800 a year—not bad for a wife and mother of four, who operated her business in her spare time, selling to customers by appointment only.

The first thing to do in considering a wig boutique is to collect as much information as you can about the field. Read books about wigs and how they are made; send for information and catalogues from wig companies; talk to local salespeople who handle wigs and beauticians who service them. Try to get an idea of what types sell best in your town, and at what price levels; ask friends what they like or dislike about wigs; hang around wig counters in department stores and watch and listen to customers trying on various types of hairpieces.

A major decision, based on this research, will be what kinds of wigs you will carry. Fortunately, you won't have to worry about tying up a lot of money in human-hair wigs; these now account for only about 5 percent of the business. Many women, even if they can afford the real thing, prefer synthetic wigs, for in addition to their economy, they are lightweight, don't change color as real hair wigs do, and hold a set better. You will have to make a choice from a number of synthetic fibers—Kanekalon, Dynel, Teklan, Venicelon and others—and a variety of wig styles.

Your investment, for at least one sample of each wig or wiglet you plan to sell and the necessary accessories may run from $200 to $300. You will not, however, need much in the way of furnishings for your "shop," other than a few tables, chairs, and a well-lighted mirror. Synthetic wigs come prestyled, but it will be helpful if you know enough about hair cutting to be able to snip here and there to adjust a particular style to the customer's satisfaction.

You should also have an arrangement with a local beauty salon who will service your customer's wigs when they need it (though synthetic wigs have their set baked in and can be simply washed and hung on a door knob to dry). The wig business is a repeat one. Not only do the same customers often buy more than one wig, but the life of even a good wig is only about two years. Consequently, it's important to see that your customers remain satisfied with their wigs, so they will come back to you when it's time for a new one.

What will your service have that bigger competitors, such as department and other stores, don't have? This personal attention, for one thing. Convenience, for another (a neighbor will be able to drop in and try on a wig while she's waiting to take the clothes out of the dryer). Still another is privacy—many women hate being stared at by standers-by (who sometimes make audible, unflattering remarks) when trying on wigs in the stores. A fourth advantage can be the relaxed, homelike atmosphere of your boutique—an atmosphere you can encourage by serving coffee and cookies to your customers.

Prices. See page 214, under "Christmas Boutique," for the general advice offered by the Small Business Administration for setting prices in any retail business.

WHERE TO GET MORE INFORMATION

Complete Guide to Synthetic Hairpieces and Wigs, Rebecca Hyman. Grosset & Dunlap, Inc., New York, N.Y., 1971.

55

ANTIQUES (OR "JUNQUE") SHOP

This is not a business one goes into simply to make money—though that's important too! Most owners of antique shops are themselves lovers of the old and the unusual, who have long made a hobby of poking into out-of-the-way places in the hope of finding a prize. They are haunters of auctions, aficionados of attics, frequenters of flea markets and junk stores—and totally incapable of ever throwing anything out.

If that description fits you, you might well look around at your community to see whether it will support an antiques shop (or another one). As the world grows increasingly more complex, objects that suggest the values of a simpler day appeal to more and more people. These objects need not be what are traditionally thought of as antiques. So strong is the present strain of nostalgia that memorabilia dating from the twenties, thirties, and even forties of the present century command premium prices.

Recently for example, *The New York Times* reported that "cultural antiques," or "junque" as these wares are sometimes called, have quietly become big business in a growing number of shops across the country. A Pepsi-Cola bottle of the twenties for $12.50 (Bath, N.C.) ; kewpie dolls from the thirties for $15 to $30 (Chicago) ; railroad lanterns for $20 to $30 (Miami) , and old gumball machines for $200 (Los Angeles) are only a few examples of the money to be made from catering to the craze for "remembering when."

Although the most successful shops of this kind are to be found in big cities, where there are more people with money to spend on such things, the *Times* reporter found that the "junque" craze has swept the country. Consequently, if you live in a resort community, or on or near a well-traveled road, the odds for success in selling antiques and/or "junque" may also be in your favor. Another promising location is a well-heeled suburb.

As an antiques buff yourself, you will be aware of likely sources of stock for your store in the surrounding area. And if you've lived there for any time, you will have an advantage that professional antique dealers from other localities lack—inside knowledge of the people and their possessions. A family may move or suffer a death of an older member. In such cases, there may be articles they want to sell. Or old buildings with interesting architectural details may be due to be torn down, and so on. Of course, if you live in an area regularly combed by dealers, you may find slim pickings are left for semi-amateur buyers like you.

Fashions in home decoration have a profound effect on the antiques business, and they should be given close attention by anyone interested in going into this field. A few years ago, Tiffany glass—vases, lampshades, bowls, and other objects of iridescent colored glass made around the turn of the century—was considered almost worthless junk. Today it's a favorite of interior decorators, and brings high prices everywhere. Another prized category is carnival glass, which has an even humbler origin—it was given away at carnivals or theaters in the twenties and thirties.

An antiques or "junque" shop can be housed almost anywhere—in a garage, shed, barn, or even in your own living room, if you want to sacrifice it for that purpose. It is essential, of course, that zoning laws permit you to post a prominent sign advertising its existence. Most of your business will come from curious passers-by, attracted by the sign. It will also pay you to call upon interior decorators in your area, and upon those responsible for window displays in department and furniture stores. Although the latter two will not be interested in buying your wares, you can sometimes work out an arrangement to supply them with unusual props on a rental basis.

Prices. The field of antiques is one in which the art of bargaining still flourishes. As a collector yourself, you know that the universal rule is to charge whatever the traffic will bear. Whether you can get what you ask will depend on (a) your knowledge of the average market value of the piece in question and (b) your bargaining skill.

WHERE TO GET MORE INFORMATION

The Antique Dealer. Rosenthal & Smythe, Inc., 101 Springfield Ave., Summit, N.J. 07901. Monthly magazine.

The Dictionary of Antiques and the Decorative Arts, rev., Louise Ade Boger and H. Hatterson Boger. Charles Scribner's Sons, New York, N.Y., 1967.

Hitting the Antiques Trail, Ann Kilborn Cole. David McKay Co., Inc., New York, N.Y., 1961.

The Official Guide to Popular Antiques and Curios, rev. ed., Hal L. Cohen. H. C. Publishers Inc., New York, N.Y., 1970. Paperback.

TRADE ASSOCIATION:

Art & Antique Dealers League of America, 807 Lexington Ave., New York, N.Y. 10022.

56

DRESS SHOP

With all the retail outlets that sell women's clothes, what chance of success does a home dress shop have? Not very much, if you go by the statistics. On the other hand, anyone who went by statistics would never attempt any kind of selling venture. And the facts are that some women *have* parlayed an interest in fashion and a head for business into a source of extra income.

In addition to a flair for picking styles women and girls in your area like, you do have to have one of two things, and preferably both: (1) a convenient location and (2) an extraspecial service.

Private houses left stranded near the center of town as encroaching businesses push other residents out, are often considered undesirable places to live. But such a location is perfect for anyone with a dress shop in mind. For one thing, it is unlikely there will be any zoning problems in converting part of the house into a commercial establishment.

Moreover, the likelihood is that the house is of an older architectural style, and that can add to the shop's appeal—a fact two housewives in Durham, N.C., capitalized on when they opened a dress store in a run-down Victorian mansion.

The special service required of a home shop can take a number of forms. Two women in a New York suburb make money selling dresses without any kind of formal "store" at all. Instead, they act almost as personal shoppers for their housebound neighbors, making regular trips to the city, where they scour wholesale dress houses for styles they know will be particularly suitable and appealing to their neighbors and friends. Then they invite everyone in for coffee and cake and put on a "fashion show" in a wood-paneled, well-lighted basement which they have fitted out with several three-way mirrors and curtained-off, try-on booths. Their guests are delighted with this service (which is also entertainment and a chance to get together with other women), and enough end up buying the specially chosen clothes to make the business profitable.

Preselection and a relaxed atmosphere are also the secret of success in a regular in-home shop. Many women are confused by the crowded racks in larger stores, and are happy to sacrifice a wider range of choice for carefully chosen styles and sympathetic personal attention. Some home dress shops also offer free home adjustments, and will do additional alterations for a small fee.

Another attraction of still other home dress shops lies in the low prices they feature. These shops specialize in buying up factory close-outs (styles the manufacturers guessed wrong on and overproduced) and then offering them at close-to-wholesale prices. This operation is made feasible by the curious time schedule big stores operate on. (By the time summer really arrives, for example, they have ceased to stock summer clothes and have begun to push their fall lines.) Consequently, both dress manufacturers and customers benefit from this kind of clean-up operation.

The dress industry is almost entirely concentrated in New York City, with a few small branches (mostly for casual clothes) on the West Coast. However, salesmen from the big buying chains and from individual manufacturers make frequent trips throughout the country, showing samples and taking orders from the many dress-shop owners who cannot make twice-yearly buying trips to New York.

The investment required to open a dress shop is higher than for almost any other kind mentioned in this chapter. That is because of the large inventory needed (every dress style must usually be carried in at least four or five sizes). Some money is also needed for fixtures (clothes racks, display cases, etc.). It is rare that the initial investment can be recovered in less than two years; obviously, a home dress shop is a bad bet for anyone who expects a quick profit. It is a natural business for a woman, however, and it does have substantial long-term possibilities.

Prices. See advice under this heading for #53, "Christmas Boutique," page 214.

57

ART NEEDLEWORK BOUTIQUE

A talent for needlework can be put to work to make money in a number of ways, some of which have already been discussed (see pages 93–111). Still another possibility is an art needlework boutique, set up in your own home.

Most women who start a business of this kind more or less fall into it as the result of teaching needlework and/or selling original designs (and the kits for making them) to needlework stores. It's a good route to follow. The first activity brings in pupils who, as they learn, become eager customers for needlework designs—and naturally favor their own teacher's. The second gives you an excellent idea of the kinds of designs most in demand, and the markup at which kits featuring them can be sold. Eventually you may find that the only sensible thing to do is to combine the two functions and open up a home needlework shop, where students who come for lessons can buy the needed materials right on the spot, and customers for kits can, if they need it, get help in making up the designs.

The chances for success in this business depend not only on how good a teacher, designer, and businesswoman you are, but on the competition you face where you live. In an area with a number of good needlework shops, it will be hard to attract enough customers to make the venture worthwhile. In many communities, though, there are no such shops at all, and it is not even possible to buy canvas, yarn, and other materials locally. Given the spectacular recent increase of interest in needlework, particularly the creative kind often described as "painting with a needle," such an area is obviously a good one for a creative at-home boutique. (Remember, though, that in any community you will face competition from the many excellent needlework kits sold through the mail.)

The best place for your boutique can be your own living room. Decorated with the products of your skill—framed designs (your own, of course) on the walls, needlepoint cushions on the chairs, pillows worked in crewel on the sofa, an afghan draped across a chaise longue—it can be a more effective showroom than a conventional shop.

How much investment in inventory you will need depends on how big a step you want to take at the start. For a regular needlework shop, the New York State Woman's Program estimates the minimum investment needed to be $2,000. A home shop (which will attract fewer customers) can be started on a tenth of this amount, since there is no necessity for it to achieve an arbitrary level of sales in order to stay in business.

Just as a strong sense of color and a real talent for creating original designs is necessary to attract customers to your boutique, so a talent for organizing your work and handling the business end of your transactions is vital if you hope to make any money from it. Making up kits is laborious business, involving not only establishing a reliable source of supply for the materials, but the tracing or stenciling of the designs and the writing of the instructions which must then be mimeographed or printed.

Prices. Pricing needlework kits is tricky, since, while you must cover all your costs (including overhead), plus an allowance for your labor and a modest profit (one widely used formula suggests allowing one-sixth of your net production cost for the latter), the result must be in the range the customer is willing to pay. Sometimes you must overprice some designs, in relation to their cost, in order to make up for the necessary underpricing of others. Learning how to do this juggling act successfully is the key to making a profit from a needlework boutique. (Some typical prices in big-city boutiques; pillow covers, $10 to $60; director's chair covers, $40 to $90; rugs (3 × 5 feet), $100 to $400; eyeglass cases, wallets, address books, $15 to $30. Prices include the wool, the design on canvas, needles, instructions, and a piece of canvas to practice on.)

If your business thrives, a natural step to consider is to attempt to sell your kits by mail order as well. See "How to Expand into Mail Order," page 41. This will entail considerable additional expense for advertising and an illustrated catalogue (to say nothing of handling and mailing costs) , and will require you to expand your sources of supply for materials. A bottleneck on the supply end has led to the failure of many a promising mail-order business, so investigate this angle thoroughly before you start.

GIVING LESSONS

"Those who can," runs an old saying, "do. Those who can't, teach." Stripped of its cynicism, the proverb offers encouragement to those with marketable abilities but no way to put them to work directly to make money. If *you* have expert knowledge in some field—and the patience and skill to teach what you know to others—you may be able to earn extra income with very little investment other than your own time.

GENERAL GUIDELINES

• Teaching is an art in itself, quite separate from knowledge of the subject being taught. Some of the world's greatest scholars are terrible teachers. If you have never taught before, you may be surprised (perhaps dismayed!) when you discover how much time, close analysis, and self-discipline it takes to organize a course in anything.
• Your competition may be not only other private individuals or schools but adult education programs in the public schools and classes organized by Y's, civic groups,

clubs, and possibly even local stores (to promote the use of their products). Check all these to determine what you'll be up against, and also to find out what others are charging for the kind of instruction you intend to offer.

• Zoning laws usually do not apply to home classes (though it is always wise to check). But any kind of sign, even a small card in a window, will probably require permission.

• See "A Word about Prices," page 5.

HELPFUL HINTS

• If you are the slightest bit rusty in the skill you plan to teach, brush up on it before you open shop. Good word-of-mouth is essential to this business; if you let your first pupils down, it may take you a long time to get any more.

• Also essential is advance lesson preparation. Before you take your first pupil, not only should the entire course be outlined and divided into lessons of appropriate length, but each segment should have its own lesson plan, with an estimate of the time it will take to cover each topic or technique to be taught. Without such a plan, it's easy to be diverted by interesting but nonessential matters, until eventually the whole course gets out of hand and your pupils do not learn as much as they should.

• For individual lessons it's traditional to charge by the hour, with no commitment by the pupil to take any specified number of lessons. Group lessons are sometimes charged for in the same way. It is preferable, however, to set a flat fee for a course containing a specified number of lessons. This fee should be payable in advance, with no refunds granted (except in the case of emergencies) after the second lesson.

• Whether the teacher or the pupils pay for the cost of materials varies. Generally, materials used primarily for demonstration purposes (food for cooking classes, flowers for flower arranging, etc.) are the responsibility of the teacher, even though the pupils consume, or take home, the result. Materials that the pupils work with and that become their permanent possessions (needlework supplies, gardening tools) are paid for by them.

HOW TO GET BUSINESS

• Run a classified ad (under "Instruction") in local newspapers; take a listing in the classified telephone directory.

• Write individual letters, or have flyers prepared, to send to schools, libraries, clubs, churches, community organizations, and any other group whose members might be interested in the subject you are prepared to teach. If an organization has a bulletin board, ask permission to post a flyer, or your business card, there.

• Giving lessons, as an educational activity, sometimes qualifies for free publicity, so write up a description of the courses you offer and send it to women's page editors of local papers. Cooking classes, classes in gardening techniques and flower arranging, and swimming lessons for young children are examples of projects whose intrinsic interest has produced feature stories even in big-city newspapers.

• Other sources of publicity (and perhaps promotional tie-ins) for some subjects may be merchants in your town. In return, for example, for permission to exhibit posters advertising your classes in the store, you might agree to give a cooking demonstration in the store of a local appliance dealer, or a swimming lesson on the premises of a swimming-pool dealer.

• Get as much personal exposure as you can in other ways too. If you teach cooking, needlework or sewing, gardening or flower arranging, display the products of your skill at local fairs or shows; if you teach music, offer to perform at church, community, and school affairs and put on student recitals. Keeping in the public eye will be your best form of advertising.

58

GARDENING LESSONS

If you have a particularly green thumb, and live in a suburb where there are a lot of recent refugees from the city, you should have no trouble attracting students eager to learn how to make their gardens grow. Needless to say, your own garden must be a showcase; it will be both your best advertisement and the laboratory for your classes.

For real novices, you could offer a course that starts in March (earlier in warm sections of the country) with the planting of new roses and the pruning of old ones, sowing of seeds in flats, testing the soil for acidity and good drainage, and so on, and continues through to late fall with the planting of bulbs, propagation of plants, sowing of seeds of hardy annuals, and all the other many attentions a garden demands.

Basic information, such as the identification of various flowers and plants and their classification, and types of garden tools and their uses, should be an important part of the course. But each lesson should also be planned to be complete in itself and to treat one or two subjects in depth, so that even experienced gardeners, who nevertheless want additional information on particular topics, such as planning a rock garden or growing plants under artificial light, will be attracted to some of the sessions.

Gardening lessons generally last from two to three hours and are held once a week, once every two weeks, or once a month, according to demand. Depending upon the duration of the lesson and the area, fees may range from $3.50 to $5 per session.

Gardening is thirsty work; at the close of the session, it's a nice touch to offer students coffee or hot tea in cool weather, iced tea in warm.

59

LESSONS IN FLOWER ARRANGING

In many cities and suburban areas, there is great interest in learning how to arrange flowers. Often the local garden club or Y offers classes. But in some communities the demand for instruction is strong enough to support private classes as well.

To teach flower arranging, you must be adept in all the various styles, from traditional to abstract and including the demanding Oriental techniques. Courses that offer all these are generally the most popular, though in some areas you may be able to specialize—or at least offer several different courses, each devoted to a single style.

If you live in a suburb, you will, of course, use flowers from your own garden whenever possible, but even so you must count on some expenditure for flowers and foliage from florists, and for suitable containers and accessories in addition to those you already have.

For an idea of what to charge, check the fees asked by others offering such instruction in your own or nearby communities. Countrywide, these generally range from about $2 an hour upward for group instruction.

WHERE TO GET MORE INFORMATION

Encyclopedia of Flower Arrangements, J. G. Conway. Alfred A. Knopf, Inc., New York, N.Y., 1957.

How to Arrange Flowers for All Occasions, Katherine N. Cutler. Doubleday & Co., Inc., Garden City, N.Y., 1967.

60

COOKING CLASSES

Everyone is more sophisticated these days, and that goes for tastes in food as in other things. In addition, for many women cooking is both a daily duty and an absorbing hobby—creative, rewarding, and capable of almost endless variation.

The result is seen not only in the proliferation of cookbooks—there are over 1,200 in print—but in the popularity of courses that treat cooking as a fine art. If you are a specialist in a particular type of cuisine—French (above all), Italian, Chinese—or in a branch of cookery, such as baking or dessert making, you might consider imparting your expertise to others, for a fee.

The best location for such a venture is a city or suburb where a good deal of entertaining goes on and hostesses vie with one another in offering gourmet meals to their guests. If you offer demonstration classes only, you won't need any special facilities other than your own kitchen; it need only be big enough for a group to gather around as you demonstrate. If, on the other hand, the students are to participate in the preparation, not only must your kitchen be roomy but you must have extra utensils and equipment.

Advance planning is particularly important for a cooking course; it means drawing up lesson plans and then performing a trial run for each. You may have to change some of your preparation methods, eliminating shortcuts you have been using for years and substituting exact measurements for instinct in determining quantities. It is important too, to time yourself in making the recipes you plan to teach—and don't forget to allow for students' questions. Some teachers distribute mimeographed copies of the lesson recipes to the class; others ask pupils to bring a notebook along for copying the instructions and making preparation notes.

In addition to gourmet cooking classes, there may be a demand in some areas for instruction in basic cooking, low-calorie cooking, or in cooking for those on special regimes such as low-sodium, diabetic, or allergy diets.

What you should charge for your classes will depend on the going rates in your area, and whether you offer demonstration or participation instruction. Generally, rates average around $5 to $10 per pupil per two-hour session, though cooks with a big reputation can sometimes charge more—perhaps as much as $15 to $30 per session.

61

SEWING CLASSES

The demand for instruction in the fundamentals of sewing is pretty well satisfied, in most communities, by such free instruction as that offered by sewing machine and pattern companies. In addition, Y's and adult education programs offer lessons in basic sewing at low cost.

More advanced instruction is something else. Correspondence schools do a big business in teaching the tricks of tailoring and couture dressmaking to women who want to go beyond the basics and turn out a professional-looking job. If you yourself are an expert sewer, you may well tap the same market for live classes.

You can rent the additional sewing machines needed; there should be one for every two pupils. You will also need one, or perhaps two, large cutting tables. Students should be expected to provide their own materials, patterns, and sewing equipment.

Fees are lower for sewing lessons than for some other types of instruction. For a special service such as yours, though, you should be able to charge more than the going rates for basic sewing lessons. Check what these are in your community and then raise yours accordingly.

62

NEEDLEWORK CLASSES

Giving lessons in various kinds of needlework—creative embroidery (commonly called crewel work) , needlepoint, crochet, knitting, rug hooking—may be carried on as part of a bigger venture (see #57, Art Needlework Boutique) or for itself alone. It has the big advantage of requiring absolutely no investment, since students usually bring their own materials. (You may, however, want to make up basic kits for teaching each technique and supply them to students at cost.)

What you can charge for lessons depends a great deal on where you live. In big cities, group instruction rates are usually about $5 per person for a two-hour class; in smaller communities, $2 to $3 is more likely. Individual instruction is rare and mostly confined to well-known needlewomen, who ask as much as $5 to $10 an hour.

63

LANGUAGE LESSONS

Every year the number of U.S. citizens who apply for passports to travel abroad runs into hundreds of thousands. Granted that some of these already know the langauge of the country to which they are going, and others expect to get along with a phrasebook, that still leaves a great many people who may be good prospects for lessons in languages such as French, Spanish, Italian, and German.

There are other people, with no immediate thought of travel, who would like to acquire a language skill for the fun of it, or to aid in the pursuit of some hobby or course of study they have undertaken. It is among this group that students are to be found for lessons in such languages as Russian, Greek, or Japanese, which are spoken in countries off the usual tourist's track.

Other prospective customers are high-school and college students who are failing language courses in school (see #66, Tutoring) , and younger children whose parents want them to learn a second language at the age it is easiest to acquire. In some ultra-sophisticated communities, even preschoolers are given language lessons, but usually the age range is from nine or ten years up.

You will find most customers for language lessons in a big city or university town, though some suburbs are also fallow ground. The particular language you want to teach (and how good you are in it) will also affect the number of students you can expect. Another factor will be whether you offer individual instruction, group instruction (at lower rates), or both.

The typical customer for language instruction takes a two-hour group lesson once a week for six to eight weeks, but occasionally a student will want to come two or three times a week or even daily, for intensive coaching. Since you will probably be getting students at several levels of proficiency, you will have to have detailed lesson plans for each level. Incidentally, a little imagination in devising teaching aids will help too. Crossword puzzles, word games, and spelling bees in the language being taught, assignments requiring the use of foreign-language newspapers and magazines, and occasional excursions to a foreign film or restaurant (students pay their own way) will enliven the lessons and make them fun.

For aid in setting rates, check those charged by local colleges, Y's, and private language schools. For a two-hour-a-week, six- to eight-week group course, the average rate tends to be around $25 to $35. Private lessons range from around $5 to $10 an hour.

64

MUSIC LESSONS

In any moderately affluent community, there are scores of parents who are willing to pay for music lessons for their offspring. If you are a particularly good teacher of a popular instrument like the piano, or the only teacher available for an exotic one like the flute, you may be able to build up a steady business. (The most popular instruments, after the piano, in order, are: violin, guitar, trumpet, accordion, saxophone, clarinet, and flute.)

One word of caution: Before you even consider music teaching, which gives rise to a certain amount of noise, check to make sure it's permitted in your neighborhood. If you live in an apartment, consult your lease or your landlord; if you own your own home, see the town clerk.

Customers for music lessons are almost exclusively children, which means, of course, that patience should be one of your strong points. Although academic background is rarely important for teaching the other subjects discussed in this chapter, parents of music students usually inquire into the teacher's credentials. It's wise, therefore, to assemble evidence (including letters of recommendation from your own former teachers) of your training and experience to show to inquirers.

Rates charged for music lessons vary widely depending upon the instrument and the area (and of course upon the reputation of the instructor). A typical charge for a half hour of elementary or intermediate instruction in guitar is $3 to $5. Piano lessons are usually higher, averaging from $4 to $7 per hour.

65

SCHOOL FOR WATER BABIES

This opportunity is strictly for a suburbanite who owns a swimming pool. Nothing very grand is needed, for you won't be teaching older children (who will probably go to the Y for lessons, if they want them). The idea is to specialize in what was once a rather startling concept but one that has gained wide currency in the last ten years: namely, that children as young as three or four can be taught to swim, and that it's good for them and lots of fun too.

Naturally you yourself should be an excellent swimmer, with a certificate as an authorized instructor and a life-saving badge from the American Red Cross or the YWCA. And if you don't already have liability insurance that covers your pool, this is clearly the time to get it.

Water-baby classes work best with a maximum of five pupils for an hour at a time (a half hour for formal instruction, a half hour for play). The object is to give the children confidence and make them feel at home in the water while getting over to them the basic techniques. Usually mothers bring their children, and some may stay for the lesson, which will save you from having to have another person on hand to keep an eye on the children you're not immediately working with. (On the other hand, it means you may have to cope with maternal kibbitzing!) In some communities, though, the teacher will be expected to pick the students up and take them home afterward.

One tip: In addition to other ways of getting business, mentioned on page 228, try to interest the pediatricians in your town in recommending your classes for their health value. And by all means, alert your local paper. A school for water babies, especially if the children are quite young, is a natural for photographic coverage.

Swimming lessons for young children are a luxury for most families, so you can't set your rates too high. Twenty-five to thirty-five dollars for a course of eight to ten lessons is typical. But take into consideration the going rates for other types of swimming lessons in your community and keep yours in line. If you are expected to pick up and return the children, you will, of course, be entitled to charge more.

WHERE TO GET MORE INFORMATION

How to Teach Children to Swim, Carolyn Kaufmann. G. P. Putnam's Sons, New York, N.Y., 1960. Out of print, but available in many libraries.

Teaching an Infant to Swim, Virginia Hunt Newman. Harcourt Brace Jovanovich, Inc., New York, N.Y., 1971.

Teaching Young Children to Swim and Dive, Virginia Hunt Newman. Harcourt, Brace & World, Inc., New York, N.Y., 1969.

66

TUTORING

Tutoring is no longer confined to students who can't make passing grades. Today, some parents begin worrying whether their children are going to get into the college of their choice when they first enter kindergarten. By the time the child reaches high school, the pressure is really on, and a tutor is often called in to help boost grades from C's to B's, or even B's to A's.

To impress anxious parents with your ability to do the job, you need former teaching experience or a sufficiently impressive academic background. A college degree is essential—and it helps if the degree is from a "name" institution (there's a lot of snobbery involved in education). As for the community where you hope to ply your trade, it must obviously be one where the majority of the students are college-bound.

If there is a tutoring agency in your community (and you don't mind going outside your own home to tutor), you might consider registering with it. (Check for such agencies in the classified telephone directory under "Tutoring.") You will probably get more pupils that way, but you will also have to pay the agency its commission. The number of pupils you can expect, either with an agency or as a free-lance, also depends on how many subjects you are qualified to teach.

Your pupils will probably be divided into two main groups: children who are having difficulty in school, and high school students preparing for College Boards. Reading difficulties are often the root of the trouble in younger children in the first group; to untangle them, some knowledge of the techniques of remedial reading, as well as a great deal of patience, are needed.

If you work as a free lance, any contacts you have in teaching circles will be very helpful in getting you pupils. If you don't have any, ask for an appointment to see the principals and/or individual teachers in local schools and discuss with them the service you offer and your credentials. If they approve of you, they will become the best source of referrals.

Current rates for tutoring range from $2 to $5 an hour, with higher rates in big cities and on the East and West coasts than in small towns and the South and Midwest.

67

BRIDGE LESSONS

Are you a bridge fiend? A terror in local tournaments? Everybody's favorite partner because you always help him win? Then you might scout the possibilities in your community for earning a little money by teaching your skills to others.

In some communities, the local Y or the town's adult education program offers bridge classes, but this needn't stop you, for many people might prefer the more social atmosphere of classes held in a private home. Your main problem will be to let prospective clients know of your existence. Dropping word of your availability to friends and acquaintances and writing to all the clubs, the PTA, and church groups in the community may bring you in your first students, after which word-of-mouth will help. You can also try running classified ads in local newspapers.

Unless you have a standard of comparison in similar classes given by others in the community, you will have to feel your way in setting fees. But even if you charge only $1 an hour and have a single foursome to instruct, you might make as much as $12 in an afternoon.

68

NATURE STUDY CLASSES

The recent concern over the environment has focused attention on the wonders of the natural world that lie all about us, and that we are in danger of destroying unless we are more careful. Consequently, the climate is particularly favorable for anyone who is able and willing to reveal some of nature's amazing workings to those newly interested in the subject.

Depending on the age level of your audience, which might be anywhere from small children to gray-haired adults, you might hold classes on local plant and animal life in your own back yard or take your students on field trips to meadows, swamps, woods, or streams in the vicinity. You won't make much money. Many people who will spend $3 or $4 to see a mediocre movie will balk at being asked for a similar amount to be shown a much more exciting drama in nature's hidden world. However, any income from this source will be in addition to the satisfaction derived from educating others to the importance of protecting a heritage that, once lost, can never be recovered.

69

SLIMNASTICS

The number of women who periodically vow to "do something" about a less-than-shapely figure must run into the millions. Many of them do go on (and off) various reducing diets. But when it comes to shaping up with exercise—firming flabby muscles and working on unsightly bulges in particular areas—most people lack the will power to persevere on their own.

That is where you can come in, if you have a basic understanding of the principles of physical training—perhaps from having taken a good exercise course yourself.

Classes that promise the morale-boosting presence of fellow sufferers exercising to music in pleasant surroundings, with the guidance and encouragement of an instructor, may well attract enough customers to provide you with a little to a lot of extra income.

The equipment needed is limited to inexpensive exercise mats and a record player; more important is your attitude, which should be both firm and supportive, businesslike yet relaxed enough to make the whole occasion seem like a social one and therefore almost fun.

It's important to tailor your exercise program to the age and physical condition of each of your clients. Refuse to take really obese women, or those with a history of high blood pressure, heart trouble or other circulatory ailments, unless they get the approval of a doctor. And don't make any promises you can't keep. Warn your students that exercise won't really take off much weight. (It would take an hour of fast bicycling, for example, to compensate for the extra calories contributed by a single piece of apple pie.) But it can help dieting produce results, and make the dieter feel and look better in the process. Have each of your students write down her weight and inch-loss goals, together with her present measurements in vital areas, and occasionally help her check her progress.

Members of reducing clubs are good prospects for classes like these; ask to visit a club session to explain your program. You might also try handing out flyers outside health food stores, supermarkets, and beauty salons. Spring—when the thought of the coming bathing-suit season panics many women—is a particularly good time to launch your project. Gauge how much to charge by checking fees for exercise courses given by the local Y and other establishments.

70

SHORTHAND AND TYPING LESSONS

Although most high schools offer typing and shorthand as electives, there are a great many girls who don't take them, and then find they can't get a job without at least knowing how to type. The result is a large pool of potential students for secretarial schools—and for you, if you have the requisite skills—to draw from.

You won't be able to compete with the latter for students who want training in a variety of office skills or who are looking for the assurance of a placement service after they finish a course. On the other hand, there are lots of girls who just want the basics—mostly a typing speed of 40 to 50 words per minute—to get them past the personnel office. If there are enough of these in your community, or of girls who want only typing and shorthand, you should be able to lure quite a few away from bigger competitors by virtue of the lower fees you will be able to charge.

You will need some money for investment, though, since you can't teach typing without having a late-model office machine for each student in the class. It will be best to rent or lease these, perhaps together with the necessary type-writer tables and chairs, and turn them in for new models at frequent intervals. You will also have to allow something for supplies. For a classroom, choose the best-lighted and ventilated room in your house and clear it of all unnecessary furniture in order to create a businesslike atmosphere.

High school girls and recent graduates will be your best prospects. Place ads in local school papers, and try to get permission to post flyers on school bulletin boards. An effective but more expensive way to reach customers is to get lists of recent high school graduates (girls) and mail each one a letter describing your service. Emphasize the price advantage you offer by quoting the rates of other schools. A typical instruction rate for a commercial typing course consisting of 1½ to 2 hours per day, 5 days a week, is around $40 a month (check these against rates prevailing in your community). By operating out of your own home, you can charge considerably less than this and still make money.

71

TRAINING FOR NATURAL CHILDBIRTH

There is no more enthusiastic supporter of natural child-birth than the woman who has herself gone through it and found that it magically does away with most—or all—of the pain, difficulties, and indignities often associated with bear-ing a child. What is more "natural," then, than that she should teach the techniques that helped her to others? You yourself don't *have* to have had a child by the method to teach it, but it is unlikely that anyone else, except a profes-sional in the field, would want to go through the necessary preparation.

There are several methods of painless childbirth. All are based upon work by Dr. Grantly Dick-Read in 1933. Dr. Dick-Read believed that the psychological tensions associ-ated with childbirth can be relieved by conditioning the mother—physically through special breathing exercises, and mentally through the power of suggestion. The difference between any two methods is a question of emphasis. The one chosen for discussion here is the Psychoprophylactic (PPM), better known as the Lamaze method, which has a formal program for training qualified persons to teach it.

If you don't have experience as a nurse or other medical background, you'll have to have the sponsorship of a local doctor or hospital to be eligible for PPM training. Several different programs have been worked out, depending on the applicant's needs and the resources of the local Lamaze chapter (there are 16 of these located throughout the coun-try). All lead first to provisional, and then full, accreditation by the American Society for Psychoprophylaxis in Obstetrics, Inc., a national organization of 14 chapters and 15 affiliated groups, with direct connection to the International Society for Psychoprophylaxis, devoted to the furtherance of the Psychoprophylactic Method of Childbirth Education.

The intensive version of the training program for Lamaze teachers runs for three consecutive days (a total of about 18 hours) at the national headquarters in New York City or at the offices of a local chapter with an active program. At the conclusion, you must pass a written examination, whereupon you receive provisional accreditation to teach for one year. This preliminary training can also be obtained through a home-study course or by working with an experienced teacher. Depending on the method selected, the fee ranges from $25 to $50.

During your year of provisional teaching, you must submit reports on five mothers you have prepared, three of whom you have observed in labor, to obtain full accreditation as a Lamaze teacher. This means, of course, that you must have the active cooperation of a local doctor and the hospital where he practices. If you have had a child yourself by the "natural" method, this is not too difficult, since your own doctor is usually glad to cooperate.

Once you receive provisional accreditation, you can start teaching classes in your own home. Usually these consist of six training sessions, held once weekly for six consecutive weeks. Ideally these should be given during the last three months of your students' pregnancies when their motivation is strong; conditioning acquired at this time is at its peak of effectiveness when labor takes place. Husbands are encouraged to attend classes with their wives so that they may serve in more than a merely passive role during the training, labor, and delivery. Classes should consist of no more than six couples, and each session should be limited to a hour and a half to two hours.

This is not the kind of course in which you advertise for students. Expectant mothers will usually be referred to you by their doctors or by friends who have themselves attended your classes. Ask any student who comes to you through a nonmedical referral for the name of her doctor, and make sure he approves of her attending your classes. To get business, visit or write to the doctors and hospitals in your community, outlining your program and your credentials; include a copy of a letter of recommendation from your doctor or hospital sponsor.

Fees. There are several methods for determining fees. For her course, Mrs. Joseph Rodriguez, of Fairhaven, N.J., charged $30, which was the going-rate per credit at the community college in her vicinity. Another woman, in Nashville, Tenn., set her fee at $20 (10 percent of the going-rate for obstetricians' fees in the area) .

WHERE TO GET MORE INFORMATION

For full details on requirements for teaching the Lamaze method, write to: The American Society for Psychoprophylaxis in Obstetrics, Inc., 7 West 96th Street, New York, N.Y. 10025.

Painless Childbirth, Fernand Lamaze. Henry Regnery Co., Chicago, Ill., 1970.

A Practical Training Course for the Psychoprophylactic Method of Painless Childbirth, Elizabeth Bing, Marjorie Karmel, and Alfred Tanz. American Society for Psychoprophylaxis in Obstetrics, Inc., 7 West 96th Street, New York, N.Y. 10025, 1961. Comes with a long-play record of breathing exercises.

ARTS, CRAFTS, AND OTHER TALENTS

There are all kinds of talent. It takes talent to cook a gourmet meal, type a perfect letter, or breed predigreed puppies. But in this section we'll be dealing with the kind of talent generally labeled "artistic"—the skill needed to create an original needlework design, do portrait sketches, or make distinctive jewelry. There's no sense beating around the bush: some of us simply don't have it. Still, many others do possess artistic talents that they have never really had a chance to develop. If *you* do, there's a good chance that an occupation you now regard simply as a hobby can be turned into a money-making proposition.

The jobs that qualify for this category are so various that no general guidelines can be given. The one thing they do have in common—individuality, or the strong impress of a particular personality—is the thing that makes it impossible to lump them together. It is also what makes them appeal to the customer who appreciates, and is willing to pay for, distinctive goods or services not often found in a society geared to mass production.

See "A Word about Prices," page 5.

72

HANDCRAFTS

According to the New York State Woman's Program, "It is possible for a craftsman to make a very adequate living, but only if he is willing to work really hard and to adapt his skills to the problems of production and marketing."

Basic artistic skill, an intensely serious attitude toward the work, and a head for business are the main requisites for a career (even a part-time one) in crafts. They make the difference between the professional artisan and the amateur hobbyist. Also essential is an efficient production method, refined by long practice to the point where an excellent product can be turned out at a reasonable cost.

If you have these requirements, the crafts field is currently a very promising one. In the last ten years or so, there has been an unprecedented burgeoning of interest in individually designed, handmade products, with the result that craft shops have sprung up all over the country. Other shops too, whose main stock in trade is commercially produced greeting cards, jewelry, clothing, or souvenirs, now increasingly show the work of local craftsmen.

Unless you live in a small, isolated community, you will find that there is a market for really good craft products almost anywhere. The best opportunities lie in the many specialty shops of big cities, which are always on the lookout for something new; of course you will also find the greatest competition there. Another excellent location for a craftsman is in or near resort communities, or on main roads leading to them. The towns of Taos, New Mexico, and

Provincetown, Massachusetts, are famous for the craft products they offer; some are of the highest quality, some S.F.T. (Strictly for Tourists) . Even in a town as small as Sugarloaf, New York, with a population of a few hundred, the blocklong main street is lined with craft shops, including a woodcarver, a lampmaker, a candlemaker, and a blacksmith; the local postmaster makes jewelry.

Incidentally, if you do live in a resort community, you will do well to develop a craft product that in some way is reminiscent of the area. Few people can go on vacation without bringing back some token that reminds them of their stay, and increasingly, public taste is being educated to reject the tawdry and crude in souvenirs. A product such as a wall plaque or a handwoven rug that is both a memento and a truly decorative object in its own right can be a steady (though seasonal) source of income.

Among popular crafts are ceramics, tile work, leather craft, stenciling, block printing, stained glass work, wood engraving, enameling, weaving, metalwork, basketry, and silk screening. Some of these require extensive training and technique. Below are three types of crafts that almost anyone with basic artistic skills can learn to do, either from reading books on the subject or attending craft courses at the local Y, a workshop, a museum, or a high-school adult-education program.

Candlemaking. Once candlemaking was a regular duty of the housewife, to supply the household's own needs, and it remains an operation that can be easily performed at home. Equipment and supplies needed are limited to wicking, dyes, wax, molds, dippers, and a large kettle for melting the wax; the main requirement is the imagination to create distinctive designs. Mrs. James S. Bourn of Arlington Heights, Illinois, is reported to make 20 different styles of candles, many of them decorated or sculptured by hand. (There is now a type of liquid wax that can be whipped up, like cream, with an egg beater, then used to decorate a conventional wax candle. Left to dry, the "cream" hardens and behaves just like regular wax.) Many candlemakers create their own decorative molds, or use milk cartons, jars, cans, and other "found" molds in imaginative ways. Mrs. Bourn's candles sell for $1 to $15 in Chicago specialty shops; of this she gets about half.

Jewelry. Despite the multimillion-dollar costume jewelry industry, which devotes itself to supplying American women with a bewildering choice of trinkets for adornment, there is still an excellent market for unusual handmade jewelry. The medium you work in is up to you; some women have made a success of ceramic earrings and cuff links; others work in metal (silver, copper, stainless steel) or beadwork; one woman sells delicate, lacy-looking pins and earrings made of crochet-work that has been stiffly starched, then sprayed with a protective coating.

Marcia Sarowitz, a young wife who lives in New York City, has created a charming collection of rings, necklaces, and key rings by painting original designs on smooth rocks that she collects at the beach. "The first big hurdle," said Marcia, "was to search out sources of supply (for the 'findings,' the clasps, chains, earring backings, etc.) that would allow me to produce the items efficiently and inexpensively." Once she had accomplished this, she made the rounds of New York City buyers. Her success can be measured by the fact that she soon began to supply large New York department stores such as Lord & Taylor and Saks Fifth Avenue, in addition to a specialty shop, "My Rich Uncle Henry's."

Tie-dyeing. Currently very popular, this is a craft for which the demand waxes and wanes according to the dictates of fashion, but seems never to disappear completely. The technique is simple enough: it consists of dyeing lengths of fabric or finished garments while they are tied in knots; the resulting unevenness with which the dye "takes" produces patterns in the fabric. The art lies in the selection and combination of colors, and in the devising of knots that produce interesting and exotic patterns. (You also, of course, have to know something about fabrics, and the way in which they react to various kinds of dyes.)

How to get business. The hardest way is to try to set up your own shop and sell directly to the public. Handcraft-marketing experts advise against it, for anyone just starting out in the business. Not only will you encounter all the problems (and expenses) incidental to operating a store, but your time, the main resource of the business, will be diverted from its most profitable use—the creation of the crafts you want to sell. Later, if your business is successful and you are able to hire help (or persuade a relative to help you), you may want to take the next step and open your own shop.

In the beginning, you should try to sell your product to retail outlets. An excellent outlet for a beginner in the field is a guild store or woman's exchange (for a list of cities in which exchanges exist, see page 24). Exchanges and guilds are cooperatives which sell all sorts of handcrafts and needlecrafts (and sometimes food products) on consignment. You are paid when your goods are sold, less a commission of from 25 to 50 percent retained by the exchange. Goods left unsold after a reasonable period of time are returned to you. If your product sells well (and you are able to produce it in sufficient quantity), the local exchange may be able to arrange for it to be offered by other exchanges.

Other retail outlets are specialty shops, gift shops (including those at airports and terminals), art shops, and department stores. Make an appointment to see the owner or buyer and take with you samples of your work, or if these are too bulky to carry, good color photographs. Be prepared to give definite answers to questions about price, production method, delivery dates, and quantities. If the store is interested, it may begin by giving you a trial order.

Don't make the mistake of promising more than you can deliver; a bad first performance can kill your chances of getting further work. A retailer pays you the full price on delivery; however, when *he* sells the product, he must realize a 50 percent markup. This means that he must price at $10 the ashtray he bought from you at $5—a fact that should be kept in mind when evaluating your chances of getting retailers to stock your products.

If you find that carting your samples around from one retailer to another takes too much time from production, it may pay you to retain an agent, with knowledge of the gift market, to do your selling for you. The disadvantage is that you must add 15 to 25 percent to the price of the product to the retailer in order to pay the agent's commission.

Prices. Pricing a craft is difficult. The buying public is willing to pay more for the uniqueness and quality of a handmade piece. But few people will pay as much as the craftsman thinks his work is worth. The art of pricing lies in compromise, and in covering your costs while also meeting your competition.

Here's a helpful summary of pricing from the New York State Department of Commerce:

"Basically a craftsman's profit lies in his labor, which should be about twice that of his costs of overhead, rent, light, heat, materials, packaging, shipping and accounting. Materials should be purchased in quantities for lowest price, wherever possible. A craftsman should estimate his labor cost by the hour, taking into account the efficiency of his production and quality of work. Thus his labor cost may vary anywhere from $1.25 an hour up to $5, or in these days of high costs even more, depending largely on his skills. It is important that a craftsman be objective about his skills and prices until he has established his reputation. His speed of production allows lower costs and therefore greater profit."

The department further advises that after analyzing your costs, you should take a look at your competitors' prices. If yours are appreciably higher (and don't forget to take the retailer's markup into account), you'll have to find a way to reduce them—perhaps by using cheaper materials or buying in greater quantity. Or you may have to come to the sad but sensible conclusion that you can't make money with that particular product. (If you work in your own home, your overhead will be low or nonexistent. But if you make no allowance for such items in your pricing, you will not later be able to expand without abruptly raising your prices.)

WHERE TO GET MORE INFORMATION

The sources suggested below are also applicable to #73.

Craft Shops/Galleries USA. American Craftsmen's Council, 29 West 53rd St., New York, N.Y. 10019. Directory of craft stores and the materials they carry.

Handcrafts and Home Businesses, Small Business Bibliography #1, Small Business Administration. U.S. Superintendent of Documents, Government Printing Office, Washington, D.C. 20402. Free booklet.

Selling Your Crafts, Norbert N. Nelson. Reinhold Publishing Corp., New York, N.Y., 1967.

73

NEEDLEWORK

Although also a handcraft, needlework, with its many variations, has so many possibilities for producing income that it
deserves separate discussion. Recently, the rediscovery of its
great decorative potential has elevated it from the status of a
useful but rather staid pastime to a position among the
lively arts. Actress Mary Martin and Sylvia Sidney have
written best-selling books on the subject; Hermione Gin-
gold sells the hooked rugs and needlepoint wall panels she
delights to make. Some modern needlepoint designs are
even to be found in museums, along with the beautiful
work of past periods.

This upsurge of interest has created an active market for
needlework designs and finished needlework products.
Most in demand are: creative embroidery (also called
crewel, though that term is more properly applied to a particular type of design), which is characterized by bold,
brushlike "strokes" made with heavy yarn; needlepoint;
crochet; and latchet-hooked rugs. There is some market too
for hand-knits, but the excellence and variety of modern
machine-made knits is a limiting factor here. Demand for
the delicate embroidery and appliqué that used to be so
popular for baby clothes and fine lingerie has dropped off to
almost nothing.

There are a number of ways to make money from needlework. The most profitable way, but one that demands a
high degree of creative skill, is to sell original designs to
needlework wholesalers or to needlework or women's maga-

zines. All these, and particularly the wholesalers (those who sell yarn and other materials and are constantly looking for designs to promote their products) , are eager to find new sources of supply but complain that most of the material they receive is unimaginative or old-hat. For designs they do accept, though, they pay well: $100 or $250 per design is not unusual, while some companies will put a designer who does a great deal of work for them on a royalty basis.

To submit a design, write to the company enclosing a color transparency or color print of the finished piece, together with a brief description of it. (A sketch is not sufficient unless the company is already familiar with your work.) If interested, the company will then ask that the actual piece be sent for consideration.

You will find the addresses of needlework magazines (*Good Housekeeping Needlecraft* is a leader in the field) listed on their mastheads. The addresses of the seven most important wholesalers are as follows: Bernard Ullmann & Co., 3020 Thompson Avenue, Long Island City, N.Y.; Paragon Art and Linen Company, 357 Southern Boulevard, Bronx, N.Y.; Dritz-Scoville Company, Empire State Building, 350 Fifth Avenue, New York, N.Y.; Spinnerin Yarn Company, 230 Fifth Avenue, New York, N.Y.; Columbia Minerva Corporation, 295 Fifth Avenue, New York, N.Y.; William Unger & Company, 230 Fifth Avenue, New York, N.Y.; and Emile Bernat & Sons, Oxbridge, Mass.

Another skill in great demand is the ability to write clear, concise, and excruciatingly accurate instructions for making up needlework designs. Although you may think it is something almost any accomplished needlewoman could do, it is, in fact, a skill rare enough to induce needlework companies and magazines to pay $40 or more per set of instructions to anyone who proves able to do it. If you think *you* can, write to a company and ask for a chance to prove it, enclosing a set of instructions you have made up for an original design. If you then pass the test they will send you, if they are interested in your work, you will have found a steady source of income. (Nor is there any reason you shouldn't try other companies for the same kind of assignment, if you want more work.)

The most usual way of making money from needlework is by making up products to order for needlework, gift, or specialty shops or for the needlework departments of department stores. Here the same considerations apply as in marketing any handcraft; for selling and pricing tips, see page 252. Pillows, footstool covers, eyeglass, cosmetic, and cigarette cases, tennis racket covers, men's and women's vests, purses, wall hangings, pictures, afghans, sweaters, dresses, stoles, scarves, and caps are only some of the possible products to consider. Check the shops in your area to find out what sells best.

It is important for any craftsman to keep up with the trends in his or her field; for the needlewoman, whose market is so closely affected by the rapidly changing styles in fashion and home decoration, it is absolutely essential. Subscribing to foreign (particularly French and Scandinavian) publications, or examining them in the library, is a good idea too, since needlework designs originating in these countries are often later adapted here.

WHERE TO GET MORE INFORMATION

Creative Stitchery, Dona Z. Meilach and Lee Erlin Snow. Reilly and Lee, Chicago, Ill., 1970.

Crewel Embroidery, Erica Wilson. Charles Scribner's Sons, New York, N.Y., 1968.

The Good Housekeeping New Complete Book of Needle-craft, Vera Guild. Good Housekeeping Books, 250 West 55th Street, New York, N.Y. 10019, 1971.

Needlepoint Design, Louis J. Gartner, Jr. William Morrow & Co., Inc., New York, N.Y., 1970.

Rugmaking: Techniques and Design, Mary Allard. Chilton Book Co., New York, N.Y., 1963.

A Treasury of Knitting Patterns and *A Second Treasury of Knitting Patterns,* Barbara G. Walker. Charles Scribner's Sons, New York, N.Y., 1968, 1970.

Also see listing under #72, "Handcrafts."

74

QUILTING

Quilting is a craft that is not creative at all, but it is so necessary to the creative art of *quiltmaking* that it has been included here for the sake of convenience. Although you may find it hard going to sell original designs for quilt covers, you will probably be welcomed with open arms if you are willing to undertake the not difficult but tedious task of sewing cover, batting, and backing together.

This is a job that only the bravest (or most desperate) woman would undertake alone; to be really feasible it calls for a minimum of two, and a group is even more practical. Of course, the more workers you have, the farther the fee has to go ($50 per quilt is typical), but the work is finished faster too. At least one of you should have had previous quilting experience, and you will need a quilting frame (easily made from four strips of wood) from which the quilt can be hung and unrolled as the work progresses.

If you are interested in doing quilting, make it known at local needlework shops and needlework departments of department stores.

75

PICTURE FRAMING

Today almost everybody buys some kind of art to adorn his walls, whether it's an original painting, lithograph, watercolor, or a reproduction of any of these or other art forms. Many of these works come without frames, or at least with the option of being bought unframed, in which event they are considerably cheaper. Readymade frames in stock sizes are available, but these are unsuitable for most good works of art. A greater threat to the quality framer is presented by museum-designed framing kits, to be found in some big cities; but these are in limited distribution. Good commercial framing is very expensive; in the case of a reproduction, the frame often costs much more than the picture itself.

As a result, there is an opportunity for a creative, reasonably priced service almost everywhere. If you are good, and you can work from your house or apartment, you can compete even in a city, where your lower overhead will enable you to undercut the prices of regular shops. In a city too you will have more potential customers, both buyers of art and artists themselves, who often have their works framed in order to get a better price for them.

A good framer should have something of an artist's eye,

for a frame should complement a picture by carrying out its mood and style. The materials and colors used (including the wide range of wood colors) should enhance, not detract from or clash with, the artist's work; some attention should also be paid to where the picture is to be hung. In addition to this, anyone going into the framing business should have some previous knowledge of the mechanics of the craft, perhaps from framing her own pictures, or from having worked for a framer or an art gallery. Additional information can be obtained from books (see below).

To go into framing on a commercial scale, you will need space to set up a workbench that can hold quite large pictures and that can be bolted to the floor for rigidity. Other equipment, which should be of professional quality, includes a miter box, glass cutter, mat knife, oilstone and compass, along with other cutting and finishing tools. You will also have to buy framing materials, and since each job will be different, it is unlikely, at least at first, that you will be able to realize the savings that come from buying in quantity. However, this is not a major consideration, since the big cost of framing lies in the labor. In estimating expenses, don't forget to allow for the cost of insurance to cover loss, theft, or damage to the pictures you frame; if these include original works of art, the policy should be for a hefty amount. And before you start, invest the time and money to make up a sample display of the types of frames you can offer—a corner of each will do.

How to get business. A sign outside your house or apartment will be essential; if you live in an area where zoning laws, or the landlord, will not permit this, the framing business is not for you. You should also advertise your service in the classified section of local and neighborhood papers and list it in the classified telephone directory. But most of your business, at least at first, will probably come from referrals.

Show samples of your work to hobby shops, art supply stores, book shops, art galleries, and antique and gift shops and ask them to tell customers who need it of your service. You will probably have to pay a "finder's fee" or commission for customers who come to you this way, but it will be worth it to get a start in the business.

Prices. Costs vary so widely, depending on the nature of the materials used and the size of the frame, that no general figures can be given. As in pricing all crafts, you must keep in mind what the competition charges (or if there is no competition, what people in your area are able and willing to pay), while still receiving enough above your costs to make your own labor worthwhile. At the start, though, you may find you will have to work for very little until your reputation is established and your skill has increased to the point where you can turn out good work in less time.

WHERE TO GET MORE INFORMATION

Better Frames for Your Pictures, Frederic Taubes. Viking Press, New York, N.Y., 1960.

How to Make Your Own Picture Frames, Hall Rogers and Ed Reinhardt. Watson-Guptill Publications, New York, N.Y., 1958.

Picture Framing, Max Hyder. Pitman Publishing Co., New York, N.Y., 1963.

Right Frame, Henry Heydenryk. James H. Heineman, Inc., New York, N.Y., 1964.

76

ART CONSULTANT

The current upsurge of interest in art, especially as a status symbol, opens up another moneymaking possibility for someone who is knowledgeable in the field, has good contacts with local artists, is thoroughly familiar with galleries and sources of good reproductions, and has a certain amount of salesmanship talent.

That possibility is an art-consultant service directed at doctors, dentists, attorneys, banks, restaurants, business executives, hotels, motels, cocktail lounges, swank dress shops, and any other profession or business whose owner wants to give his clients something interesting to look at (and something, not-so-incidentally, that will elevate his status in their eyes) while they are waiting for his services.

How to get business. The best location for this service is a city big enough to have a sizable business community with a fairly sophisticated clientele. You can easily spot potential customers by going around to businesses that seem prosperous and earmarking those whose décor in reception rooms, sales rooms, and offices would be greatly improved by the addition of carefully chosen works of art. Pick out a few of your top targets (don't forget interior decorators with business clients) ; before even approaching them with the idea, work out a custom-tailored plan to present to each. Then write, on your business stationery, to the owner, president, or public-relations director of the firm and ask for an appointment to discuss your service. If he is interested enough to grant you an interview (and that will largely depend on how well you sell yourself in your letter), your chances of success are high, provided you can tactfully discover his own tastes in art and integrate them with your plan for his office.

Whether you offer original art or reproductions, and whether, if the art is original, you sell or rent it, will depend largely on the client's tastes and budget. Your best source for originals will be promising young artists whose prices are low enough to appeal to economy-minded businessmen. For the same reason, you may find that good reproductions, imaginatively framed, will be a popular offering.

This is a word-of-mouth and personal contact business; apart from a listing in the classified telephone directory, advertising will be of little value. Since works of art are sold on consignment, the investment needed is minimal, consisting mostly of expenses for business cards and stationery, and for insurance for works of art while they are in your possession for showing to potential customers, or for art placed on a rental basis.

Prices. For an original work, the artist or gallery sets the price; if you sell it, you get a 40 percent commission. The usual monthly rental fee for a work of art is about 10 percent of its value, of which you take half, the other half going to the artist or gallery. (Your share is not clear profit, however; a rented painting must be insured during its period of rental, a cost which you must bear unless the artist or gallery agrees to share it.) You of course set the price of a reproduction, charging enough above your costs to return a reasonable profit. In practice, your client will usually set a maximum budget for the job, and you will have to find suitable pictures within those limits.

77

INTERIOR DESIGNER (DECORATOR)

If you have had training in the fine arts, *if* you have an appreciation of line, color and form, *if* you are knowledgeable about furniture, fabrics and finishes, *if* you delight in decorating your own home and are often called upon by friends for advice with their decorating problems too—*then* you might want to consider making money from what you have previously thought of only as an avocation. As noted, a great many "ifs" are involved; it is not a job for everyone. But the special qualifications it takes also mean that, if you live in the right area, you won't have too much competition.

The right area for this job is definitely *not* a big city, where not only are there scores of well-established professional decorators, but also many department and furniture stores give free decorating advice. ("Interior decorator," incidentally, is the older term; many professionals, feeling that it has been abused, prefer to be called "interior designers.")

You will do best with this service in a smaller city or town or in a suburb, especially one where young wives whose husbands are just beginning to "make it" are anxious to create a setting whose tastefulness and style will reflect the family's new status. It must be a community where you are reasonably well known, since advertising your service will do you little good; most of your business will come to you by personal recommendation from people who know and like your work.

Unless you have had specific training and/or experience

in interior design, it is unlikely that you will be able to offer a full range of design services, from making architectural renderings (which may include structural alterations or built-ins) to ordering custom-made furniture. However, relatively few people require such extensive help (or have the money to pay for it), and those who do usually prefer to turn to well-known designers.

You will probably find the demand to be greatest for a consulting service that involves visiting the client's home, examining her decorating problems, and then advising her how to solve them. This might include planning a color scheme, drawing up a floor plan, making watercolor sketches of the proposed result, helping the client decide on a furniture style, advising her on how she can integrate new pieces with what she already has, suggesting window treatments, showing her rug, fabric, and wall covering samples, and helping her choose among them.

In addition, some clients will need help with their shopping, or will want you to do it for them. For this you will need a thorough knowledge of retail and wholesale sources in your area, as well as of wholesalers who will deal with decorators through the mail. You will also have to establish your professional status with these sources (in order to gain entrée to showrooms closed to the general public), to obtain manufacturers' sample books, and to qualify for the decorator's discount, which in some cases (see below) will represent the amount of the fee you charge for your services.

Very little investment is needed to start a consulting service; your expenses will be largely limited to business cards, stationery, and transportation to your clients' homes. (If your formal training has been weak, you might also want to consider first taking a course in a school approved by the professional organizations in the field.)

If you shop for the client under an arrangement whereby

you order the merchandise and bill her later, you will have to establish a credit rating in the field. To do this, you must open a commercial checking account for a sizable amount at your bank, and register with two companies that act as collection agencies for decorating wholesalers: Lyon Furniture Mercantile Agency, 185 Madison Avenue, New York, N.Y. 10016, and Allied Board of Trade, 342 Madison Avenue, New York, N.Y. 10017. They will investigate your credit rating and furnish, to wholesalers who inquire, an appraisal of the nature and extent of your financial responsibility. (Incidentally, you too should check into the credit rating of your customers before you accept assignments, particularly if these involve shopping.)

Fees. Designers have different ways of charging for their services. Among them:

- *Hourly and per diem fees.* This is the method used for a consulting-only service. Established designers in big cities charge from about $25 an hour to $60 or more. You will probably have to set your fees considerably lower, especially at the start. (But don't set them too low, or clients will not have any faith in your abilities. Be partly guided by the income level of the community.)
- *Retail basis.* The designer buys furnishings at wholesale but charges the retail price. His fee is the difference between the wholesale and retail costs, less his overhead.
- *Cost-plus-percentage markup.* The designer adds a certain percentage, which may be from 20 to 50 percent, to the cost of materials he purchases for the job.
- *Percentage off retail.* The retail price of furnishings is charged, but a discount of about 10 percent from the manufacturer's suggested retail price is allowed.
- *Flat-fee basis.* The fee is based on the amount of work involved and the client's budget. The designer should give

an estimate of the fee to his client before accepting the assignment.

How to get business. Apart from taking a listing in the classified telephone directory, it is not customary (and is usually futile) to advertise a design service. Instead it must become favorably known through word-of-mouth. So tell all your friends and acquaintances; make it a point to get to know local builders, real estate brokers, architects, and stores dealing in home furnishings; take an active interest in social, civic, and community affairs where you will get to know influential people in the community. You might also try to sell your services to small businesses, such as beauty salons and dress shops, whose operation might benefit from a fresh new décor. For the first such assignment, it might be worth while to donate your own services, charging the client only costs, in order to be able to use the result as a showcase of your skills.

WHERE TO GET MORE INFORMATION

Good Housekeeping Complete Book of Decorating, Mary Kraft. Good Housekeeping Books, 250 West 55th Street, New York, N.Y. 10019, 1971.

Inside Design, Michael Greer. Doubleday & Co., Inc., Garden City, N.Y., 1962.

New Encyclopedia of Furniture, Joseph Aaronson. Crown Publishers, Inc., New York, N.Y., 1967.

Pahlmann Book of Interior Design, William Pahlmann. Viking Press, New York, N.Y., 1968.

Your Future in Interior Design, Michael Greer. Richards Rosen Press, New York, N.Y., 1963.

PROFESSIONAL ORGANIZATIONS:

American Institute of Interior Designers, 673 Fifth Ave., New York, N.Y. 10022.

National Society of Interior Designers, Inc., 157 West 57th St., New York, N.Y. 10019.

TRADE JOURNALS:

Interior Design, 78 E. 56th St., New York, N.Y. 10022.

78

SKETCH-YOU

If you have art training, and a talent for sketching likenesses of people and/or animals, you may be able to make quite a lot of pin money, and even more serious sums, at home. In spite of the popularity of photography, a drawing of a child or a pet or a beloved adult has strong appeal for many people; at fairs, the booth occupied by the sketch portraitist usually has a line of waiting customers.

Your main problem will be in letting people know of your service. A good way at the start will be to ply your art for free at bazaars, church suppers, and other charitable fund-raising affairs; in return (and in proportion to how good you are) , your fame will be spread among the "doers" in the community, and commissions may begin to come your way. If possible, you might also make a fee-sharing arrangement with a local store to set up your easel for an hour or so on their premises; take the opportunity to hand out your business card to every passer-by or shopper who merely stops to watch your work. An ad, in local papers, showing a sample of your work (and, if you draw animals, in pet-club newsletters) should bring in business—and may even interest the newspapers in commissioning work from you. And be sure to make your service known to clubs, fraternal organizations, business firms, popular hostesses, and others who give parties or put on entertainments where a sketch portraitist might be a welcome novelty.

As for fees, like every artist, you will have to find out for yourself what people are willing to pay for your work.

79

WEDDING PHOTOGRAPHER

With all the cameras sold today—some households have as many as three or four—you might think there would be no market for a commercial photographer who specializes in candids. Anyone who has ever been to a wedding knows differently: There is always a camera-for-hire clicking steadily away throughout the festivities. Despite the competition, there is room in this field for you too, if your work is up to professional standards. And as a woman, you have a special advantage you can exploit to get jobs a man can't.

The reason lies in the popularity of elaborate albums that record every phase of a wedding; some brides spend more on these than they do on their wedding gowns. Usually, wedding photographers cover only the great day itself, taking pictures from the time the bride arrives at the church to the departure of the couple on their honeymoon.

Although they are well aware of the even greater appeal of complete coverage of the whole happy time, from the engagement on, most photographers can't fit all the events, including showers, parties, and the rehearsal, into their schedule. Moreover, if they are men, their presence would be awkward at some of the intimate occasions that give rise to the best pictures—such as all-girl showers or the bride's bedroom when she is being helped to dress by her bridesmaids.

This is where you, as a woman and a community resident, can offer a special service. Together with the fact that you can probably also charge less because of lower overhead, it will give you an edge over other wedding photographers. After a while the bride-to-be and others will tend to forget you are there, and the pictures you get will be real "candids," with all the charm of family photographs but the technical excellence of professional ones.

If you are good enough to compete with professionals, you no doubt already have all or most of the equipment you will need. Some photographers have their own darkrooms, but unless you do a great deal of work, it will be less expensive to deal with a good commercial lab. (The kind of mass photo-finishing available through drugstores won't do; send your films to a custom lab. You pay a little more, but it's worth it. If there's no custom lab near you, you can do business through the mails.) You will need a first-class portfolio of samples of your work—which should, of course, include a complete wedding sequence of the kind described above.

How to get business. Wherever you go, keep an ear cocked for hints of forthcoming engagements and weddings, in order to get in on the scene as soon as possible. And let all your friends, acquaintances, and members of organizations you belong to know of your availability. But your steadiest source of prospects will be the engagement announcements in local newspapers. As soon as you see one, call or write the engaged girl, asking for an appointment to discuss your service; emphasize, on this very first contact, its uniqueness.

You might also arrange to pay a commission to caterers, printers, wedding-gown saleswomen, or others for clients they send to you. Ads in local newspapers may also produce results.

Prices. As a rule, wedding photographers get from $5.50 to $7.50 per candid color photograph, size 8″ x 10″; $3.50 to $4.50 for 5″ x 7″; $3 to $4 for 3½″ x 5″. The same sizes in black and white average $3 to $3.50, $2.50 to $3, and $1 to $1.25, respectively. Many photographers contract for an album containing a number of different pictures—sometimes as few as 12, usually for 20 or 24, with the cost of the album itself (from around $8 to $20 and up, depending on quality) being added to that of the pictures. Others quote a price on a complete package, e.g., one 8″ x 10″ album of 30 pictures for $215; duplicate 5″ x 7″ pictures in a separate album for $4.50 per picture, plus the cost of the album.

If this sounds like a lot of money, it is; the wedding photography business is a profitable one. Not all the money is profit, of course; for every picture the bride agrees to buy, the photographer has probably snapped four, to make sure he has what she wants. This involves a lot of expensive film, proofs of all the negatives for the customer to choose from, and the final developing of those she selects. A great deal of time is also involved, especially if you undertake the kind of coverage outlined above and turn up at each of the functions preceding the wedding. All this has to be taken into account in setting your prices. If enough work comes your way, though, you will find that you can make quite a bit of money from romance.

WHERE TO GET MORE INFORMATION

Most of the sources suggested below are also applicable to #80, #81, #82, and #83.

Professional Photography Literature Packet (about 90 service publications—black-and-white and color photography, processing and photographic techniques for portrait, commercial, and industrial photography). Eastman Kodak Company, Department 454, Rochester, New York.

The Color Photo Book, Andreas Feininger. Prentice-Hall, Inc., New York, N.Y., 1969.

Complete Photographer, by Andreas Feininger. Prentice-Hall, Inc., New York, N.Y., 1966.

Life Library of Photography (*The Camera, Light and Film, The Print, Color;* 4 more titles in preparation). Time, Inc., New York, N.Y. 1970–.

Photographic Dealers and Studios, Small Business Bibliography #64. Small Business Administration. U.S. Superintendent of Documents, Government Printing Office, Washington, D.C. 20402. Free booklet.

Photography in Your Future, Jacob Deschin. The Macmillan Co., New York, N.Y., 1965.

Successful Wedding Photography, Michael K. Arin. Chilton Book Co., Philadelphia, Pa., 1967.

Wedding and Party Photography, Barney Stein and Les Kaplan. Chilton Book Co., Philadephia, Pa., 1968.

Your Future in Photography, Victor Keppler. Richards Rosen Press, New York, N.Y., 1965.

PROFESSIONAL ASSOCIATIONS:

Professional Photographers of America, 152 West Wisconsin Ave., Milwaukee, Wis.

American Society of Magazine Photographers, 60 East 42nd Street, New York, N.Y. 10017.

80

CHILD PHOTOGRAPHY

Child photography is another specialty well suited to women who are skilled with a camera. Studio photographs, which require a special setup and lighting equipment, aren't the only possibility. Today more and more parents are recognizing the often superior quality of professionally made, enlarged "candids," which show the child in natural situations.

Child photography of this kind is usually linked to special occasions, such as christenings, first communions, confirmations, Bar Mitzvahs, and birthday parties. The latter can be a specialty in itself; one woman in Kansas has made a reputation for herself (and won several camera contests) with charming candid portraits of children blowing out candles or reacting with unself-conscious joy as they open presents.

These are exactly the kind of shots parents themselves constantly attempt, but seldom achieve with the same degree of artistry and technical perfection. For one thing, enlargements from 35 mm. film, which most amateurs (as well as many professionals) use, emphasize any faults or blurs. In addition, a children's party is usually a hectic occasion, where pictures, if taken at all, are caught on the run by the harried hostess. Any felicities of mood, lighting, or composition that result are usually an accident.

How to get business. Like the wedding photographer, you should keep a close watch on the women's pages of local newspapers, in your case for news of births. You can find out about confirmations, christenings, etc. from church calendars. Sources of business for birthday photographs are the same as for #79; see page 268. You might also get lists of graduating classes from local elementary and high schools; in addition to, or instead of, the rather stiff formal portrait usual on these occasions, some parents may commission candids from you. Local baby shops—for toys, furniture, clothing—are a good source of referrals. Leave your business card with the proprietors, with the understanding that they will receive a commission for any clients they send your way.

Prices. These are usually considerably less than for wedding photographs (see page 270), but your expenses are lower too. For an album (less elaborate than the gold-tooled leather or leatherette type used for wedding pictures) containing four or five 8″ x 10″ color pictures, you might charge $35 to $40; for black-and-white, $15 to $20. Child photography, unlike wedding photography, is a repeat business. If the parents like your work, they will probably engage you to take more pictures of their child at a later stage of development.

WHERE TO GET MORE INFORMATION

How I Photograph Children, Suzanne Szasz, Chilton Book Co., Philadelphia, Pa., 1966.

The Photographic Portrait, O. R. Croy. Chilton Book Co., Philadelphia, Pa., 1968.

Also see sources listed under #79, "Wedding Photography."

81

PET PHOTOGRAPHY

If you happen to be an animal lover as well as a shutter bug, pet photography is a way to put both interests to work. It's a specialized area, though; at least at first you will probably have to work through a local pet shop or grooming salon which agrees to display samples of your work and send you customers in return for a share of your profits. If you are really good, you should be able to place some of your pictures with local newspapers. In addition to the payment for their use, the advertising value will be immense.

Still another opportunity lies in local pet shows. Although there is almost always an official photographer at these events (an assignment you might go after yourself, incidentally), the winners and runner-ups usually get all the coverage. But the owners of the also-rans are proud of their pets too, and might be good customers for *your* pictures. Dog-license bureaus are another good source of prospective clients.

Christmas cards featuring a picture of the prospect's pet are an especially good item for this market. In October, send a sample card showing your work to a selected list of prospects; enclose a return postcard on which the client may indicate a desire to see your portfolio and discuss your service. You might also try your luck at selling to pet magazines. Never submit just one or two pictures; send a whole batch to permit choice. Address the carefully wrapped package to the art editor, and be sure to include return postage.

WHERE TO GET MORE INFORMATION

Animal and Pet Photography, 2nd ed., Mildred Stagg. Chilton Book Co., Philadelphia, Pa., 1969.

Cats in Pictures, Jeanne White. Chilton Book Co., Philadelphia, Pa., 1965.

Free-Lance Magazine Photography, Lou Jacobi, Jr., Hastings House, New York, N.Y., 1970.

Also see sources listed under #79, "Wedding Photography."

82

COMMERCIAL PHOTOGRAPHY

If portraits—of people or animals—are not the kind of pictures you do best, there is still an opportunity to make money with your camera by supplying real estate brokers and homeowners with pictures that make their property look especially attractive. (Some brokers take their own pictures, but many do not, relying on free-lance photographers or the property owners for this service.)

Other sources of business are local advertising agencies, lawyers, and insurance companies (for pictures of accidents or of loss or damage to property) ; local retail stores not big enough to have an ad agency; businesses and factories that want pictures of their premises or operations for booklets or brochures; construction companies (for pictures of construction progress) ; local newspapers with too small a staff to supply all their photographic needs.

To get business, scour your community for these and other businesses that make use of photography and visit them in person with your portfolio. Prices will have to be a matter of negotiation between you and your client; it is not possible to suggest even a rough guide applicable to so many varying situations.

WHERE TO GET MORE INFORMATION

See sources listed under #79, "Wedding Photography."

83

FILMMAKING

This is another limited specialty, but one that may appeal to you if you have made many films of your own and learned professional techniques of lighting, filming, and editing. There are two possible markets—private individuals, who may want films of superior quality of such important events in their lives as a wedding, housewarming, child's graduation from college, or other event in which they are involved to an extent that prevents them from making films themselves. Here 8 mm. equipment is probably sufficient and may be necessary in order to keep costs low enough to attract any customers.

The second market is made up of groups such as clubs, fraternal societies, community organizations, businesses, schools, camps, and professional societies that use films for promotional, instructional, or entertainment purposes. Since this kind of movie is meant for projection in auditoriums or other big rooms, the larger 16 mm. film with its sharper image and superior sound capabilities* is needed. Films for these purposes are usually not a simple recording of events but require a script, props, indoor shooting location, and special lighting equipment.

The kind of equipment you have, as well as the nature of your community, will determine which market to try. In either case, you will need a short demonstration film to show to prospective clients. Direct solicitation by means of a personal letter, directed to lists gleaned from wedding announcements, social news, directories of graduating students, listings of officers of organizations, business directories, and so on, is the best means of getting business. Ask for an appointment to show your demonstration film; in some cases you may have to bring along your own projector and screen.

Fees. To make a 10-minute 8 mm. film, figure on a budget, exclusive of equipment, of $100. A 16 mm. film of the same duration would cost at least $50 more. Make sure to include rental or purchase charges for special equipment, film and development costs, an allowance for overhead and your own time, and a small profit, if possible, in arriving at an asking price.

WHERE TO GET MORE INFORMATION

The American Cinematographer's Manual. American Society of Cinematographers, 1782 North Orange Drive, Hollywood, Calif.

Creative Filmmaking, Kirk Smallman. Collier Books, New York, N.Y., 1969. Paperback.

---

* Now on the market, however, is an 8 mm. camera that produces lip-synchronized movies. The soundtrack is incorporated in the processed footage via magnetic sound stripping.

Guide to Filmmaking, Edward Pincus. New American Library, New York, N.Y., 1969. Paperback.

8 mm/16 mm Movie Making. Henry Provisor. Chilton Book Co., Philadelphia, Pa. 1970.

A LITTLE ABOUT A LOT OF THINGS

The ways for making money that are suggested in this chapter are so various that they can't be lumped under any one subject area or type of skill. Some of them, like #84 (Convalescence Baskets), call mostly for imagination; for others, you must have specialized training or experience (see #91 Real Estate Sales), or very special personal qualifications (see #86 Executive Relocation Service). All of these businesses can be undertaken at or from home, and under the right circumstances can produce extra income ranging from a few dollars a week to sums that those with full-time jobs outside the home might well envy.

See "A Word about Prices," page 5.

84

CONVALESCENCE BASKETS

Baskets for convalescing adults represent the same idea as #38 (Emergency Play Kits for children), but on a more sophisticated level. They're a moneymaking possibility because they are a solution to a common problem. Haven't *you* sometimes wandered through a gift or department store, looking for something for a sick friend—one who's bored and restless at having to stay in bed? And if so, wouldn't you have welcomed an attractively packaged kit containing a selection of items related to your friend's special interests?

This business consists of assembling inviting baskets for gardeners, gourmet cooks, stamp collectors, needlework devotees, puzzle fans, Sunday painters, and anybody else who has an identifiable interest. Each item is individually wrapped and placed in a wicker basket, then, like a child's Easter basket, the whole thing is swathed in cellophane. (If some of the items are too big to fit in a basket, the latter can be omitted and only the cellophane wrapping used.)

Convalescence baskets are directed at a very special market, and are therefore best sold through department stores, gift stores, and gift shops in hospitals and nursing homes. The key to success lies in the imagination with which the contents are chosen, and in the ability to put together a selection that, after the retailer's markup, can still sell at roughly the same prices people are willing to pay for flowers for sick friends.

Your service can operate on two levels: on the first, you would fill orders for standard baskets in the most popular subject areas; on the other, given 24 hours' notice, you would assemble a gift basket especially tailored to the personality and interests of the particular patient. For a gardener, for example, in addition to a paperback book on gardening, flower holders for arrangements, a pretty jar and instructions for making scented potpourris, an old botanical print, and a small ceramic flower in its own pot, you might include bulbs for forcing or a kit containing seeds already planted and needing only water to start growing. Or, in a needlework basket, include stamped designs, together with materials, that, when worked, would make appropriate presents for the patient's doctor and other attendants.

Standardize the contents of all your kits as much as you can, in order to take advantage of the savings involved in buying in quantity at wholesale prices.

85

ROOMMATE BUREAU

Strictly for the big city, with its high rents, chronic housing shortages, and loneliness, the roommate-bureau business also has a specialized clientele—young people (mostly girls) who are new in town. Their big problem is generally housing. A nice apartment in a good neighborhood invariably costs more than a girl fresh out of college can swing by herself. Yet finding someone compatible to share expenses with isn't easy. Notices on office bulletin boards scare up too few contacts; newspaper ads often bring responses from unsavory characters.

In many cities the resulting vacuum has been filled by agencies that specialize in matching roommates. Most of these are run by women, and some (with the permission of the landlord) operate out of apartments in residential buildings. Usually a single room is devoted to the office—an office that deliberately retains a homelike atmosphere to put clients at ease. A typewriter, some filing cabinets, and a telephone are the only tools of the trade needed.

Basically the job consists of interviewing girls who come in search of roommates and giving each, on the basis of an

analysis of her personality, character, and interests, a list of
five or six other girls who might be compatible with her. It
is then up to the client herself to meet these girls and decide
whether she'd like to room with one or more of them. In
addition, most roommate bureaus act as an unofficial clear-
ing house for news of job openings, sales of used furniture
and rugs, social activities, and so on. You'll also find yourself
being looked upon as a kind of housemother, handy for
lending a shoulder to cry on, or looked to as a source of
advice on anything from getting a job to finding a doctor.

Skill as an interviewer and an ability to make quick but
accurate judgments of people are essential to success in this
business. Most agencies use a questionnaire which asks the
applicant's age, job, religion, interests; whether she smokes;
what time she goes to bed; whether she likes to entertain
often; whether she is tidy or messy; whether she wants to
buy her own groceries or split the cost of food; and so on.
But whether two people will get along together or not is
also heavily dependent upon character, and the ability to
judge this accurately is a matter of instinct and experience.
Some agencies will not take girls unable or unwilling to
supply personal references, and all turn down any girl they
suspect of taking drugs or drinking excessively.

Building up your initial clientele will be the hardest part
of the venture. After that it will be easier, since marriage,
job changes, or moves are constantly breaking up roommate
combinations, whereupon, typically, the odd girl out returns to the same agency that found her roommates before.
In the beginning, though, you will have to work hard persuading women's residences, YWCA's, churches, visitors'
bureaus, alumnae groups, real estate agents, and others to
recommend your service. It may also be helpful to place ads
in small neighborhood newspapers and to try to get a notice
of your service in the employee publications of big business

firms. When and if the growth of your business permits, you should have brochures printed to send to vocational placement bureaus at major colleges and universities across the country.

Fees? In cities like Boston, New York, Chicago, and Los Angeles, the going rate ranges from $10 to $20, with some agencies charging less for their services to the person who already has an apartment and is looking for someone to share it with than to the girl who wants a roommate *with* an apartment. If the match doesn't work out within a few days, it's understood that another referral will be made without charge.

86

EXECUTIVE RELOCATION SERVICE

In most big companies, a young executive on his way up is asked to transfer to another community at least once in his career and usually more often. Such a move creates problems both for the man and his family—finding a place to live, making new friends, locating needed services and facilities in the community. Recently, corporations have come to recognize the strain relocation puts upon their employees and to make efforts to help relieve them.

The help given is in the form of a willingness to pay others to assist relocated executives in every way possible. This assistance might include furnishing detailed information about local schools; neighborhoods; transportation and recreational facilities; helping a family find a suitable house or apartment; taking them on a guided tour of local landmarks; introducing the wife to other young women in the neighborhood and making sure she is aware of community activities.

This kind of service is of course strictly limited, but it is an opportunity particularly suited to women. For it to be a possibility for you, you must live in a community where the home or branch offices of a number of socially responsible corporations are located. You must also have a thorough knowledge of your own community, the kind of contacts that usually come only from long residence in an area, and social poise that enables you to feel at ease with people of any background.

Your only expense will be to have business stationery printed. On it, write to the president or vice-president in charge of public relations of each company you have selected to approach. (You can find company addresses in such reference books, available at many public libraries, as *McRae's Blue Book, Thomas's Register of American Manufacturers, Dun and Bradstreet Reference Book,* and the *Conover-Mast Purchasing Directory. Poor's Register of Corporations, Directors and Executives* may be helpful in finding the name of the person to write to.) Describe briefly the services you can offer to executives transferred to your community, and ask for an appointment with the company's local representative to discuss the matter further.

Fees for this kind of service are paid directly by the corporation and can be high. A Boston woman has made a success of a two-day, $200 Exec-Tour of historic and literary landmarks in the city and the surrounding area. But in most areas a great deal more time and work would have to be invested to earn a comparable amount.

87

"BIRD DOG" TRAVEL AGENT

To be a regular travel agent with a service of your own requires more investment in time and money than most women can afford. Extensive preliminary training and experience are needed, as well as authorization from the conferences (associations) of the carriers (airlines and rail and steamship lines) whose services you will be selling.

A much more attainable goal, if you have family responsibilities, is to become a "bird dog" travel agent, one whose job it is to find prospective clients for an agency on a freelance basis. If the clients you refer actually do use its services, the agency pays you a commission.

You don't need any particular qualifications to be a bird dog, but at some point, perhaps in your carefree unmarried days, you should have traveled widely yourself. Your sales spiel for Williamsburg or Disneyland, London or Rome, will carry much more conviction if you have actually visited these places yourself. Most important of all, you should have a wide circle of acquaintances in the community, particularly among people who do a lot of traveling.

To become a bird dog, visit the travel agencies in your community to see whether they are interested in your services and if so, which one will offer you the best commission on referrals. (Be sure, however, that the one you choose has a reputation for good service, or your missionary work on its behalf will not carry much weight.)

Then thoroughly familiarize yourself, by studying the material the agent will give you, with the itineraries and costs of various tours and private travel arrangements to popular vacation destinations. Keep abreast of developments in the travel industry by subscribing to trade journals, and attend if you can one or more of the travel orientation seminars for agents sponsored by various airlines (the agency with which you are affiliated can make the arrangements).

In addition to selling friends and acquaintances on the benefits of travel, you might work up presentations for clubs and similar groups in your community. Color films and slides can be obtained free or for a token rental fee from airlines, steamship companies, and other travel industries.

How much you will make as a bird dog depends entirely on how much business you can scare up and on your bargaining powers in dealing with regular travel agents. Some agents pay bird dogs a flat "finder's fee" for each client brought in; others turn over a percentage of the amount the client spends.

WHERE TO GET MORE INFORMATION

TRADE ASSOCIATION:

The American Society of Travel Agents, 360 Lexington Ave., New York, N.Y. 10017.

TRADE JOURNALS:

ASTA Travel News, 360 Lexington Ave., New York, N.Y. 10017.

Travel Agent Magazine, 2 West 46th St., New York, N.Y. 10036.

Travel Weekly, 641 Lexington Ave., New York, N.Y. 10022.

88

FIX-IT SERVICE

Can you rehabilitate a battered doll? Restring pearls? Mend a piece of fine china so skillfully the crack can't be seen? Repair a broken zipper? If so, you possess talents (and patience) that many other people lack and for which they are often willing to pay.

Repairs most often requested are those mentioned above, plus fixing broken umbrellas and Venetian blinds that need new cords and tapes. (Pocketbook repairs are also in demand, but for most leather work special equipment is needed. Repairing and refinishing furniture—see #89, following—is a specialty in itself.) The chances are that if you have a basic knowledge of repair techniques and are a careful worker, you'll be able to cope with almost anything repairable that comes into your shop.

Even if you have had no experience with certain jobs, there are books (see below) that explain the methods to be used. If you find there's a demand for reweaving—repairs to woven or knitted garments necessitated by cigarette burns, tears, etc.—you may want to look into one of the several correspondence courses that offer training in that technique. Be sure that anyone you choose is approved by the National Home Study Council (see page 17) .

Apart from a place to work and a few basic tools, you need very little to start a business of this kind. Your major expense will be for advertising, which must be continuous.

People need you only when something breaks or breaks

down, and when they do they must be able to find you. A regular ad in the classified section of local newspapers, and in neighborhood shopping guides, plus a listing (and perhaps a display ad) in the classified telephone directory will bring the best return. You might also try telling local merchants, such as jewelers and gift-shop owners about your service; leave your business card as a reminder. If zoning laws permit, post a sign on your property.

Pricing a repair service, like any other, is a matter of balancing what the customer is prepared to pay against the cost of materials and the value of one's own labor. Some typical fees: repairing pocketbook zipper, $3; rewiring lamp, $3.50 to $5; replacing umbrella rib, $2.95; reweaving small cigarette burn, $10 and up. Electrical and more intricate repair jobs obviously bring higher fees.

One word of advice: Ask for a token deposit on each job to be done, and specify on the receipt the time within which the object must be picked up. Some people never return for repaired articles, in which case you should be free to sell them.

WHERE TO GET MORE INFORMATION

The Furniture Doctor, George Grotz. Doubleday & Co., Inc., Garden City, N.Y., 1962.

How To Fix Almost Everything, Stanley Schuler. Pocket Books, New York, N.Y., 1970. Paperback.

How To Mend China and Bric-A-Brac, Paul St.-Gaudens and Arthur R. Jackson. Charles T. Branford Co., Newton Centre, Mass., 1953.

Small Appliance Repairs, Robert W. Newnham. McGraw-Hill of Canada Ltd., Toronto, Ont., Canada, 1967.

89

FURNITURE REFINISHING

In many areas there is a modest but continuing demand for a furniture doctor, a person who can magically remove the scratches and stains from a favorite table, supply a rush seat for a chair, or restore a prized antique. The woman who delights in collecting and refurbishing old furniture for her own home might well consider turning her hobby into a source of at least occasional income.

Repairing antiques requires the most specialized knowledge, including a thorough familiarity with various period furniture styles and the ways in which the pieces were made. It is unlikely that the owner of a really costly antique would entrust it to anyone except an expert to restore. But there are other collectors with less valuable pieces who might gladly employ a local restorer to refinish their finds.

Sometimes this can be as simple as scrubbing the piece down with soap and water to remove traces of old wax and imbedded dirt, touching up small scratches, then giving the piece a thorough rubbing with a good furniture polish. Sometimes it calls for painstaking treatment with fine steel wool or abrasive powders, to remove multiple layers of old finish, and to repair deep scratches, cracks, and gouges.

Repairing and refinishing old furniture that has no particular value as an antique is less taxing, since the whole idea is to make it look like new, not preserve the patina of age. If you can also recane old chairs, or weave new rush seats for them, you will have still another string to your bow. (Although pretty much a lost art nowadays, neither is particularly difficult to do; if you don't already know how, the technique can be learned from a book.) And if, in addition to making old furniture look like new, you can make new furniture look old (via "antiquing," distressing or spatterdashing) , or are skilled in stenciling or découpage, you can appeal to still another taste.

Apart from overhead (which should include insurance to cover loss or damage to furniture while it is in your possession) and advertising, the expense of operating a refinishing business is low. The tools needed are few and the materials relatively inexpensive. You should require customers to deliver the furniture to you and pick it up when it is ready.

How to get business. Word-of-mouth, particularly if you have many friends who have always admired your work, will get you some business, but you may also have to advertise on a continuing basis in local papers and take a listing in the classified telephone directory. Tell antique shops of your service, and exhibit samples of your best work at bazaars, fairs, and other community functions. If the zoning laws permit, hang a sign on your home, and prepare a "before-and-after" exhibit featuring restored furniture.

Fees. No specific advice can be given, other than that your charges should be based on the amount of time and skill involved—an art that can be learned only through experience.

WHERE TO GET MORE INFORMATION

The Complete Book of Furniture Repair and Refinishing, Ralph Kinney. Charles Scribner's Sons, New York, N.Y., 1950.

The Popular Mechanics Home Book of Refinishing Furniture, Arthur M. Mikesell. Hawthorn Books, Inc., New York, N.Y., 1967.

90

LIFE INSURANCE SALES

Selling life insurance is a field in which, up to now, women have been conspicuous mostly by their absence. According to the Institute of Life Insurance, of agents who make half or more of their income from life insurance, only 3 percent are women. The reason, says the Institute, is not male prejudice against women, either by the companies or by life-insurance buyers, the majority of whom are men. Rather, it is the failure of more women to think of life insurance as a possible source of income.

Yet selling life insurance is a chance for women who want to, or have to work irregular hours to make really substantial amounts of money. Companies are always on the look-out for agents, male or female, and are not only willing to train those persons they think might qualify, but to pay them a salary while they're learning. Once trained, you make your own appointments and work at your own rate.

One word of warning, though: Selling life insurance is definitely not a part-time job. It's true that, once the initial training period is over, you don't have to spend a set number of hours per week, or of weeks or months per year. But you *do* have to bring in a minimum amount of business to keep the company interested in retaining you as an agent. For one big company, this means the equivalent of an average weekly sale of a policy with a face amount of $5,000 or more. Some agents can average this amount over the course of several months; others can take an entire year to do it. It's all up to you.

To investigate your chances of a job selling life insurance, talk to your own insurance agent. Or get in touch with a local agency or write to the home office of an insurance company in your state. You will be given an aptitude test and a personal interview. If you pass both, the company will train you at its own cost, while paying you a salary to cover expenses. The amount varies with the insurance company and, in some cases with the preference of the applicant. In one company the beginning salary ranges from $300 to $800 a month. The higher the salary, though, the more life insurance you must sell to earn it.

The initial training is directed at helping you pass the state examination for life insurance salesmen. Once you have your license (usually after two to three months), you are sent out with an experienced agent to learn the ropes, then given prospects of your own to approach. Required once-a-week training sessions continue for up to two years; during this time you also usually report to the district manager on how many hours you spend selling by telephone, how many in personal calls on prospects. Your salary is continued all this time, with commissions from any sales you make being applied against it. Once the two years is up, you are paid on a straight commission basis.

Mrs. Marion Robke, of Upper Brookville, Long Island, is an agent for New York Life, and loves it. Married at 19, Mrs. Robke had no previous work experience when she decided to try selling life insurance. Although one of her two sons was still in elementary school, she managed to fit her training as an agent into her family's schedule. Now, five years later, she devotes from 30 to 50 hours a week, pretty much at her own convenience, to her job, and earns a substantial income. (The average earnings of New York Life five-year agents is $10,563.)

WHERE TO GET MORE INFORMATION

Life and Health Insurance Handbook, Davis Weinert Gregg. Richard D. Irwin, Inc., Homewood, Ill., 1964.

Your Future in Insurance, Armand Sommer and Daniel P. Kedzie. Richards Rosen Press, New York, N.Y., 1965.

For booklets on insurance careers, write to: Institute of Life Insurance, 277 Park Ave., New York, N.Y. 10017; Insurance Information Institute, 110 William St., New York, N.Y. 10038.

91

REAL ESTATE SALES

The real estate business, especially that part of it concerned with selling houses, is a natural for women. When a couple buy a house, it's often the wife who has the final say. And a sales*woman* usually knows better than a sales*man* just what it is that women look for in a home—good traffic patterns, closet space, efficient kitchen layout, unbroken wall space for furniture arrangement, and so on. In some counties, in fact, where the property is overwhelmingly residential, women comprise from 25 to 65 percent of all real estate brokers and salespeople.

Some of these women work from broker's offices and have the equivalent of a full-time job; some are brokers themselves (many of these work from their homes). But in many areas there are also opportunities for women who want part-time jobs selling real estate. Much of the work can be done from home, though you will, of course, have to spend con-

siderable time examining properties in your area and showing them to prospective buyers.

To get started in the real estate business, you must find a
broker who is willing to hire you. (This usually isn't too
much of a hurdle, since he pays you nothing out of his own
pocket. You earn a commission on any sales you bring in.)
You must also be willing either to learn the ropes on the
job—by going on calls with the broker to observe how he
gets listings, analyzes property values, motivates prospects to
buy, and negotiates and closes sales—or by taking a correspondence or regular course in real estate. (Check the
rating of any schools you consider with your local board of
realtors.) The training, and the sponsorship of a broker, is
necessary to enable you to pass the state examination for the
salesman's license. To become a broker yourself, you must
pass another, more advanced examination.

This is how the Small Business Administration describes a
real estate salesman's job:

> The real estate salesman scouts his community for owners want-
> ing to sell who will list their properties with him. A listing ob-
> tained, he analyzes the land and building, the mortgage on it, the
> zoning ordinances governing the building's use, the neighborhood
> trends—every feature that may interest a prospective buyer.
>
> Using current prices, he recommends to the owner an asking
> price. With the owner's agreement, the salesman then prepares a
> sales presentation which he puts to prospective buyers. When he
> finds one seriously interested, bargaining with the owner through
> him begins.
>
> If the sales presentation has been skillful and the buyer and
> seller agree on a price, the sale is almost ready to be made.
>
> But while some properties are sold free of debt, most carry a
> mortgage. Sellers usually want payment in cash above the mort-
> gage, but not all buyers have the full amount available. When
> they don't, the salesman must know the banks, insurance com-
> panies and savings and loan associations which invest in property
> mortgages and will finance the purchase.

The salesman assists the purchaser to qualify for a new mortgage loan by helping him assemble the credit data required by the lending institution. When the institution commits itself to the financing, there comes a "settlement" at which time the sale is closed.

Obviously, this is a skilled job, requiring a good head for business as well as persistence and the ability to get along with all kinds of people. But the rewards are also great. Says the Small Business Administration (speaking of brokers) : "Fantastic earnings have been made in real estate selling. Even comparative newcomers in the business sometime earn $40,000 to $50,000 yearly."

Of course, a salesman or saleswoman, especially one who works only part time, is not going to make anywhere near this amount. Still, since the usual commission rate on residential property is 6 percent, a single sale of a $20,000 house can bring you $1,200. Any woman, therefore, who is looking for a long-term source of income and is able to undertake training might seriously consider real estate.

WHERE TO GET MORE INFORMATION

How Any Woman Can Make $10,000 a Year in Real Estate, Miriam Wald. Prentice-Hall, Inc. Englewood Cliffs, N.J., 1965.

How to Operate a Real Estate Business, rev. ed., Stanley L. McMichael. Prentice-Hall, Inc., Englewood Cliffs, N.J., 1967.

Real Estate Business, Small Business Bibliography #65, Small Business Administration. Superintendent of Documents, U.S. Government Printing Office, Washington, D.C. 20402. Free booklet.

92

TELEPHONE SELLING

If you have a good telephone voice and a forceful (but pleasant) personality, you have the only requirements necessary for telephone selling, or soliciting. As you no doubt know from your own experience in receiving such calls, many companies—notably, diaper services, magazines, newspapers, book companies selling encyclopedias or other multivolume sets, vacuum cleaner agencies, and others—use this sales technique to locate prospective clients or customers. The majority of these companies require solicitors to work on their premises, perhaps only for a few hours a day, or on Saturday mornings. But there are also some companies that "farm out" telephone selling assignments to persons working from their own homes.

Under either arrangement, you'll be given a list of numbers to call (or assigned a section of the telephone book), together with a standard message and answers to typical questions. Experienced solicitors can make as many as 60 calls an hour (these include no-answers), but as a beginner you'll find that you average far fewer. As you become more experienced, you'll learn not to waste time on someone who is obviously disinterested or who just wants to talk, to take in your stride people who are rude to you, and to set aside calls to which there is no answer by the third ring (to be tried again later in the day).

If you work on a company's premises, you will probably be paid by the hour—the minimum rate is usually $2. If you work from home, it is more usual to be paid a commission

.on those calls that net an appointment for a salesman. (Your telephone expenses won't be reimbursed, so it's important that you have unlimited service for the area in which you'll be making calls.)

Although telephone selling is rife in the suburbs, the companies that use it are usually located in big cities. To locate such a job, look under "Telephone Sales" in the want-ad sections of newspapers in the city nearest you. Or you can try your luck in calling the sales managers of the kinds of firms, such as those mentioned above, that typically make use of the telephone-selling technique. Telephone solicitors are also used by market-research firms. (See #33, Market Research.) In this case, you will be asked not to sell but to gather information for the firm's clients.

Unless you are employed full-time by a company, telephone selling cannot be counted on as a steady source of income, however small. Typically, it is an on-again, off-again activity, limited by the duration of special promotional drives undertaken by various firms. It is also a field in which some women have been exploited by companies who promise big money but in reality pay very little for extensive telephone work. If you have any doubts about the reputation of a particular company, check with your local Chamber of Commerce or Better Business Bureau.

WHERE TO GET MORE INFORMATION

How to Get the Most out of Promotional Telephone Selling, T. Griffin. Prentice-Hall, Inc., New York, N.Y., 1966.

93

PARTY SELLING

Party selling is based on the idea that the best time to sell a woman something is when she is relaxed, having a pleasant time, and is in the company of other women who are buying. Some of the many products sold through the party plan include cosmetics, china, cookware, appliances, flatware, hosiery, baby furnishings, household gadgets, costume jewelry, reducing equipment, and lingerie. Your opportunity for making money in this field lies in becoming the local representative of a company that uses such a plan. It works like this:

As the company's representative, you find a woman who is willing to throw a party for her friends and neighbors for the express purpose of giving *you* a chance to sell them pots and pans or cosmetics or whatever. (For her services, the hostess receives a gift; frequently the guests get a small prize too.) Since the guests are aware beforehand of the nature of the party, you are presented with a captive audience already predisposed toward your product (or they wouldn't have bothered to come in the first place). After a general period of conversation (and games too, perhaps), and after refreshments—usually coffee and cake—are served, you pass out order blanks and begin your demonstration. The guests write down their orders as the various items are presented; most of them buy at least one item.

Then—and this is a vital part of the technique—you approach a few of the guests and ask them to become hostesses for similar parties with different guests. At this second round of parties, you take further orders, prospect for further party givers, and so on.

To be successful in party selling, you must have a friendly, sociable personality and be a good organizer. Also, since this is a very personal type of selling, you should pick a product that you can be sincerely enthusiastic about. You don't, however, need any previous selling experience; the company that hires you will train you, either through formal classes (expect to spend 30 hours or more, spread over several weeks, on such instruction) or by starting you as a party hostess and taking you along to other parties as an observer until you are ready to go it alone. The company will also supply you with leads to prospective party hostesses and help you with every detail of the party planning.

The easiest way to locate companies that sell through the party plan is to send for the Membership Roster of the Direct Selling Association (see "Where to Get More Information," below). This lists 91 active members; these include a number of party-plan firms. Or you can answer magazine advertisements or newspaper want-ads for persons to sell through party plans.

Party-plan representatives work on a commission which may amount to from 25 to 45 percent of their total gross sales. Those who are well established in the field, and have a sufficiently large "territory," can often make a steady income. However, it may take several years to work up to this point.

WHERE TO GET MORE INFORMATION

Membership Roster, Direct Selling Association, 1730 M Street, N.W., Washington, D.C., 20036. Free.

Your Future in Direct Selling, Foster E. Goodrich. Richards Rosen Press, New York, N.Y., 1965.

94

ROADSIDE STAND REVISITED

The words "roadside stand" conjure up a vision of a busy highway or a country lane. And it is, of course, true that not everyone can have, or would want, such a stand on his front lawn. Nevertheless, if you do live in an area with fairly relaxed zoning laws and have food or plant products to sell, you might well consider this throwback to the thirties (when farmers, hard hit by the depression, went in for selling as much of their produce as they could to roadside buyers). The disappearance of small produce stores, and the belief that anything from a local source is better than its supermarket counterpart, has made suburban roadside stands, where they are permitted, extremely popular.

Fresh vegetables and fruits in season are the biggest sellers; plants and cut flowers also sell well. If your own garden doesn't supply enough to make the venture worthwhile, you might offer to sell your neighbors' produce on a consignment basis, retaining 15 to 30 percent of the proceeds for your trouble. Other local products to sell on consignment might be regional foods (syrup, jellies, honey), homemade bread and other baked goods, eggs, homemade candies, candles, handcrafts, and souvenir items.

To make any money, you must live on a fairly well-traveled road, and have enough frontage so that you can provide parking space for at least two or three cars at a time. Your stand, particularly if the stock is well displayed, will be its own advertisement.

95

WEDDING PLANNER

Weddings, even the simplest, take a lot of work. And when they're complicated, as all formal and many semiformal affairs are, both the bride and her mother may wind up being too busy and too tired to enjoy themselves.

Consequently, if you live in a city or a heavily populated suburban area and have had some experience in this field— perhaps from having married off a daughter or two of your own—you might entertain the idea of starting a wedding planning service. The community need not be a particularly wealthy one for such a service to succeed, since if there is one thing people with even modest incomes will extend themselves for, it's a daughter's wedding.

More important than the location are your own qualifications as a wedding planner. You must know, or be willing to learn, every detail of bridal etiquette and of the practices of the major religions in regard to weddings. You must have an excellent grasp of detail. And you must be thoroughly familiar with your community's resources.

If called upon to do so, you must be able to plan the entire affair, from the engagement announcement to the honeymoon trip, a task which means dealing with printers, musicians, photographers, caterers, clergy, florists, limousine rental agencies, travel agents, and assorted other actors in the wedding drama. This includes the ability to estimate the costs in advance, to make up a budget for the client, and to handle the payment of bills.

As with any business, the first thing to do is to get as much advance information as you can about the chances for its success in your area. Would it have any competition, and if so, on what level? How much help would brides-to-be and their families want, and what would they be willing to pay? Would local suppliers—florists, caterers, printers, photographers—be cooperative? Only after questions like these have been answered satisfactorily does it make sense to start your business. Also, before you start, you should have a card file of sources of services and supplies, with notes on prices charged and time needed to deliver.

Your only initial expenses will be for business stationery and cards announcing your service. Since your market is so clearly defined, the best way to get business is to watch for engagement announcements in local newspapers and send a personal letter, together with your card, to each engaged girl. Once you have done a few weddings, and done them well, you should get a considerable amount of word-of-mouth business, particularly from bridesmaids in weddings you arranged who themselves become engaged.

Although later you may be able to specialize, at first you should (and will no doubt want to) take every job offered to you, even if it's limited to attending the rehearsal and then the ceremony to see that all the arrangements the bride's mother has previously made go smoothly.

The fees charged by wedding planners vary, but usually amount to 10 percent of the cost of that part of the wedding which they arrange. Thus for a simple informal ceremony and home reception, you might make only $50; whereas your income from an elaborate "do" might be as much as $300 to $1,000. May, June and September are generally the busiest months for weddings; you will earn the bulk of your income then. It is not unusual for even a successful business to go for several months without a single wedding.

WHERE TO GET MORE INFORMATION

The Bride's Book of Etiquette, the editors of Bride's Magazine. Grosset & Dunlap, Inc., New York, N.Y., 1967.

The Wedding Planner, Diana Bright. Nash Publishing, Los Angeles, Calif., 1970.

The Wonderful World of Weddings, Elizabeth L. Post. Funk & Wagnalls, New York, N.Y., 1970.

96

PARTY PLANNER

A party planner has much the same job as a wedding planner, except that she is spared the many details of the ceremony itself. On the other hand, something is often added—the necessity to provide some kind of professional entertainment, from an electric guitarist to a strolling astrologer. This means that in addition to sources of supply for food, flowers, decorations, rented tables and chairs, and so on, a party planner must know what local talent is available and how to match it up with specific occasions. She should also have imaginative ideas for party themes, decorations, and activities.

A party-planning service is more restricted than one devoted to planning weddings. Weddings take place everywhere, but parties elaborate enough to call for the services of a professional planner are far more frequent in some communities than others. Often a complete party-planning service develops from a successful smaller operation, such as a catering service, so that the planner already has a good idea of the potentials in her community. If you do not, you can get some idea by talking to caterers, florists, party supply rental agencies and others. These sources may also be willing to supply names and addresses of their customers for your mailing list, in return for your agreement to use their services for any parties you arrange.

If you must start cold to get customers, you will need an attractive brochure describing your service, which you can send out to prospective customers—both individuals and organizations. You should also have a prominent listing or an ad in the classified telephone directory under "Party Services." For so specialized a service, other paid advertising is not very productive. You will need to do a great deal of face-to-face selling of your service through social contacts and club memberships and by following up leads supplied by party supply services. A party or parties interesting enough to be described in detail in the local paper (including, ideally, a mention of your service in planning the party) will be a great asset. Eventually word-of-mouth should help too.

Party planners have various ways of charging for their services. Some ask a "per head" fee for each guest who attends, or a flat fee based on the elaborateness of the party (the fees asked by a one-woman service in White Plains, New York, run from a minimum of $150 to $1,000). Other planners charge a percentage (10 to 15 percent) of the total cost of the party, or set an hourly rate for their time.

WHERE TO GET MORE INFORMATION

The Party Planner, Bernice Hogan. Fleming H. Revell Co., Westwood, N.J., 1967.

97

COLLEGE-TOWN CRAM KITS

The French have a proverb that says, "The more things change, the more they remain the same." Certainly it's true of college students who, however their moral and political convictions may differ from those of earlier generations, still suffer from midterm and final examinations. Like their predecessors, they welcome with open arms the best aid yet designed to get them through. This is called variously a "cram kit," "survival kit," "care package," and "exam pack."

Whatever the name, it's a box of goodies, delivered to the student's door at the beginning of the exam period. The idea is that you supply them, the student eats them, and his parents pay for them. The parents could supply the food themselves, of course, but would have the trouble and expense of mailing their packages, whereas you, as a resident of the town, can simply drop yours by.

To launch this business, you obtain a list of names and addresses from student directories, freshman handbooks and yearbooks. Then, six weeks or so before exam time each semester, you mail a printed or mimeographed letter to each student's parents, describing the traumatic times approaching for their child and recommending your service. Enclose an order blank listing a selection of two or three kits varying in content and price; set a deadline, at least two weeks before exams, by which all orders, with accompanying checks, must be received.

With the orders in hand (and the reply ratio for some cram-kit services is as high as 30 percent), you buy the food wholesale, make up the kits, mark them with the names of the recipients and parent-donors, and deliver them at the appointed time. Typical kits contain crackers, peanut butter, an assortment of cheeses, fruit juices, cookies, and candy; additions for higher-priced versions might be nuts, dried fruits, canned meats, and gourmet delicacies.

Your markup on the kits should be high enough to cover the cost of your promotional expenses (the mailings to parents) , and overhead, including the cost of delivering the kits, plus an adequate return for your labor. Usually, this will work out to a selling price roughly three times the wholesale cost of the food. At that, it will cost the parent-customer little more than if he bought the food, packed it up, and mailed it himself, a point you should emphasize.

This business is a seasonal one, geared to the school year; it works best at large residential colleges with a high proportion of out-of-town (and preferably out-of-state) students. It is totally unsuited, for obvious reasons, to commuter colleges, or to colleges within easy reach of a shopping center.

98

BIRTHDAY CAKES FOR COLLEGE KIDS

Also perfect for the college town is a variant of the cram-kit idea, this time directed at birthdays, occasions seldom forgotten by doting parents. Rare is the American middle-class household where the birthday cake is not an institution. When their children go off to college, some mothers try to keep up the tradition by mailing a birthday cake. But the expense (it can cost as much as $3 or $4 to send a cake whose ingredients come to less than 40¢) and the battered, stale condition the offering is likely to arrive in, discourages many others from trying.

But suppose they could order for the occasion a freshly baked, homemade cake, delivered the same day it was made? Correctly anticipating almost any mother's reaction to the idea, some women who happen to live in the vicinity of a college or university with many out-of-town students have built up a profitable home business. Birthday cakes are the staple, but by no means the only offering of such businesses. Once the student tastes a luscious, fresh cake, he is likely to hint to his parents back home that he could make more frequent use of baked goods from the same source.

To launch a college-town birthday-cake business, follow the same procedure as for cram kits. (See #97.) At the beginning of the school year, write to parents and include an order blank. Along with prices for various sizes and types of cakes, state prices for other adolescent favorites—brownies, cookies, gooey sweet rolls. Ask for the birthdate of the student and specify that an order for a cake for the occasion must be placed at least two weeks in advance. In the meantime (or if the student's birthday happens to fall during a school holiday), you can point out that some of your other baked goods would undoubtedly be welcome. Specify that checks should accompany orders to avoid a later billing charge. Keep a file on orders received, and send out occasional follow-up letters to parents asking for new orders until the student is graduated.

Prices. Although you should keep an eye on what local bakeries charge, you won't be in competition with them (your customers are the parents back home), so you can afford to charge a bit more. Reasonable prices for birthday cakes might range from $1.50 to $3 and up, depending on the size and elaborateness of the decoration. Cookies might range from $.70 to $1.00 a dozen; brownies and rolls, from $1.25 to $1.50 a dozen.

99

WRITING FILLERS FOR NEWSPAPERS AND MAGAZINES

The number of people who make money from writing is relatively very small. The number of people who *try* must run into the millions. The big reason for the discrepancy is that the ability to write well is a special talent, usually developed only after intensive practice. Another major cause of rejection slips is aiming too high too soon.

If you have an interest in writing and want to make some money from it, it will pay you to look into what is called the "filler" market. This market is composed of newspapers and magazines that carry features made up of a number of small items on various subjects—children's sayings, jokes and anecdotes, little-known facts about famous people, recipes that have an interesting story attached to them, helpful household hints, and so on. Most of these items are contributed by outsiders who are paid for their contributions. Depending upon the publication and the nature of the item, a single "filler," consisting of no more than a few lines or a few paragraphs, can bring from $2 to $25 or more.

If you are interested in trying your hand at writing fillers, carefully study those that appear in various newspapers and magazines and attempt to analyze what each publication looks for in the fillers they accept. Look through books on writing at your local public library for help on "angling" fillers and for suggestions on sources of ideas for them.

Two periodicals (see below) aimed at writers, from beginners to established professionals, will also be of interest. Each frequently publishes news on markets for writers plus an annual yearbook. Writer's Digest also issues *The Writer's Market,* which contains a complete list of publications in Canada and the U.S.A., specifically what kind of material each publication looks for, and the rates each pays.

Another possible market for relative beginners in the writing field is what is known in the magazine trade as "regionals." These are quite short features, often about subjects of more local interest than those with which the magazine's main articles are concerned. They appear in regional editions of the magazine distributed only in those sections of the country where the products of certain regional advertisers are sold. (Regionals are *in addition* to the magazine's regular content, which is the same everywhere. They are used to fill the additional editorial space created by less-than-full-page regional ads.)

Another tip: If you are just starting out, don't concentrate exclusively on big, well-known publications. Granted, they pay better, but the competition is also great. Try the smaller periodicals, where a beginner has a far better chance of being published. And wherever you send your submission, make sure it is neatly typed (always use double spacing) on 8½ x 11 bond paper, and accompanied by a stamped, self-addressed return envelope.

WHERE TO GET MORE INFORMATION

The Writer, 8 Arlington St., Boston, Mass., 02116. Monthly.

Writer's Digest, 22 East 12th St., Cincinnati, O. 45210. Monthly.

100

WRITING GREETING CARDS

Another field open to those with a flair for words but relatively little writing background is the huge greeting-card industry. It is estimated that over two-and-a-half billion cards are printed every year, in thousands of variations on seasonal themes (Christmas, Valentine, Easter, Mother's Day, and so on) and every-day occasions (birthdays, weddings, new births, anniversaries).

To supply the ideas and verses for this unending stream of greetings, the card companies employ staff writers—some major firms have as many as 150. But many firms also buy contributions from free-lance writers. It must be said that the rate of acceptance is not high. One free-lancer who has been writing for several companies for years estimates that only about one out of 20 of her submissions are ultimately accepted (and this after they have been sent out, in turn, to a number of markets). On the other hand, the pay for those that *are* bought is good: from 50 cents to $2 or more a line for the four- to eight-line verses known in the trade as "sentiments" to $10 to $30 for just the idea (often necessarily accompanied by a rough sketch) for a "studio" card.

In trying the greeting-card market, your biggest investment will be for postage to keep submissions circulating from one company to the next until, it is hoped, at least some of them are bought. (This means, of course, that you must keep careful records—a card file is a good idea—or you will never be able to keep track of what you have sent to whom.) Experienced free-lancers advise waiting until you have at least 10 or 15 verses or ideas and submitting them in batches, rather than one at a time. There's more chance of a sale that way, and postage costs are kept down.

WHERE TO GET MORE INFORMATION

The Greeting Card Writer's Handbook, ed. H. Joseph Chadwick. Funk & Wagnalls, New York, N.Y., 1970.

101

MAGAZINE SUBSCRIPTIONS

A tried-and-true method of making money at home, widely used by everyone from shut-ins to college students, is selling subscriptions to magazines. It's a method particularly well suited to women with family responsibilities, because you can spend as much or as little time on it as you wish; there are no quotas to fill. Nor is any investment required. Everything you need is provided by the company you sell for.

Most magazine subscriptions are sold through big wholesale brokers like International Circulation Distributors (a division of the publishers of *Good Housekeeping*). These brokers handle a great many periodicals and are in constant need of community representatives. If you indicate you'd like to be one, you'll receive all kinds of material to help you sell: price lists, order forms, free envelopes, letterhead stationery, circulars, sales tips, help with sales letters, even sample copies of magazines to show potential customers. Regular mailings keep you up to date on price changes, special offers, and new sales plans and ideas.

Your easiest sales will be to your own friends, relatives, and acquaintances. It costs them nothing to order through you, and will earn you a handsome commission. Even if they are already taking all the magazines they want, you can place all their renewals—and renewals earn the same commission as first orders. The next step is to expand beyond your immediate circle to other groups in the community. There are many ways of doing this, as the sales literature you receive will point out: obtaining the membership lists of clubs and other organizations; watching the newspapers for notices of marriages, births, social events; copying names off mailboxes; checking professional directories. Then you either visit prospects or reach them by telephone or mail. Whichever way you choose, you'll get selling tips from the company that sponsors you. ICD, for example, even has a form letter for use by shut-ins, who can't go out to sell in person.

One attraction of magazine selling is that you get your money right away. When you sell a subscription, the subscriber gives *you* the money; you deduct your commission before forwarding the balance to the company. The commission rate differs for different magazines, but is generally between 10 and 25 percent of the subscription price, with special commissions and bonuses for those who maintain a high level of sales.

If you'd like to sell subscriptions to *Good Housekeeping* and its sister magazines, as well as many other leading publications, write to the Agency Bureau, International Circulation Distributors, 250 West 55th Street, New York, N.Y. 10019. For the names and addresses of other brokers, check the classified telephone directory under "Magazines—Subscription Agents," or write to the Central Registry of Magazine Subscription Solicitors at 575 Lexington Avenue, New York, N.Y., 10022.